A PSYCHOLOGY OF HOPE

A PSYCHOLOGY OF HOPE

A Biblical Response to Tragedy and Suicide

REVISED AND EXPANDED EDITION

Kalman J. Kaplan *&* Matthew B. Schwartz

WILLIAM B. EERDMANS PUBLISHING COMPANY
GRAND RAPIDS, MICHIGAN / CAMBRIDGE, U.K.

First published 1993 by Praeger Publishers, an imprint of Greenwood Publishing Group, Inc.
This revised and expanded edition published 2008 by
Wm. B. Eerdmans Publishing Co.
2140 Oak Industrial Drive N.E., Grand Rapids, Michigan 49505 /
P.O. Box 163, Cambridge CB3 9PU U.K.
www.eerdmans.com

Printed in the United States of America

13 12 11 10 09 08   7 6 5 4 3 2 1

Library of Congress Cataloging-in-Publication Data

Kaplan, Kalman J.
    A psychology of hope: a biblical response to tragedy and suicide /
    Kalman J. Kaplan & Matthew B. Schwartz. — Revised and expanded edition
        p.   cm.
    Includes bibliographical references (p.   ) and index.
    ISBN 978-0-8028-3271-9 (pbk.: alk. paper)
    1. Suicide — Biblical teaching.   2. Suicide — Religious aspects — Christianity.
    3. Suicide in literature.   4. Suicide — Psychological aspects.
    5. Suicidal behavior.   I. Schwartz, Matthew B.   II. Title.

    BS680.S855K37   2008
    241'.697 — dc22

                                                        2008022122

The material forming chapter 10 herein previously appeared in a slightly different form in
"Jacob's Blessing and the Curse of Oedipus: Sibling Rivalry and Its Resolution," *Journal of
Psychology and Judaism* 22 (Spring 1998): 71-84. The authors and publisher are grateful to the
Journal of Psychology and Judaism for permission to reprint this material here.

To the memory of my beloved parents,
Lewis C. Kaplan (Yehuda Leib ben Moshe haCohen)
and Edith (Yehudith) *Saposnik Kaplan,*
both writers in their own right,
who raised me with a psychology of hope,
and to all the Kaplans and Saposniks
and their kin (mishpachot).

KJK

To my dear wife, Nehama.

MS

Contents

Foreword to the First Edition, by David Bakan ix

Foreword to the Revised and Expanded Edition,
  by Nicholas Wolterstorff xii

List of Illustrations xv

Acknowledgments xvii

Introduction xix

I. The Problem of Suicide

1. To Be or Not to Be: The Question of Suicide 3

2. Suicide in Greco-Roman Thought 14

3. Suicide in Judaeo-Christian Thought 34

**II. Individual Case Studies from Greek Tragedy
and Biblical Narratives**

4. Cycle vs. Development: Narcissus vs. Jonah 65

5. Suicide in Greek Tragedy 80

6. Suicide and Suicide Prevention in Biblical Narratives 107

III. **Marriage and Family Case Studies from Greek Tragedy and Biblical Narratives**

7. Couples: Polarization vs. Growth, Prometheus-Pandora vs. Adam-Eve   123

8. The Suicide-Promoting Structure of the Greek Family: Oedipus and Electra   139

9. The Life-Promoting Structure of the Biblical Family: Isaac and Ruth   158

10. Oedipus's Curse vs. Jacob's Blessing: Sibling Rivalry and Its Resolution   179

IV. **Contemporary Confusions about Life and Death**

11. Kevorkian, Hippocrates, and Maimonides: Watching Over Patients' Life and Death   195

12. Zeno vs. Job: The Biblical Case against "Rational Suicide"   206

V. **Conclusion**

13. From Tragedy to Therapy: The Case for Biblical Psychotherapy   223

    References   233

    General Index   248

    Index of Selected Classical Writings   256

    Scriptural Indices   258

Foreword to the First Edition

In the course of the development of psychoanalytic psychotherapy, Freud went through some interesting steps with respect to his dealing with history. First, he focused on the memory of the individual as the major determinant of human experience and conduct, especially its sufferings and the failures of the normal volitionary mechanisms. He allowed that most of the content of memory was unconscious and that the recall of historical events in the life of the individual comprised the essential therapeutic operation.

However, this history began with the birth of the individual. Freud's next step was to conceive of history as something that went back further. In order to truly understand and help the individual one had to look to the history that extended way back, back even before the beginning of civilization and especially the crises of the beginning. Freud thus went from individual to the group, from the short history that began with the birth of the individual to the long history of culture. He went from works such as his contributions in *Studies in Hysteria* and highly temporally local considerations such as those that fill the pages of *The Interpretation of Dreams* to the larger history as expressed in such works as *Totem and Taboo, Civilization and Its Discontents,* and *Moses and Monotheism.*

Durkheim came upon a somewhat different consideration in his *Suicide;* yet, in a certain way, the position of Durkheim bore a similarity to the second position of Freud noted above. A single phenomenon caught the attention of Durkheim — the extraordinary constancy of the suicide rate over time in various groups. The finding led to his notion of the "social fact," the trans-individual characteristic of groups not identifiable in individuals. This notion would become the ground for a science of sociology for him. His reasoning was that if suicide were an individual phenomenon, the suicide rate of any group would change over time, since the suicidal individuals were separated from the group by their act of suicide. However, the suicide rate remained constant. It even remained constant in groups that had major population turnover, such as the army. Thus Durkheim concluded that the suicide rate was an essential reflection of some characteristic of the group as such. That characteristic of the group reflected itself in the determination of the relative numbers of people committing suicide in the group. He took a strong position against the relevance of psychological considerations for the understanding of suicide.

I find this work by Kaplan and Schwartz an intellectually remarkable synthesis of these two lines of thought, combined with direct applicability to psychotherapy with suicidally inclined people. Both the Freudian and the Durkheimian positions strain credibility. The Freudian approach went towards the uncomfortable assumption of some kind of genetic inheritance of history, a kind of Lamarckianism, which even alienated some of Freud's closest supporters. The Durkheimian approach went against the obvious truth that individual psychological factors play a role in suicide. Kaplan and Schwartz have transcended both of these difficulties, and they bring what is credible in both positions together.

Kaplan and Schwartz recognize the continuity of cultural history and have placed the individual within it, albeit born into it. They see the facticity of suicide as embedded in our collective culture including its very complexities. They have identified the two great historical cultures of Western civilization, the Greek and the Hebraic, that have given rise to the culture in which we live. They take full cognizance of the fact that contemporary culture derives from both of them and carries within it both syntheses and abiding conflicts. Most important, they identify social forms and attitudes that bear on suicide in the historical cultures. Every person living in our society draws his being from the culture that combines the two cultures. It is not that the culture is carried genetically, as Freud suggested. Nor is it a mysterious transcendental social fact with respect to which psychological considerations are irrelevant, as Durkheim argued.

And from this arises a moral direction, a practical direction and some research directions, all very valuable.

The moral direction is the implicit recognition that suicide is a casualty of our collective culture, of the culture which each of us is *in*, each of us *is*, and of which each of us is the *agent* of the future. The rate of suicide is an index of the health of the society at large. When anyone commits suicide we must look to the nature of the culture which is generating that suicide, and take steps to rectify it. When, for example, the rate of suicide in some sub-group is high, we should move to improve the conditions in that sub-group. And should the rate of suicide rise for the whole group, or for any particular group within it, we should take it as a major signal calling for rectifying action.

The practical direction is the ready emergence of guidelines for psychotherapy with suicidal individuals that are indicated in this work. I have little doubt but that the application of these guidelines can save lives that might have been lost otherwise. Hopefully, this work will encourage more therapists to undertake therapy with suicide-prone individuals.

Of the research paths that seem to open, two are clear. First, there is a great need for more critical study of history as the basis of contemporary psychological conditions, including suicide proneness. History, in this sense, is the patent extension of the psychoanalytic method. The study of history should be the act of the culture in the conduct of its own psychoanalysis towards promoting its perfection. Second, it would be hoped that there be continued work in the assessment of the guidelines indicated and their improvement.

DAVID BAKAN

Foreword to the Revised
and Expanded Edition

This is one of those unusual books in which the background is as important as the foreground, maybe more so.

The central question that Kaplan and Schwartz address is what the therapist can do to prevent suicide. The proposal they develop for a "suicide prevention–therapy" is set by them within the context of a theoretical analysis of the dynamics characteristic of suicide.

In order to arrive at mature well-being, all of us must develop two fundamental dimensions of our existence. We must arrive at some degree of individuality and autonomy; and we must develop attachments to family, to surrounding members of society, to institutions, to our environment. Kaplan and Schwartz call these two dimensions *individuation* and *attachment*. In the typical case of suicide, the negotiation of these dimensions has gone tragically wrong. The individual finds himself excessively disengaged, excessively enmeshed, or helplessly caught between engagement and enmeshment; and he feels that there's nothing to be done about it. There's no way out other than death.

The therapy that Kaplan and Schwartz propose aims at showing the patient that there is a way out, and helping him to set foot on that way. Hence the title of their book, *A Psychology of Hope*. Suicide-prevention is placed within the context of life-promotion.

All of this belongs to what I called the *foreground* of the discussion. It would be hard to exaggerate its importance. Their analysis of the dynamics of suicide, informed by the literature on suicide, is penetrating and compelling, And any therapy that carries the promise of preventing the dynamics of suicide from following their course in a patient is obviously important.

What, then, is the *background* that I say is just as important if not more so? The background is their contrast between the attitude toward suicide in the literature of ancient Greece and the attitude toward suicide in the biblical writings. The authors point out that in the great plays of classical Greece, suicide is common and dramatic; in the biblical writings, it is rare and low-key. They ask, why the difference?

I must confess that over the years I have become wary of discussions that pit supposedly Greek ways of thinking against supposedly Hebrew or biblical ways of thinking; all too often the contrast depends on the selection of evidence. So I was apprehensive when the authors moved on from their theoretical analysis of suicide to this intellectual archaeology. But Kaplan and Schwartz do not begin up in the air of generalization but on the ground of the particulars. The bulk of their book consists of detailed analyses of the cases in Greek and in biblical literature. Their generalizations arise cautiously out of the cases. My own judgment is that their analysis of the cases make their generalizations compelling.

The ancient Greek writers had a tragic view of life. Theirs was a culture of honor and shame; they admired the hero. But the hero often found himself hopelessly enmeshed in a situation where death provided the only alternative to living in shame. The fates had decreed; there was no other way out. Sometimes the heroism of the hero even consisted in his determination to accept death over a life of shame and disgrace.

Kaplan and Schwartz substantiate the striking claim that nowhere in the biblical literature is it suggested that continued life is sometimes a dead end. The reason it's never a dead end is that the biblical God is not one who decrees our fate but one who has created each of us as a creature of worth, and who loves us, inscrutable as that love sometimes proves to be. In this world, heroism is not called for; it's enough that we be grateful and make good use of the life that's given us.

After contrasting these two attitudes toward suicide and the frames of thought that lie behind them, the authors go on to argue that the modern psychoanalytic tradition has been Greek in its basic orientation rather than biblical, this in spite of the fact that Freud was Jewish. And they pointedly note that much of the modern discussion about assisted suicide and euthanasia operates with the Greek rather than the biblical mentality.

I too hold that there are fundamentally different attitudes toward human well-being and dignity, toward injustice and pain, toward the place of God in our lives, in the classical Greek writers and in the biblical

writers. Kaplan and Schwartz have highlighted and detailed one important dimension of that multifaceted contrast, the contrast between the
tragic view of life and the covenantal view, as they sometimes call it. I
think that's their most important contribution. Once one sees that contrast, and once one chooses the *covenantal* view, then everything falls into
place. Then one will see the role of the therapist, confronted with a patient contemplating suicide, to persuade her that her situation is not
hopeless, to show her the way forward, and to help her to set foot on that
way. Such a therapy is a therapy in which suicide-prevention occurs
within the context of life-promotion. It's a therapy of living in hope
rather than a therapy of submitting to tragic fate.

NICHOLAS WOLTERSTORFF

*Noah Porter Professor Emeritus
of Philosophical Theology,
Yale University*

*Senior Fellow, Institute for Advanced
Studies in Culture,
University of Virginia*

Illustrations

Figures

1.1 A Bidimensional Distancing Representation of Suicide Types   11

1.2 The Individual Clinical Axis   12

1.3 The Individual Developmental Axis   13

7.1 The Couple Clinical Axis   125

7.2 The Couple Developmental Axis   126

7.3 Prometheus and Pandora   128

7.4 Deucalion and Pyrrha   131

7.5 Adam and Eve   133

7.6 Noah and His Wife   136

7.7 Marital Pathology and Completed Adolescent Suicide   137

8.1 The Oedipus Complex, Pathology, and Suicide   148

8.2 The Electra Complex, Pathology, and Suicide   156

9.1 The Akedah Motif, Healthy Development, and Life Promotion   169

9.2 The Ruth Motif, Healthy Development, and Life Promotion   177

Tables

4.1 Individual Development for Narcissus and Jonah   75

5.1 Self-Destruction in Greek Tragedy   83

6.1 Suicide in the Hebrew Bible   108

6.2 Suicide Prevention in the Hebrew Bible   114

8.1 Greek Parent-Child Narratives   141

9.1 Biblical Parent-Child Narratives   161

10.1 Paternal Blessing and the Relationship between Brothers
     in Biblical Narratives   181

10.2 Paternal Threat/Curse and the Relationship between
     Brothers in Greek Narratives   188

Acknowledgments

This is a revised and expanded second edition of an earlier edition published by Praeger Publishers in 1993, and we acknowledge the help of important people at two publishers. Our first edition benefited from the devoted labor of the staff at Praeger, especially Mr. Paul Macirowski, acquisitions editor, Ms. Susan Wladaver-Morgan, copy editor, and Ms. Diane Spaulding, production editor.

As to the second expanded edition (2008), we thank Bill Eerdmans and Reinder Van Til, who are both stimulating comrades and raconteurs—knowledgeable, wise, and responsive—for their support of this endeavor. We also thank the staff at Eerdmans for helping bring this work to fruition, especially Linda Bieze and Jenny Hoffman.

Dr. Kaplan also thanks the John Templeton Foundation, especially Dr. Paul Wason and Andrew Rick-Miller, for providing the resources and guidance to develop the Program in Religion, Spirituality, and Mental Health (RSMH) at the University of Illinois, Chicago. Elizabeth Jones, coordinator of the RSMH, has been invaluable in helping us edit this work and having a crucial role in the filming of the online educational program. We are also indebted to the following people, all of them at the College of Medicine of the University of Illinois, Chicago (UIC): Dr. Joseph Flaherty, professor of psychiatry and dean; Dr. Henry Dove, professor of clinical psychiatry and interim head of psychiatry; Dr. Martin Harrow, director of psychology in the department of psychiatry; Dr. Les Sandlow, senior associate dean and chair of the department of medical education; and Diane Rudall, assistant to the chair of medical education. We also thank Gerald R. Stapleton, director for distance learning, and Phillip

Bertulfo , multimedia manager, for their skill in adapting the ideas in this book to an online venue.

Finally, we acknowledge the late David Bakan, a pioneer in the interface of biblical thought and psychology, for his foreword to the first edition; and the late Erich Wellisch, who provided the inspiration for this book in his seminal work *Isaac and Oedipus*, which in 1954 called for a biblical psychology.

Introduction

Ask any group of people this question: "Is it more difficult to kill yourself or not to kill yourself?" Invariably, two equally strong opinions emerge. The "kill yourselves" and "not kill yourselves" groups are similar in size, and each camp finds it difficult, if not impossible, to comprehend the other's point of view. This variation tells us a great deal about the lack of unanimity in our culture concerning the question of suicide, and we may wonder about the source of these opinions.

This book is about suicide and suicide prevention in both ancient and modern times. The focus is at once historical and psychological, theoretical and practical. The development of a suicide-preventive therapy in modern society can gain much from the ancient sources. After all, the question of suicide is linked to the larger issue of human existence, both at the level of individual psychopathology and within a more general societal milieu.

Sigmund Freud noted the pervasive "death instinct" in the human being. He says, in *The Ego and the Id,* that "the aim of all life is death," or a return to an early inanimate state that existed before the animate one. In that book Freud argues that the superego could become "a pure culture of the death instinct," which could turn its strength against the ego. In *Mourning and Melancholia,* Freud suggests that suicide, like depression, results from the turning inward of anger and aggression toward the outside world.

Historians, too, have pointed to an apparent cycle in human affairs in which primitive but warlike peoples conquer great civilizations, then become highly civilized but less vigorous themselves, and in the end they collapse before new waves of primitive aggressors. Greece, Rome, and the other ancient Mediterranean cultures and empires all rose and fell. And scholars of our own time have seen possible signs of the collapse of Western civilization in the wholesale destruction of the two world wars and in the rise of radical Islam.

Our work has led us to the conclusion, surprising to us, that these historians have not merely created an artificial theoretic structure; they have correctly sensed a trend of rising and falling that characterizes the history of most nations. However, they have fallen short of an important finding. This pattern is established neither by universal forces nor by some predetermined cosmic doom. We argue that there is instead a feeling of despair, alienation, and worthlessness that eats at the inner core of a civilization even as it reaches its peak of military and cultural strength.

This response is in large part not a realistic *Weltanschauung* but a suicidal pattern that closely parallels that of an individual who moves toward hopelessness and self-destruction. Nations as well as individuals often need a "stopper," a saving intervention to restore them to the road toward healthy self-fulfillment. For the Stoics of classical Greece and Rome, the right to kill oneself represented the highest degree of human freedom. In contrast, biblical thought presents freedom as fulfilling the divine command to live. The way an individual — or, indeed, a society — deals with this issue is manifest in every fiber of its being and does much to form its character and progress. If life has little or no meaning, then wisdom will not help.[1] Further, does not ending such a life become a viable and sensible alternative? Some have answered this last question clearly in the affirmative and look on self-destruction favorably; others answer with an equally strong no and are unalterably opposed to it.

In this book we bring together our training and knowledge as a psychologist and a historian, respectively, to study Greco-Roman, biblical, and postbiblical views on suicide in order to connect the influence of these civilizations to modern thought. A new specialty has emerged in the mental health field — suicidology. In the last several decades it has grown quickly to deal with both individuals and families. The clergy have been quite prominent in this movement, and many crisis centers and hotlines are affiliated with churches and synagogues. Yet there has been very little systematic use of biblical materials by the churches and synagogues in dealing

---

1. This reflects the classical Greek bias against self-knowledge, which emerges in Sophocles' *Oedipus Rex:* "What good is wisdom if it does not benefit the wise?" See also the myth of Narcissus: "He will live a long life so long as he does not come to know himself."

with suicide. It is as though the clergy have put aside their religious backgrounds when they practice suicide prevention; instead, they adopt the dominant psychological and psychiatric models in the culture, many of which are subtly based on a Greco-Roman view of life. The treatment of the "psyche" and the emphasis on the Oedipus complex are but two examples. This curious self-limitation may be especially relevant when we investigate suicide and suicide prevention. The study of Greco-Roman and biblical precedents is fundamental both for an understanding of intellectual history and for practical treatment in individual counseling situations.

Earlier social thinkers who have written on these matters, such as Henry Romilly Fedden and Alfredo Alvarez, have been consistently and quite correctly faulted by historians for their lack of care with historical sources.[2] Émile Durkheim has been criticized for viewing religion as "an elaborate reflection of more basic social realities" rather than as an important motivating force in human life (Pope 1976). Thus, Durkheim argues that Protestants have higher suicide rates than Catholics do because of the lower level of social integration provided by the Protestant church and the potentially suicidal aspects of the highly individualized Protestant desire for knowledge. Durkheim says that Jews, because of their persecuted status, have greater social integration and thus show lower suicide rates than do either Protestants or Catholics.[3] This may be, but Durkheim reveals his lack of familiarity with biblical and Jewish historical viewpoints on suicide. For example, he incorrectly says that the Hebrew Bible contains no law forbidding a man to kill himself, and that the only Jewish proscription against suicide is mentioned by Flavius Josephus in the *Jewish War* (3.25).

Durkheim's limitations with respect to the biblical materials may well be typical of a general antireligious bias among social scientists. R. Stark, D. P. Doyle, and J. L. Rushing (1983) have argued this forcefully:

> Despite Durkheim's reputation as a founding father of the sociology of religion, we found his writing to display amazing innocence of ele-

2. For example, David Ladouceur (1987, 113) has referred to the uncritical approaches of Henry Romilly Fedden and Alfredo Alvarez in their treatment of Roman and Jewish suicides.

3. The single exception to this rule, curiously, was Bavaria, where Jews killed themselves twice as often as did Catholics. This anomaly led Durkheim (in 1897) to ask prophetically, "Is there something exceptional about the position of Judaism in this country [Bavaria] we do not know?" The rise of Adolf Hitler there some thirty years later provided a tragic affirmative answer to Durkheim's speculations.

mentary facts about religion in Europe at the time he wrote. Time and again in *Suicide* (1897) his open contempt for religion and his lack of knowledge of it led him to frame obviously wrong arguments. Nor were these directed towards peripheral concerns. Critical parts of his analysis rest on arguments that never should have passed even moderately informed inspection. That these matters were not recognized long ago probably reflects the persistence among social scientists of the same biases and unfamiliarity that led Durkheim himself into error. (Stark, Doyle, and Rushing 1983, 120)

Such an antireligious bias is especially unfortunate given Durkheim's brilliance, as well as his own statement that "a religious nature . . . is very different from the egoistic involvement . . . which leads man to suicide" (Durkheim 1897, 336).

A more serious attempt to explore the relationship between religion and suicide has been made by A. Bayet (1922) in his work *Le Suicide et la Morale.* In this work, Bayet attempts to distinguish two kinds of morality. The first and primitive kind, *morale simple,* is founded on religion and represents the basis for the morality of common people; the second, *morale nuancée,* is the morality of the educated and intellectual minority and has its roots in reason. Bayet then seeks to apply this idea of twin moralities to an understanding of the fluctuation in attitudes toward suicide. As reason increases, he suggests, the penalties for suicide decrease; as religion increases, the penalties for suicide increase. Thus the classical Greek and Renaissance tolerance of suicide follows the defeat of the *morale simple* of earlier times and of the Age of Faith. A fuller and more direct comparison of the place of suicide in biblical and Greek societies can be expected to help illuminate this issue.[4]

In our examination of these contrasting views of life, death, and suicide, a number of important questions stand out: What is the meaning of life and death? To whom does life belong? Why do people terminate their own lives? What kinds of internal or external circumstances may be involved? Is there something that a person may know or may not know that brings her to suicide? Finally, do the biblical and classical civilizations provide different kinds of wisdom for the treatment of these problems?

In the Bible, God is the guide, protector, and indeed partner of hu-

---

4. See also Arthur Droge and James Tabor, *A Noble Death* (1992).

man beings. No matter how bad things get for humans, they need never lose hope. God has placed a rainbow in the clouds as a sign of his covenant (Gen. 9:12-17). This hope provides a stopper that is simply unavailable to humans in Greek mythology, on whom Pandora loosed all the ills from the box of Epimetheus. Hope alone is locked up inside the box (Hesiod, *Works and Days*, 90-96).

The widespread incidence of suicide and the obsession with self-destruction in the classical literature are astonishing. Clearly, self-destruction was a pervasive motivating theme in Greek and Roman thought. The Greek world seemed consistently undone by a tragic confusion implicit in the heroic impulse and by a commitment to unsatisfactory choices that were always destructively rigid and harsh. In this world, *hubris* brings *nemesis,* and families are often pathological, which makes matters worse. The gods are capricious: narcissistically preoccupied with their own affairs, they are incapable of providing any stopper in the individual's rush to self-destruction. Suicide often seems to be the only way out. These themes appear uncomfortably similar to many varieties of suicidal thought in modern society.

The "right-to-die" debate has been raging in America for some two or three decades now. The questions of euthanasia (itself a combination of two Greek words that mean "good death") and physician-assisted suicide have been posed by the Hemlock Society with respect to the philosophical idea of a right to die. Left untouched in much of this debate, however, is the religious question of why an individual would want to end his life and the therapeutic issue of how to restore hope.

In contrast to the Greek worldview, the ancient biblical writings speak little of suicide and approach duty and freedom in vastly different and more realistic terms. God is an involved parent who cares for his children. Heroism in the Greek sense is not needed, nor is the individual compelled to choose between impossible and unlivable alternatives. Biblical families are typically supportive; and even when they are not, there is still hope. God protects his children and allows them to develop, to recover when they err, and to avoid the polarities of egoism and altruism, of hubris and nemesis, even in the absence of supportive families.[5] Many of these

---

5. What is often required is a regression from this impossible axis and a return to a more harmonious yet possibly less developed position. Anna Freud (1936) referred to this as "regression in the service of development."

ideas may be critical to preventing suicide and the obsession with self-destruction in the modern world.

This book is divided into four sections — (I) The Problem of Suicide, (II) Individual Case Studies from Greek Tragedy and Biblical Narratives, (III) Marriage and Family Case Studies from Greek Tragedy and Biblical Narratives, (IV) Contemporary Confusions about Life and Death — followed by a conclusion. In each of the first three sections, we begin by discussing the issue of suicide and suicide-prevention in a comparative framework (chapters 1, 4, and 7); then we discuss the suicide-promoting effects of the Greco-Roman societies (chapters 2, 5, and 8); finally, we look at the suicide-preventing effects of the biblical world (chapters 3, 6, and 9). The third section also examines the issue of sibling rivalry and its resolution in the Greek versus the biblical narratives (chapter 10). The fourth section continues this contrast of Greek versus biblical worldviews with regard to contemporary confusions about life and death, first comparing the Hippocratic Oath with Maimonides' "Physician's Prayer" (chapter 11), and then comparing the narratives of Zeno and Job concerning the issue of "rational suicide" (chapter 12). The concluding chapter summarizes much of the above material and briefly outlines the dimensions of a biblical psychotherapy to suggest a psychology of hope that may help overcome the tragic confusion of modern humans in the Western tradition.

I. The Problem of Suicide

1. To Be or Not to Be: The Question of Suicide

To be or not to be, that is the question, whether 'tis nobler in the mind to suffer the slings and arrows of outrageous fortune, or to take arms against a sea of troubles, and by opposing end them.

Shakespeare, *Hamlet*

There is but one truly serious philosophical problem, and that is suicide.

Camus, *The Myth of Sisyphus*, 3

Hamlet's ponderings are found in the best-known soliloquy in Western letters. This musing on suicide grows clearer in each succeeding line. First a hint: "Whether 'tis nobler in the mind to suffer the slings and arrows of outrageous fortune, or to take arms against a sea of troubles, and by opposing end them." He then addresses the question of death head on: "To die: to sleep; no more; and, by a sleep to say we end the heartache and the thousand natural shocks that flesh is heir to, 'tis a consummation devoutly to be wished." Finally, he poses the question of suicide directly: "For who would bear the whips and scorns of time . . . when he himself might his quietus make with a bare bodkin [dagger]?" (Shakespeare, *Hamlet*, Act 3, Sc. 1, lines 55-75).

Seldom has the question of life and death been posed so earnestly. Hamlet places life and its attendant suffering in one hand and death and the supposed cessation of suffering in the other. The centrality of the question of suicide in the human agenda has also been stated very directly in the quotation above by the French existentialist Albert Camus, which he follows with this sentence: "Judging whether life is or is not worth living amounts to answering the fundamental question of philosophy" (Camus 1955, 3). There has been no agreement on this question in Western society and hence on the permissibility of suicide.

Views of Suicide

Dante's *Divine Comedy* places the "violent against themselves" in the wood of the suicides in the second round of the seventh circle of Hell. The souls of the suicides are encased in thorny trees where the leaves are eaten by harpies, causing their wounds to bleed. Only as long as the blood flows are the souls of the trees able to speak. They are permitted to speak only through that which injures and destroys them (Dante Alighieri, *The Inferno,* canto 13).

In Germany some centuries later, Immanuel Kant (1785) argued strongly against suicide because he felt that it was incompatible with the affirmation of a universal law of self-love. At about the same time, however, Johann Wolfgang von Goethe (1774) romanticized suicide in his novel *The Sorrows of Young Werther.* Indeed, the publication of Goethe's book was followed by a veritable epidemic of romantic suicides throughout Europe.

Many of the greatest names in French philosophy were sympathetic to suicide. Voltaire (1973), for example, argued that at times suicide must be defensible, even though his own temperament was opposed to it. While regarding it as abnormal, he admitted the possibility of its social and moral validity. Paul d'Holbach (1770) strongly favored the permissibility of suicide on two grounds: first, suicide is not contrary to the laws of nature; second, suicide is not antisocial. The individual's contract with society is based on mutual benefit. Therefore, if society can give him nothing, the suicide has every right to consider the contract void. Jean-Jacques Rousseau, too, was sympathetic. The twenty-first letter in his *Nouvelle Héloise* (1761) contains an extensive apologia for suicide from a young man disillusioned with life. Like d'Holbach, he says that, first, suicide is not against the laws of nature: that is, it is up to us to leave life when it no longer seems good. Second, suicide is not akin to deserting one's post (see Plato's argument in chap. 2 below) but is like moving to a more hospitable town.

4

Third, suicide does not remove one from the providence of God; it destroys one's body but not one's soul, which actually comes closer to God through death. Fourth, suffering sometimes becomes unendurable. Fifth, the scriptures have no word to say against suicide.

At the same time, France produced a great voice against suicide. Madame Anne Louise de Stael, in her 1814 essay *Reflections on Suicide*, reverses the support for suicide she had shown in an earlier essay she wrote, entitled *On the Influence of Passions* (1796), by offering a threefold argument: first, pain serves to regenerate the soul, and thus to escape from pain through suicide is a refusal to recognize the possibilities of one's own nature; second, God never abandons the true believer, so there is no reason or right to commit suicide; finally, suicide is not consonant with the moral dignity of humankind.

The English poet and churchman John Donne (1608) expresses a very different point of view in his classic work on suicide, *Biathanatos* (1648, 29). He argues that, under certain limited conditions, suicide might not be a sin: "[F]or we say . . . that this may be done only, when the Honor of God may be promoted by that way and no other" (136). However, Donne did present a general plea for charity toward suicides, and he offered a proof that no set of rules can govern all instances (145).

David Hume goes even further in *An Essay on Suicide*. For suicide to be criminal, he argues, it must be a transgression of duty against God, one's self, or one's neighbors. That it cannot be the first stems from Hume's assertion that all our powers are received from our creator. Therefore, suicide can be no more ungodly than any other form of death. That suicide cannot involve a transgression against one's self seemed obvious to Hume, as no one has ever thrown away his life while it was worth keeping. That suicide does not involve transgression against one's neighbors was also obvious to him. All one's obligations to do good to society, according to Hume, imply something reciprocal. Therefore, as long as one receives benefit from society, one is obligated to promote its interests; but when one withdraws altogether from society, one is no longer so bound.

A very different point of view was taken by an English clergyman named Adams at the beginning of the eighteenth century. In a publication entitled *An Essay Concerning Self-Murder* (1700), Adams declares that human life is God's own property that he entrusts to humans only for a certain end. Therefore, human beings have no liberty to destroy it. Adams extends this viewpoint into the political realm. A person may hazard her life for her country, but she may not destroy herself for it.[1] Another English clergyman, the Reverend Tuke, attempted to bridge this gap by differentiating between two kinds of suicide, one permissible and the other not.

> There be two sorts of voluntarie deaths, the one lawful and honest such as the death of Martyrs, the other dishonest and unlawful, when men have neyther lawfull calling, nor honest endes, as of Peregrinus, who burnt himself in a pile of wood, thinking thereby to live forever in men's remembrance.[2] (1613, 21)

Views in contemporary Western society are similarly mixed. The American psychiatrist Thomas Szasz (1971) has attacked the view that suicide is necessarily a manifestation of mental illness. Suicide, he has argued, is a product of choice by an agent, not a symptom of disease. Such a choice, he says, must be respected by psychiatrists, police, and others who might attempt to intervene in suicide. To do otherwise involves the infantilizing and dehumanizing of the suicidal person.

On the other side, an equally compelling antisuicide position has been taken by Austrian psychiatrist Erwin Ringel, the founder of the International Association for Suicide Prevention. Ringel (1981) has argued that suicide cannot be freely chosen, and thus he opposes libertarian attitudes toward suicide, including those that would allow planned deaths for the terminally ill. Arguing that every human life is important, he presents the purpose of suicide prevention as the reinvigoration of human life — through the help of psychiatry and crisis intervention — for all human beings.

R. B. Brandt (1975) and Lebacqz and Englehardt (1977) have taken middle-ground positions. Brandt, a past president of the American Philosophical Association, has attempted to distinguish between rational and irrational suicide. His opinion is that a person may, on utilitarian grounds, reach a rational decision to take his life but that the rational decision process is often distorted by emotional disturbances. He has argued that intervention to prevent suicide may be justified if the decision to take one's life is an irrational one. However, if the decision is rational, such an intervention is not justified; furthermore, Brandt has even argued for an obligation to assist a person attempting a rational suicide. Lebacqz, a professor of

---

1. The clergyman Adams is referred to by Henry Romilly Fedden (1938, 216-17).
2. The Reverend Mr. Tuke is discussed by Faber (1967, 31-32).

Christian ethics, and Englehardt, a professor of the philosophy of medicine, have taken a slightly different approach. While acknowledging on libertarian grounds that people may have a *prima facie* right to commit suicide, they have maintained that this right is nonetheless usually overridden by contravening duties that grow out of our covenantal relationships with others. Still, there may be a right to suicide in at least three kinds of cases: voluntary euthanasia, covenantal suicide, and symbolic protest, for in these cases suicide would affirm the covenants we have with others.

These views, of course, represent only a sample of those existing in past and present Western society. However, they do reflect the confusion and vacillation with regard to many issues involving suicide.[3] Is suicide to be viewed as mental illness, when judgment is, by definition, distorted and irrational, or can the choice be based on a rational decision? What implications would this definition have for mental-health professionals, religious leaders, and concerned laypeople? Should they respect an individual's "right to die" and even assist that person? Or are they morally bound to attempt to preserve life even against the expressed will of the potential suicide? To whom does an individual's life belong — to herself, to the state, or to God?[4] And, finally, how is suicide related to the basic idea of freedom? Suicide must be understood in the context of the larger issues of life and death and the historical antecedents to this problem.

3. Studies of the attitudes of African and Asian societies toward suicide also indicate variation (Bohannan 1960; Elwin 1943; Hankoff 1969b; Thakur 1963; Yap 1958; Ohara 1961). India practiced *suttee,* the custom in which widows were placed on the funeral pyres of their husbands (Thakur 1963). Japanese history is filled with incidents of suicide, ranging from the traditional story of the forty-seven *ronin,* in which servants killed themselves en masse on their master's death, via the practice of *hara-kiri* or *seppuku* (conducted by the Samurai warriors), to the modern Kamikaze pilots, who dive-bombed to their deaths in World War II (Ohara 1965; Tatai and Kato 1974). Suicide in China has never been ritualized to the same extent as in Japan and has thus attracted less attention. Yet suicide has played an important role throughout Chinese history, and an astounding number of eminent men and women are reported to have taken their own lives. These suicides were often committed as expiation for violations of loyalties, even if they were committed inadvertently (Yap 1958; Lindell 1973; Rin 1975).

4. Ross and Kaplan (1993) have developed a questionnaire designed to measure an individual's "life-ownership" orientation. The Life-Orientation Ownership Questionnaire (LOOQ) assesses whether an individual feels his life belongs to himself, to the state, or to a divine being. Ross and Kaplan have begun to investigate the influence of this orientation on attitudes toward abortion, suicide, and capital punishment.

Definitions of Suicide

In his book, *Definition of Suicide,* Edwin Shneidman (1985), the father of the suicidology movement in America, has offered what many regard as a state-of-the-art definition of suicide: "Currently in the Western world, suicide is a conscious act of self-induced annihilation, best understood as a multidimensional malaise in a needful individual who defines an issue for which suicide is perceived as the best solution" (Shneidman 1985, 203). Shneidman's emphasis on "currently" reflects his awareness that the meaning of suicide may vary from one historical period to another; his emphasis on "Western world" implicitly recognizes that the meaning of suicide may be a function of the cultural matrix in which it occurs; the word "conscious" limits suicide to *human* acts, while the word "act" calls for a narrowing of our use of the term "suicide" to a particular behavior that leads to death. As such, this passage seems to suggest that the word "suicide" not be so readily used to refer to attempts and/or threats. The word "self-induced" indicates a death by one's own hand, and "annihilation" is meant to imply the end of experiential aspects of life and of the actual cessation of life itself. Suicide thus represents the permanent cessation of individual consciousness.

Nevertheless, Shneidman's definition fails to capture many nuances apparent in the suicides that we explore in this book. First, Jewish law, for example, addresses the question of when a person is compelled to accept death rather than to actively commit suicide. Second, many Greek suicidal themes, especially in the plays of Euripides, take the form of ritual murder, in which the victim does not literally take his or her own life. Iphigenia, for example, allows herself, without protest, to be sacrificed by others (Euripides, *Iphigenia in Aulis*). Another example is Macaria, who refuses the chance to escape her sacrifice by means of a lottery (Euripides, *Heracleidae*). Third, Shneidman's definition leaves open the relationship between martyrdom and suicide: where does one end and the other begin? Our examination of Greco-Roman, Jewish, and especially Christian materials shows how complicated this question can be. Fourth, many of the suicides in ancient narratives may not be fully "conscious." Sophocles' Ajax is a good example of this: he kills himself while in a state of severe depression and agitation (Sophocles, *Ajax*). Finally, the question arises as to whether the individual equates suicide with total "self-annihilation." What if he believes in an afterlife?

Still, Shneidman and Farberow (1957) have argued that "suicidal logic" presupposes a belief in one's immortality after death. Thus a potential suicide thinks that she will be able to experience others' reactions to her death. She may think, "You'll be sorry after I kill myself." Equally destructive is the belief that the world ends with one's own death. Such a breakdown is evident in Eugene Ionesco's play *Exit the King* (1963). Here the dying King Berenger shows no investment in the future: when told by his wife that "the younger generation's expanding the universe," the king replies, "I'm dying." When he is told that they are "conquering new constellations," he again replies, "I'm dying." Finally, when he is informed that the younger generation is "boldly battering at the gates of Heaven," he responds, "They can knock them flat for all I care" (67). Berenger has lost any investment in the world beyond him.

Many of the assumptions underlying Shneidman's definition of suicide are thus tenuous. More useful for present purposes is Durkheim's definition in his classic study *Le Suicide* (1897/1951): "all cases of death resulting directly or indirectly from a positive or negative act of the victim himself, which he knows will produce this result" (44). Durkheim's inclusion of the word "indirectly" in his definition of suicide suggests that martyrs may sometimes be classified as suicides.[5] Durkheim's taxonomy of suicide types is also extremely valuable.[6] In *Le Suicide* he suggests three common types of suicide: *egoistic, altruistic,* and *anomic.*[7] Egoistic suicides are people insufficiently bonded to the society around them. Altruistic suicides lack the autonomy to differentiate themselves from the surrounding milieu. Anomic suicides occur when there is confusion or disruption in an individual's relationship to the society around him. In addition, this work suggests a nonsuicidal category (which Durkheim labels "religious") that unites the individual personality with society (336). Durkheim's thinking seems overly influenced by outmoded utopian idealism, and his reference to religion is vague. Nevertheless, he seems to be groping toward the possibility of a category where there is unity or congruence between *individuation* and *attachment.*

---

5. In contrast, van Hooff (1990) has not counted martyrs "as self-killers because they cause their own deaths indirectly" (54).

6. A number of other classification systems of different types and motives for suicide have emerged in the professional literature over the past century (Douglas 1967; Shneidman 1968; Baechler 1979; Hill 1983).

7. Durkheim also suggested a fourth, "rare" kind of *fatalistic* suicide, which is likely to occur when there is excessive regulation and rigidity in an individual's relationship to the society around him.

An understanding of the processes of individuation and attachment is essential to the problem of healthy versus pathological human development and specifically to the problems of suicide and suicide prevention. The dimension of individuation–deindividuation refers to the degree to which an individual can stand on her own two feet — that is, can show autonomous or independent thought, feeling, and action. An individuated person is separated or differentiated from those around her but is not necessarily isolated from them. (Figure 1.1 denotes this person as having a strong or articulated self-definition or ego boundary thus — O.) A deindividuated person, by contrast, is not capable of independent thought, feeling, and action and is not separated or differentiated from those around him (Figure 1.1 denotes this person as having a weak or inarticulated self-definition or ego boundary thus — ☺.)

The attachment–detachment dimension describes the degree to which an individual can extend her hand to another — that is, can show a capacity for bonding or cooperating with others in thought, feeling, and action. An attached individual is integrated or involved with those around her but is not necessarily enmeshed with them. (This person is represented as having a permeable or flexible defensive structure or wall ⬚.) A detached individual, in contrast, is not integrated or involved with those around him (he is denoted by an impermeable or rigid defensive structure or wall □).

These two dimensions should be seen as separate and independent of one another. A number of different positions are visible in this drawing and may be placed on one of two axes. The first, labeled the AC axis (Figure 1.2) throughout this book, represents fixation and a pathological incongruence or disintegration between individuation and attachment. The suicide of an individual at position A is, by Durkheim's definition, "altruistic" — a suicide insufficiently differentiated from the environment around him. Position C, in contrast, represents Durkheim's "egoistic" suicide — an individual insufficiently integrated with her environment. An "anomic" suicide is represented by position A/C, an afflicted individual torn between enmeshment and disengagement. Someone fixated on this AC clinical axis cannot move ahead in development, but oscillates or cycles between one unsatisfactory alternative and another, and ultimately settles in a conflicted "split" position (Markus-Kaplan and Kaplan 1984; Kaplan 1988; Kaplan and Worth 1992-1993; Kaplan and O'Connor, 1993).

The second axis, labeled BED (see Figure 1.3), represents healthy congruence or integration between individuation and attachment. Positions B,

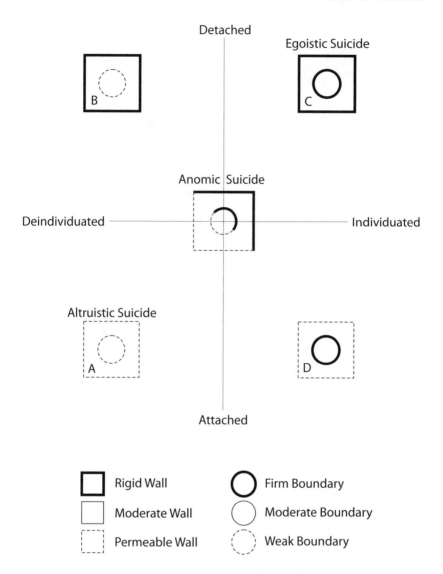

Figure 1.1
A Bidimensional Distancing Representation of Suicide Types

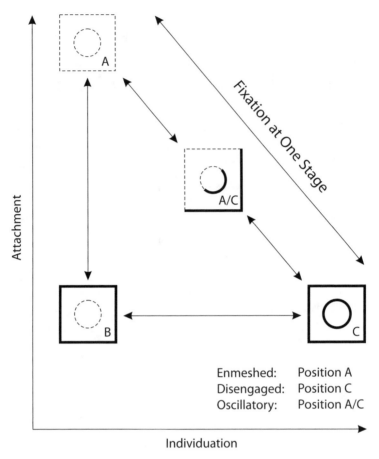

Figure 1.2
The Individual Clinical Axis

E, and D denote levels of developmental progression along a maturity dimension at a given life stage. Level B represents an individual not sufficiently differentiated from others to integrate with them. This position, if
permanent, has aspects of Durkheim's fatalistic suicide (see chap. 1, n. 3). As
a temporary position, however, this B level may actually represent a
suicide-preventive haven from the AC axis. Such protection allows the individual to mature at his own pace through E (a state of semi-individuation
— O — and semi-attachment — □) to D (a state of full individuation and
attachment). D, of course, represents exactly the nonsuicidal position that

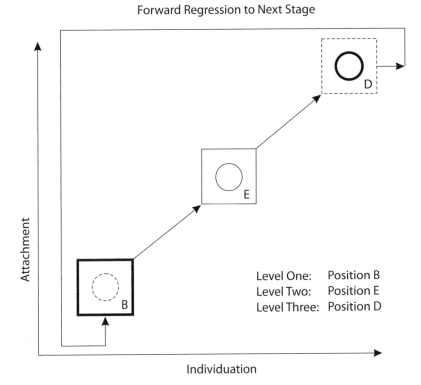

Forward Regression to Next Stage

Level One: Position B
Level Two: Position E
Level Three: Position D

Figure 1.3
The Individual Developmental Axis

Durkheim seems to have been groping for in his aforementioned attempt to define a religious, nonsuicidal position.[8]

We have come to see the entire BED axis as a suicide-preventive and thus life-promoting alternative to the suicidal AC axis. Individuation and attachment are congruent and integrated rather than incongruent and disintegrated. This book will attempt to demonstrate that the suicide-preventive BED axis emerges from the biblical, covenantal perspective. This perspective contrasts with the suicide-promoting AC axis, which, we argue, emerges from the classical (Greco-Roman) narcissistic culture.

8. As we have mentioned above (in the Introduction, note 5), this conception corresponds to Anna Freud's conception of "regression in the service of development," and the colloquial expression "going one step backward for every two steps forward."

2. Suicide in Greco-Roman Thought

Those who pursue philosophy aright study nothing but dying and being dead.

Socrates, *Phaedo,* 64a

For, if pure knowledge is impossible while the body is with us, one of two things must follow, either it cannot be acquired at all or only when we are dead; for then the soul will be by itself apart from the body, but not before.

Socrates, *Phaedo,* 68d

You see that yawning precipice? It leads to liberty. You see that flood, that river, that well? Liberty houses within them. You see that stunted, parched, and sorry tree? From each branch, liberty hangs. Your neck, your throat, your heart are so many ways of escape from slavery. . . . Do you inquire the road to freedom? You shall find it in every vein of your body.

Seneca, *De Ira,* 3.15.3-4

The philosopher may choose his own mode of death as he chooses a ship or a house. He leaves life as he would a banquet — when it is time.

Seneca, *Epistle,* 70.11

Many famous individuals took their own lives in ancient Greece and Rome. John Donne lists three pages of suicides in his *Biathanatos*. The works of ancient biographers such as Plutarch and Diogenes Laertius recount many suicide tales: Pythagoras, Socrates, Zeno, Demosthenes, the statesman Marc Antony, Seneca and his wife, Paulina, and many more. In addition, Greco-Roman literature provides a number of examples of collective suicide in the ancient world, in which men slaughtered their families and then themselves. Cohen (1982) has discussed sixteen Greco-Roman accounts of mass suicides. However, only one of these cases involved the Greeks themselves: the Phocians' nonactualized pact to slay their families and free themselves in order to avoid capture by the Thessalians in the 480s BCE (Pausanias 10.1.6-9). One other involved the Romans: the inhabitants of the city of Norba set fire to the city and slew themselves after being betrayed to Aemilius Lepidus in 82-81 BCE (Appian, *Civil War*, 1.94). Six cases concerned townspeople in Asia Minor, and eight instances involved "barbarians."[1] In any event, certain ideas and perceptions in Greek and Roman life tended to make suicide a suitable action.[2]

The Homeric Period

The Epic Hero

The epic hero of the Homeric period is consumed by the search for glory. A prime example is Achilles, who achieves greatness by slaying Trojans, particularly Hector, their great prince. Achilles does this even though he knows via a prophecy that slaying Hector will hasten his own death (Homer, *Iliad*, 18.95-96). Ajax, perhaps the second greatest warrior in the Achaean host before Troy, kills himself out of shame after recovering from

1. S. J. D. Cohen's (1982) list of suicides includes Xanthians, Cappadocians, Isaurians, Abydenes, Taochians, Sidonians, Gauls, Illyrians, and four instances by Spaniards, including the people of Sagantum, the Astapaeans, tribesmen of Vaccaei, and citizens of Numantai.

2. The German classicist R. Hirzel (1908) attempted to impose order on some of these data. He suggested that the Homeric period was not especially plagued by suicide — this despite a strong sense of the heroic. Suicidal thoughts, argued Hirzel, did emerge as a problem during the times of political upheaval in the first millennium BCE. The fifth century BCE, however, produced a veritable epidemic of suicides. Hirzel suggested that this period combined pessimism with an extreme cult of individualism.

a fit of madness when he is judged the loser in an athletic contest with Odysseus (Sophocles, *Ajax*). Generally, the *Iliad*, like most epics, glories in describing how warriors destroy each other in the field of battle, cleaving and hacking each other's flesh and bones, piling corpses all around them.

In Homer's world, the warrior-hero is the loftiest of individual types. Though always a nobleman and often descended from a god, the warrior-hero is fundamentally flawed and can never really win. Ultimately, no amount of heroism is enough, no pinnacle of glory is sufficient to bring him satisfaction or give any value to his life. In the last book of the *Iliad*, Achilles is reduced to tears by the seeming pointlessness of his life (24.505). Other Achaean heroes also come to unhappy ends. Agamemnon returns home to be brutally murdered by his wife, Clytemnestra, and her lover, Aegisthus. Ajax the Lesser is punished by the gods after he rapes the prophetess Cassandra on the altar of Zeus. Odysseus wanders the seas for ten years, consumed by a terrible homesickness (Homer, *Odyssey*, 1.59), until he finally reaches his homeland, Ithaca. And his wife, Penelope, also suffers from the heroic trap of Odysseus. Though Hirzel (1908, 884) makes much of the fact that neither Penelope nor Odysseus commits suicide to end the anguish, it is significant that Penelope begs the gods to give her death to preserve her faithfulness to her husband (*Odyssey*, 26.61). In addition, Homer portrays Hades as a place of horror. The *Odyssey* offers the scene of the shades of heroes lapping blood and speaking of their miseries (*Odyssey*, 11).

One can achieve success and recognition in the Homeric world only by means of heroism and competition, but the heroic life typically ends in miserable destruction. A good example of the potentially suicidal aspect of heroism lies in the legend that the coach of the first American Olympic team told his athletes in Athens in 1896. The legend he recounted was that of the already spent runner Pheidippides, who ran twenty-six miles from the battlefield of Marathon to the city of Athens to give the news of the Athenian victory and to warn the Athenians of a possible Persian naval attack directly on the city. After blurting out the story, he fell dead of exhaustion. One must wonder why Pheidippides ran himself to death rather than take a horse, as did Paul Revere, who was carrying a more pressing message, 2300 years later.[3]

---

3. In fact, the Pheidippides story first appears about six centuries after the Battle of Marathon, and there appears to be no evidence for its historicity; so the story may be entirely fictitious (Hooper 1967, 159).

Finley (1959, 128-29) has pointed out that the Greeks extended the idea of competition from the realm of physical prowess to that of intellect, poetry, and dramatic composition. "The Greeks used to stage contests in everything that offered the bare possibility of a fight" (Huizinga 1955, 73). Slater (1968, 36) has argued that nothing had meaning for the Greeks unless it involved the defeat of an opponent. A number of factors in Homeric thought contribute to this pattern. The hero is more than a great but tragic warrior; his behavioral pattern also seems to contain a strain of sadomasochism. As powerful and destructive as he is on the field of battle, he is more essentially a passive-aggressive personality. The first episode of the *Iliad* describes how Achilles refuses to go into battle after the general of the Greek forces, Agamemnon, takes a captured slave girl from him. The theme of that epic poem is expressed in its very first line: "Sing muse of the wrath of Achilles."

The hero typically brings misery on himself by his own acts. For example, Theseus reacts in haste to a false message and curses his innocent son, Hippolytus; soon after that, Hippolytus is killed when he is thrown from his chariot. In another myth, King Aegeus of Athens hastily jumps into the sea and drowns when wrongly convinced that his son, Theseus, has been slain by the Minotaur. Similarly Erigone hangs herself after discovering the murdered body of her father, Icarius.

These kinds of stories are manifold in Greek literature. However, the great problem is not that Greek heroes make errors; rather, it is that there seems to be no recourse, no way out of the so-called heroic pattern. Even worse, though the errors often seem to be quite minor and accidental, they spell a pattern of doom. There is no stopper in Greek society — no way out. If this view is carried to its ultimate, especially for a serious thinker, the most logical conclusion of human life is suicide.

The Classical Period

Suicidologist Henry Romilly Fedden (1938, 70-85) has placed Greek attitudes toward suicide into three camps: Pythagoras, Aristotle, and the Epicureans were opposed to it; Plato and Socrates took a guarded middle position; and the Cynics and Stoics accepted it. Although this view is oversimplified, it provides an acceptable beginning for a discussion of these schools of thought.

17

Pythagoras

Athenaeus (prominent around 200 CE) declares the Pythagorean position as follows:

> . . . that the souls of all men were bound in the body, and in the life which is on earth, for the sake of punishment. . . . On which account all men, being afraid of those threatenings of the gods, fear to depart from life by their own act, but only gladly welcome death when it comes in old age. (Athenaeus, *The Deipnosophists,* 2.216)

For the Pythagoreans, suicide is a rebellion against an almost mathematical discipline set by the gods. Death comes when it should, and at that time it can be welcomed. There is a set number of souls, according to Pythagoras, that is available in the world at any one time. Killing oneself creates a gap by upsetting this mathematical equilibrium, and thus we must reject it. Despite this philosophy, several accounts portrayed Pythagoras as letting himself be killed or actively committing suicide. According to one account, Pythagoras allowed pursuers to catch and kill him in preference to trampling on a field of beans (Diogenes Laertius, 8.45).

Socrates and Plato

Three general themes in the teachings of Socrates eased the road to suicide in the classical period. First, he made several references to the nature of the afterworld. For Socrates, Hades (if it existed at all) was not so frightening a place as it was to the Homeric hero. In the closing section of Plato's *Apology* (41a-42a), Socrates asks rhetorically:

> If on arrival in the other world, beyond the reach of our so-called justice, one will find there the true judges who are said to preside in those courts, Minos and Rhadamanthes and Aeacus and Triptolemus . . . to meet Orpheus and Musaeus, Hesiod and Homer . . . would that be an unrewarding journey? . . . What would one not give . . . to be able to question the leader of that great host against Troy, or Odysseus, or Sisyphus?

At the conclusion of Plato's *Republic*, Socrates recounts the myth of Er, which describes the wonderful gifts and rewards awaiting the good man in the life after death (*Republic*, 10.3; 1.614).

Second, the idealized harmony of humans that is evident in the statues of classical Greece gave way in Plato's thinking to a sense that the relationship between body and soul is conflictual and unfortunate. "The soul is a helpless prisoner chained hand and foot in the body compelled to view reality not directly but only through its prison bars, and wallowing in utter ignorance" (*Phaedo*, 83a). The evil acts of the body pollute the soul by preventing the soul from achieving a complete and clean separation and returning to the world of "Ideal Forms." Only the soul can perceive "Ideal Truth," but it cannot do so as long as it must perceive reality through the use of the five bodily senses. Thus, the real attainment of truth can come only in the higher world when souls can perceive directly — without the interference of the body. This position does not necessarily lead to a direct call to suicide, but it does foster a habit of thought that belittles earthly life and encourages the philosopher to believe that separation from earthly life is the only road to the "Ideal" human existence.

The third point that may have facilitated suicide was Socrates' general view, which he expressed in different forms on a number of occasions, that philosophy is "preparation for death." While awaiting execution after his trial, Socrates maintains in an argument to Simmias and Cebes:

> Other people are likely not to be aware that those who pursue philosophy aright study nothing but dying and being dead. Now if this is true, it would be absurd to be eager for nothing but this all their lives, and then to be troubled when that came for which they had all along been eagerly practicing. (*Phaedo*, 64a)

In a subsequent passage, Socrates again says that philosophers desire death, even though people do not understand why: "For they do not know in what way the real philosophers desire death, nor in what way they deserve death" (*Phaedo*, 64b). Later in this dialogue, Socrates explains that death frees the soul:

> For, if pure knowledge is impossible while the body is with us, one of two things must follow. Either it cannot be acquired at all or only when

we are dead: for then the soul will be by itself apart from the body, but not before. (*Phaedo,* 66e)

True philosophers practice dying and thus fear death less than other people do (*Phaedo,* 68a). The argument continues along the line that, unlike the ordinary person, the philosopher understands that death is not a great evil. "You know, do you not, that all other men count death among the great evils" (*Phaedo,* 68d). Given the concern with death as compared to life, it seems only a short step for Cebes to ask Socrates what the grounds are for saying that suicide is not legitimate (*Phaedo,* 62a). Socrates concedes Cebes's point (*Phaedo,* 62b) and gives the famous guard-post allegory as an argument against suicide. Life is a sorry business, but we must not leave our guard-post unless we are relieved:

> We men are put in a sort of guard-post, from which one must not release one's self or run away . . . the gods are our keepers, and we men are one of their possessions. . . . If one of your possessions were to destroy itself without intimation from you that you wanted it to die, wouldn't you be angry with it and punish it, if you had any means of doing so? . . . So if you look at it this way I suppose it is not unreasonable to say that we must not put an end to ourselves until God sends some compulsion like the one which we are facing now. (*Phaedo,* 62b-c)

The *Phaedo* is hardly a ringing endorsement of life; indeed, it is said to have inspired the suicides of King Cleombrotus of the Spartans and of the Roman Cato.

There is no question that Plato expressed different ideas about suicide in different writings. On the one hand, he called for the denial of a regular burial for a suicide (*Laws,* 9.12). On the other hand, at least according to Olympiodorus, Plato seemed to admit that "suicide may be proper to the worthy man, to him of a middle character, and to the multitude and depraved." To the worthy person, as in the *Phaedo* (62b-c); to one of a middle character, as in *The Republic* (3.406d), if he "is afflicted with a long and incurable disease, as being useless to the city"; and to the vulgar character, as in *The Laws* (8.838), if he is "possessed with certain incurable passions, such as being enamored of his mother . . . and who is incapable of governing himself" (Plotinus, *On Suicide,* 1a).[4]

This view generally permeated Socrates' reaction at his trial. In his concluding speech to the jury after his conviction for atheism and for corrupting the minds of the youth of Athens, Socrates describes death in a speech that may remind us of Hamlet's soliloquy:

> Death is one of two things . . . like a sleep in which the sleeper does not even dream, death would be a wonderful gain. For I think if anyone were to pick out that night in which he slept a dreamless sleep and, comparing with it the other nights and days of his life, were to say after due consideration, how many days and nights in his life had passed more pleasantly than that night . . . if death is, as it were, a change of habitation from here to some other place, and if what we are told is true, that all the dead are there, what greater blessing could there be, judges? (Plato, *Apology,* 40c-e)

That this speech is not simply Socrates in denial and rationalizing about his own upcoming death is supported by an earlier statement he makes before he knows that he will be convicted.

> For to fear death, gentlemen, is nothing else than to think one is wise when one is not: for it is thinking one knows when one does not know. For no one knows whether death be not even the greatest of all blessings to man, but they fear it as if they knew that it is the greatest of evils. (Plato, *Apology,* 29a)

Socrates' disciple Xenophon says that Socrates was gerophobic and feared the suffering of old age: "I know I must now suffer evils of old age, sight, hearing, learning slow, and forgetfulness. If I am discontent in life, where can I find any pleasure in continuing to live?" (Xenophon, *Apology,* 6) The trial seemed to be a golden opportunity to terminate his life "not only at a proper season but in the easiest manner" (*Apology,* 7).

Xenophon pointed out two curious aspects of Socrates' defense plea. First, Socrates seemed to go out of his way to antagonize the jury by boast-

---

4. Is Plato suggesting here a relationship between suicide and unresolved Oedipal conflicts? We take up this subject in chapters 8 and 9 below.

ing that the oracle at Delphi had termed him the wisest of men (*Apology*, 14). Second, he further angered the jury by proposing as his penalty free meals at the city hall rather than a fine (*Apology*, 23, n. 1). This served to push the jury to vote for the death penalty. Clearly, Socrates "thought that the proper time was then come for him to die." Seeing his friends weeping after the trial, Socrates said to them: "How is this? Do you now weep? Do you not know that from the moment I was born, death was decreed for me by nature?" (27).

It would be difficult to find a person with a greater *joie de vivre* than Socrates. Still, he seems to have epitomized Greek thinking in his view of death. All of his life is only to die; all of philosophy is but preparation for death. Indeed, life is permeated and clouded over by the inevitability of death. Xenophon offered his view of Socrates' trial in his usual direct, matter-of-fact style: he completely agreed with Socrates that at that point "to die was better for him than to live" (Xenophon, *Apology*, 31).[5]

Aristotle

Aristotle seemed less obsessed with the idea of suicide than Plato, his mentor, was; the subject occupies only a few lines in his many extant writings. He argues that, for certain reasons, suicide is the act of a coward: for example, suicide as an escape from "poverty or disappointed love or bodily or mental anguish is the deed of a coward. . . . The suicide braves death not for some noble object but to escape ill" (*Ethics*, 3.7). Aristotle adds that suicide is an injustice against the state, which the state may punish. Unlike Socrates' allegory in the *Phaedo*, Aristotle does not mention that humans are the property of the gods, but only as obligated to the state.

> But the man who cuts his throat in a fit of temper is voluntarily doing an injury which the law does not allow. It follows that the suicide commits an injustice. But against whom? Is it not the State rather than himself? For he suffers of his own volition, and nobody suffers injustice voluntarily. It is for this reason that the State attaches a penalty, which takes the form of a stigma put on one who has destroyed himself, on the ground that he is guilty of the offense against the State. (*Ethics*, 5.11)

5. See I. F. Stone, *The Trial of Socrates* (1988).

Durkheim (1897/1951, 329-32) argues that Aristotle is the key to understanding the Greek laws on suicide. Suicide is illegal when it is not authorized by the state and legal when it is so authorized.

Greek Law

In Athens, Cyprus, and Thebes, a suicide was denied regular burial; furthermore, the hand (seen as alien to the body) was cut off and buried separately, a practice that perhaps originated in some primitive superstition. This rule was even more severe in Sparta (Aeschines, *Against Ctesiphon,* 244.8; Plato, *Laws,* 9.12; Dio Chrysostom, *Orations,* 4.14). On the other hand, suicide was tolerated and even assisted when it had received prior state approval. In Athens, as well as in Massilia and Ceos, such a suicide was actually supplied with hemlock (Valerius Maximus, 2, 6.7-8). According to Libanius (quoted by Durkheim), the laws in Athens read as follows:

> Whosoever no longer wishes to live shall state his reasons to the Senate: and after having received permission shall abandon life. If your existence is hateful to you, die; if you are overwhelmed by fate, drink the hemlock. If you are bowed with grief, abandon life. Let the unhappy man recount his misfortune, let the magistrate supply him with the remedy, and his wretchedness will come to an end.

The Greek views of suicide were related to their attitudes toward life, death, and freedom. For Plato, death represented "the entry to the far superior world of Ideals compared to which earthly reality is a mere shadow." Therefore, suicide was never far from the surface, and attempts at suicide prevention were ambivalent. Humans were the chattel of the gods or the state, but when the state allowed it, suicide was permitted and even abetted.

Hellenistic Philosophers

Although there was no single monolithic doctrine on suicide in the later Greco-Roman philosophical traditions, it is clear that suicide was widely accepted as within the limits of normal options. We have already mentioned that some of the greatest names in Hellenistic philosophy are reported to have committed suicide. Let us discuss some of these.

Diogenes, the founder of the school of Cynicism, voluntarily held his breath until he died (Diogenes Laertius, 6.76). Zeno, the founder of Stoicism, did the same after wrenching his toe (7.28). Cleanthes, Zeno's successor, was told by doctors to fast for two days for a tooth ailment, but he continued his fast so that he could experience the entire passage to death (7.176). It is usual in these accounts for suicide to seem an almost normal response to discouraging circumstances or even to some relatively minor imperfection. To fail to commit suicide seemed a display of bad character, certainly a lack of heroism. Indeed, Zeno the Stoic counseled suicide as a reasonable end for a wise man (7.130).

This rash of philosophical suicides seems to have been associated with a generally pessimistic view of human existence. The human being is not an exalted creation; and the gods are limited in power and not loving to man. Fear of the seemingly unavoidable changes in the cycle of life pushes people to destruction and oblivion, no matter how great their accomplishments are. There is a fatalistic preoccupation with the end of life in a hostile universe.

Plotinus: The Neoplatonist

Plotinus, the third-century (CE) neo-Platonist, agreed with Plato's view that death is to be welcomed by the philosopher, but not sought before its proper time: "You should not expel the soul from the body. For in departing, it will retain something (of the more passive life), which is necessary in this case to its departure" (Plotinus, *On Suicide*, 1.9). Plotinus followed Plato in suggesting that there may indeed be times when suicide becomes necessary: "The soul is not to be separated from the body while a further proficiency is yet possible." Porphyry noted that when he himself was contemplating suicide, Plotinus convinced him that it was not a rational decision but was based on too much black bile.

The Cynics

Beginning with Diogenes of Sinope, the Cynic school taught the importance of living simply and renouncing all attachments. They lived as wandering beggars with no possessions of their own, maintaining the sparest of dress and diet.

> Poor to begin with, or renouncing their property voluntarily they lived as beggars. Possessing no houses of their own, they passed the day in the streets, or in other public places; the nights they spent in porticos, or wherever else chance might find them. Furniture they had none. A bed seemed superfluous. The simple Greek dress was by them made still simpler. . . . In scantiness of diet, they even surpassed the very limited requirements of their countrymen. (Zeller 1885, 317-18)

Diogenes undertook self-mortification when his teacher was not sufficiently severe. The Cynics tended to welcome reproaches from enemies, on the grounds that they teach people to know themselves and to amend their faults. Should life become unsupportable, they reserved for themselves the right of suicide. When the seriously ill Antisthenes cried out, "Who will release me from these pains?" Diogenes answered, "This," and showed him a dagger. "I said," replied Antisthenes, "from my pains, not from life." About this, Diogenes Laertius commented: "It was thought that he showed some weakness in leaving his malady through love of life" (Diogenes Laertius, 6.18). Although there are contradictory accounts, Diogenes Laertius reported that Diogenes committed suicide by holding his breath (6.76), as did two later Cynics, Metrocles (6.95) and Menippus (6.100). Perhaps the most striking example of a Cynic suicide is that of Peregrinus, who cast himself into a pyre erected at the Olympic festival. Halliday (1970) has considered the death of Peregrinus as an instance of the same passion for martyrdom that was exhibited in early Christianity.

The Epicureans

The Epicureans operated according to a moderate pleasure principle. Epicurus, the father of Epicureanism, put it simply: "Pleasure is the beginning and end of living happily" (Diogenes Laertius, 10.128). On the surface, Epicurus seems to have been indifferent to questions of death and suicide: "Death is nothing to us, since when we are, death has not come, and when death has come, we are not" (10.125). At times, he seems to have been opposed to suicide: "The wise man will not withdraw himself from life"

(10.120). But close examination indicates a somewhat more complicated position. Epicurus defined happiness in terms of internal rather than external states. Whereas Plato justified suicide under intolerable external circumstances, Epicurus seemed to do so in terms of avoiding internal suffering. Self-sufficiency does not consist of using little, but in needing little. One thereby gains freedom, which adds to the enjoyment of life. A self-sufficient person should have no reason to destroy herself, but she might do so if there is no other way to avoid unendurable suffering (Cicero, *De Finibus*, 15-49). Still, Epicurus was no less severe with those who desired death than with those who feared it. Seneca (*Epistle*, 24.23) quoted Epicurus thus: "It's ridiculous to run to death through weariness of life when it's by your manner of life that you've forced yourself to run to death." In another passage in the same epistle, he quotes Epicurus as saying, "Can anything be more ridiculous than to seek death when it's by fear of death that you've destroyed your peace in life?" One may add a third saying to those two: "Such is the blindness, nay, the insanity of death that some men are driven to death by the fear of it" (Seneca, *Ep.*, 24.24).

Unlike Epicurus, Hegesias of Cyrene concluded that life contains more pain than pleasure; therefore, the only logical outcome is suicide. The "preacher of death" argued his viewpoint so well, according to Cicero, that a wave of suicides took place in Alexandria, and Ptolemy II had to banish Hegesias from the land (Cicero, *Tusc. Disp.*, 1.34.83).

The Stoics

The Stoics seemed to regard neither life nor death as very important. At the same time, they seemed almost obsessed with the idea of suicide as a way of overcoming their fear of death. In a sense, the Stoics attempted to conquer death by choosing it on their own terms. At best, the philosopher should commit suicide not to escape suffering but to avoid restrictions in carrying out life, since he should be as unaffected by suffering as by any other emotions.

A central problem prompting the Stoic view of life was a pervasive fear of a loss of control — ultimately, control over life itself. For the Stoics, cheerfulness was a philosophical duty, not an indication of natural optimism. The Stoics did not accept the idea of a caring and loving deity, and they were also too deep as thinkers to place much permanent value on so limited a prospect as human success. They knew that they must fulfill their moral and social duty, but they could never desire reward, recognition, or love, and could never even feel secure that their good acts would produce a good result.

Zeno, the founder of the Stoic school, defined the goal of life as living in agreement with nature (Diogenes Laertius, 7.87). If such an agreement exists, life is good; if it does not exist, suicide becomes the wise choice (7.130). Therefore, Zeno was said to have killed himself out of sheer irritation (perhaps because of imperfection itself) when he wrenched his toe by stumbling on his way home from the stoa. He held his breath until he died (7.20). His successor, Cleanthes, fasted to death. Initially, he fasted to cure a boil on his gum; ultimately, however, "he had advanced so far on his journey toward death, he would not retreat," and he starved himself to death (7.176).

The Roman Stoics basically agreed with their earlier Greek counterparts — with one important shift. The question, as Alvarez (1970, 62) has suggested, was no longer whether to kill oneself when the inner compulsion became irresistible, but how to do so in the right way. This attribute can be seen in a sampling of the writings of Cicero. Suicide, Cicero argues, is no great evil.

> When a man's circumstances contain a preponderance of things in accordance with nature, it is appropriate for him to remain alive: when he possesses or sees in prospect a majority of the contrary things, it is appropriate for the wise man to quit life, although he is happy, and also for the foolish man to remain in life although he is miserable. . . . And very often it is appropriate for the wise man to abandon life at a moment when he is enjoying supreme happiness, if an opportunity offers for making a timely exit. For the Stoic view is that happiness, which means life in harmony with nature, is a matter of seizing the right moment. So that Wisdom her very self upon occasion bids the wise man to leave her. (*De Finibus,* 3.60 and 61)

According to Cicero, "appropriate" means "in accordance with nature, as is self-love"; thus suicide is useful to the wise man.

In the *Tusculan Disputations,* Cicero depicts death as freeing humans from chains. The gods in their benevolence have prepared for humans a haven and refuge after their departure from worldly life (1.18). Some philosophers disagreed with this, and some Stoics even felt that the soul is not immortal. Indeed, while earthly life is not wholly evil, the afterlife holds far more joy (1.84).

Cicero cites the deaths of Socrates and Cato as examples that suicide is permissible, but only when the gods themselves have given a valid reason. One must not break the prison bonds except in obedience to the magistrate. The human soul should be dissociated from the body during life by means of philosophy and virtue, for such a life will best prepare the soul for the afterlife. It is highly desirable for one to quit the sorrows of this world to gain the joys of the next (1.71-75).

Much the same view can be seen in a sampling of the declamations of the elder Seneca (ca. 40 CE). These declamations were a series of arguments on a variety of subjects and were widely used as training for law students. Whatever may have been the various opinions in individual cases, it is clear that suicide was hardly shocking to either the speakers or the listeners.

A man whose wife and three children have died in a fire tries to hang himself, but he is cut down and saved by a passerby. Is the passerby guilty of an offense? The passerby argues that a person must have hope and that, in any case, if the man had truly wanted to hang himself, he should have done so immediately after the fire. The accuser argues: "It is a wrong done me if I have to die at your will when I should have died at mine." The one who attempted suicide is not accused; rather, the one who stopped him is accused (Seneca, *Controversiae*, 5.1).

Should a suicide be allowed a burial? One speaker argues for burial on the grounds that "death should be undisturbed. There is equal cruelty in killing those who wish to live and forcing life on those who wish to die." The opposition argues that burial for a suicide is an outrage: "Some guilty conscience made him take refuge in death; one of his crimes is that he cannot be convicted. . . . One capable of killing himself might have dared anything" (Seneca, *Controversiae*, 8.4).

In this case also, suicide is not criminal because it is immoral or because it destroys human life; rather, the criminal act is that the suicide upsets the judicial processes or that it seems to show bad character on the part of the suicide. For example, a tyrant orders two sons to beat their father. At the command, one son leaps to his death; the other son beats the father, but later he kills the tyrant. One opinion on the former brother's suicide is this: "This is not sparing one's father — it's sparing oneself." The discussion focuses on the question of the extent to which one should obey a tyrant (Seneca, *Controversiae*, 9.4).

A curious story appears in the preface to Book 10 of *Controversiae*, in the form of a letter addressed by the elder Seneca to his sons regarding Titus Labienus, a writer whose books were burned by his enemies: "Labienus did not take this insult lying down, nor did he wish to outlive his genius. He had himself carried to the tombs of his ancestors and walled up. . . . [H]e not only finished his life, he buried himself" (Seneca, *Controversiae*, 10: preface).

Suicide is also a major subject in the letters of Lucius Anneaus Seneca, the brilliant Roman writer and statesman. The younger Seneca's writings show a deep concern and awareness of death. Man is always no more "than a moment ahead of the universal doom" (Seneca, *Ep.*, 71.15). Hope for the betterment of the human condition is false. "Truth doesn't grow and neither does virtue" (*Ep.*, 71.16). One must continue to try but not because there is any hope of success. Pacurius held his own wake every night, believing that anyone who can say "my life is lived" rises daily from his bed to a sense of something gained (*Ep.*, 12.8-10).

One may hope for good but must always be prepared for the worst. People discover too late that they "stand in the shadow of death, of exile and suffering" (*Ep.*, 24.12-15). The thinking man does well to feel terror before so dire a fate. Death provides a release from these horrors. Every day we stand nearer the end; every hour urges us toward the bank from which we must fall. One should not be afraid to leave the present field of action (120). Death is so far from being terrible that "by its grace all things lose their terrors." For Seneca, it seems, life is what is terrifying and death is what provides release (24).

According to the younger Seneca, the events of earthly existence are paltry and not worth any emotional involvement. The questions of who wins the Battle of Pharsalus or an election are insignificant (Seneca, *Ep.*, 71). A person may leave the world if he feels that he has overstayed his welcome (120). The human body is an unpleasantness to be endured only as long as one wishes, and when one thinks fit, one may dissolve the partnership with this puny clay (65.22).

The Stoic felt bound by necessity and sought a sense of freedom and release. In this area, among others, the philosophy of Stoicism seems to suffer from a sort of constipation. One should escape from this life whenever she chooses, and she should die when the means are at hand: "Choose any part of nature and tell it to let you out" (Seneca, *Ep.*, 117.23-24). One should pick the means by which to quit life, for the option of suicide leaves the road to freedom open. To grumble is pointless, since life holds no one fast. "Do you like life, then live on. Do you dislike it? Then you're free to return to the place you came from" (70.15). The philosopher may choose his own mode of death just as he chooses a ship or a house. He leaves life as he would a banquet — when it is time (*Ep.*, 70.11; Plotinus, *On Suicide*, 1.9).

Stoicism always emphasized duty and derogated pleasure and passion. While reason is good, emotion is evil. Pleasure is best deferred. Apples taste sweetest when they are going rotten. The drinker drinks the last draft — the wave that drowns his senses — and puts the finishing touch on his drunken bliss. Every pleasure defers its most intense thrill to the last (*Ep.*, 12).

Consequently, death is not to be viewed as an evil, and suicide is suitable. Nonetheless, suicide should not be an act of passion or emotion. Whether one dies badly or well — in the manner of a philosopher — is the important point (*Ep.*, 70.5-6). Seneca would not destroy himself merely to avoid pain, for the philosopher must be above pain: "I shall make my exit, not because of actual pain but because the pain is likely to prove a burr to everything that makes life worthwhile" (58.36). The person who dies because of pain is weak; the person who lives to suffer is a fool. Ultimately, a person is not trapped:

> You see that yawning precipice? It leads to liberty. You see that flood, that river, that well? Liberty houses within them. You see that stunted, parched, and sorry tree? From each branch, liberty hangs. Your neck, your throat, your heart are so many ways of escape from slavery. . . . Do you inquire the road to freedom? You shall find it in every vein of your body. (Seneca, *De Ira*, 3.15.3-4)

Seneca and his wife, Paulina, put these thoughts into action, calmly cutting their wrists at the order of the Emperor Nero, Seneca's former student. This consistency between thought and action the younger Seneca also exemplified in the advice he gave to the incurably ill Marcellinus, who was contemplating — and ultimately did commit — suicide.

> Be not tormented, my Marcellinus, as if you were deliberating any great matter. Life is a thing of no dignity or importance. Your very

slaves, your animals possess it in common with yourself, but it is a great thing to die honorably, prudently, bravely. Think how long you have been engaged in the same dull course: eating, sleeping, and indulging your appetites. This has been the circle. Not only a prudent, brave, or a wretched man may wish to die, but even a fastidious one. (Seneca, *Ep.*, 77.6)

Epictetus, another major Roman Stoic writer, lived as a slave during the first century CE. He did not view suicide as a criminal act either.

If Thou dost send me to a place where men cannot live as their nature requires. I shall go away, not in disobedience but believing that Thou dost sound the note for my retreat. I do not abandon Thee, heaven forbid! But I recognize that Thou hast no need of me. (Epictetus, *Discourses*, 3.24)

A sufficient degree of unpleasantness in one's existence indicates that the gods no longer need him and that it is time to make one's departure (3.24).

A person may simply decide that he "will not play the game anymore." Epictetus saw human life as of little account and hardly worth preserving: "Thou art a little soul bearing about a course" (10.41). Still, suicide must not be performed frivolously:

Only let me not give up my heart faintheartedly or from some casual pretext. For again, God does not so desire; for he has need of such a universe and of such men who go to and fro upon earth. But if he gives the signal to retreat as he did to Socrates, I must obey him who gives the signal, as I would a general.[6] (1.29)

---

6. Droge and Tabor (1992, 29-39) have found a precedent for rational suicide in this passage. Voluntary suicide is condoned when it is necessary *(ananke)* and rational; it is condemned when it is irrational. A rational suicide receives a divine signal that the time to die is at hand. "For the stoics the cosmic deity was the Logos of which human reason was a part. An individual's logos, therefore would allow him to determine the divinely (or more strictly rationally) appointed time for his exit from life" (32). In other words, Zeno killed himself by holding his breath, not because he broke his toe, but because he thought that this event represented the divine signal to depart (31). While provocative, this line of historical reasoning is highly speculative. By Droge and Tabor's own admission, there is nothing in the account preserved by Diogenes Laertius that supports this theory explicitly. Furthermore, even if

Marcus Aurelius, emperor of Rome from 162 to 181 CE, is famed for his *Meditations,* a classic text of Stoic thinking. To Marcus, the only evil in suicide is doing it in passion — emotionally. Indeed, "[i]f you cannot maintain rationality, equanimity, magnanimity . . . depart at once from life not in passion but with simplicity, freedom, modesty after doing this one laudable thing at least in thy life to have gone out of it thus" (Marcus Aurelius, *Meditations,* 10.8). If one is too restricted, "then get away out of life, yet so as if thou went suffering no harm. Why dost thou think that this is any trouble?" (5.29). If circumstances cause the loss of one's self-control, then it is not worthwhile to live, and it is in one's power to wipe out this judgment (8.47). If one cannot live as one wishes, then leave life. "This house is smoky, and I quit it" (5.29).

Roman Law

Suicide is not specifically mentioned in the fragments of the law of the Twelve Tables. Nevertheless, several later sources note the refusals to allow suicides to be buried and even of the crucifixion of their corpses (Pliny, *Natural History,* 36.24). Quintilian, however, claims that the ban on suicide could be lifted in certain cases, given prior approval by the Senate (Quintilian, *Inst. Orat.* 7.4.39).[7] Motives were important in Roman law. For example, suicide was not punishable if caused by "impatience of pain or sickness" or "weariness of life, lunacy or fear of dishonor" (Justinian, *Digest,* 48.21.3.6). These laws tended to reflect both the earlier Aristotelian concept that humans were possessions of the state and the suicidal pessimism of the later Roman Stoics. Thus was the suicidal pessimism of Greek thought and law carried into Roman society as well. When the second-century philosopher Lucian realized that he was no longer able to take care of himself, he declared: "Here endeth a contest awarding the fairest of

---

Droge and Tabor are historically correct, the psychological question remains as to why Zeno interpreted his broken toe as a divine signal to depart. After all, there is a very large leap from the pain and inconvenience of breaking one's toe to killing oneself. Zeno's decision, like that of Socrates, was likely provoked by a sense of loss of control; he attempted to regain control by his means of suicide, holding his breath. It presses the point to see Zeno's act as rational rather than as rationalized, masking underlying psychodynamic issues of gerophobia, depression, and feelings of hopelessness, helplessness, and loss of control.

7. See a more detailed discussion by Durkheim (1986, 331).

prizes: time calls, and forbids us delay." Then, refraining from all food, he took his leave of life in his habitual cheerful humor. A short time before the end, he was asked, "What orders have you to give about your burial?" He replied: "Don't borrow trouble! The stench will get me buried" (*Lucian on Demonax*, 65, 66).

Demonax had an even more biting wit. Someone asked him what it was like in Hades, to which Demonax replied, "Wait a bit, and I'll send you word from there." Admetus, a poet, read him an epitaph that he had composed for himself. Demonax scornfully replied, "The epitaph is so fine that I wish it were already carved!" (*Lucian on Demonax*, 65, 66). Demonax's favorite quotation from the *Iliad* was: "Idler or toiler, 'tis all one to Death" (9.320).

3. Suicide in Judaeo-Christian Thought

See I have put before you today life and death, blessing and curse, and you shall choose life so that you and your seed shall live.

Deuteronomy 30:19

Then the Lord God formed man of the dust of the ground, and breathed into his nostrils the breath of life: and man became a living soul.

Genesis 2:7

Read not *harut* [carved] but *herut* [freedom]. One is not free unless he devotes himself to the study of Torah.

Avot, 6.2

This world is like a portico before the world to come. Prepare yourself in the portico so that you may enter into the banquet hall. An hour of repentance and good deeds in this world is better than all the world to come and better is one hour of the peace of spirit of the next world than all of this world.

Avot, 4.21-22

Many contemporary suicidologists (e.g., Fedden 1938, 30; Alvarez 1970, 51; Shneidman 1985, 30) have argued that there is no specific anti-suicide teaching in the Hebrew Bible. However, in fact, Hebrew thought opposes not only suicide but also self-wounding. In this chapter we will deal with the question of suicide and martyrdom, first in the Jewish tradition and then in Christian thought. Both religions place the issue in terms of the larger context of views of life versus death.

Rabbinic Judaism

The Talmudic tradition condemns suicide as a most heinous sin. But the subject evokes little discussion. The minutiae in the laws of Sabbath observance or animal sacrifices in the Temple occupy far more space in the literature. For example, in the eight volumes of the *Aruch Hashulchan,* only one page covers the subject of suicide (*Yorah Deah,* 345).

The biblical basis for the injunction against suicide has been derived from the Noahide laws: "For your lifeblood too, I will require a reckoning" (Gen. 9:5).[1] This statement has been seen as a prohibition not only against suicide but also against any form of self-mutilation (*Baba Kamma,* 91b).[2] The Hebrew Bible contains several additional prohibitions regarding self-mutilation, for example: "Ye are the children of the Lord your God: Ye shall not cut yourselves, nor make any baldness between your eyes for the dead" (Deut. 14:1). Much the same prohibition is given specifically to the priests in Leviticus: "They shall not make baldness upon their head, neither shall they shave off the corners of their beard, nor make any cuttings in their flesh" (Lev. 21:5).

The prohibition against suicide is clear in rabbinic law. For example, a suicide is not given full burial honors. Rending one's garments and delivering memorial addresses and certain other rites to honor the dead are not performed for a suicide. The definition of a suicide, however, requires in-

1. Curiously, the prohibition against suicide actually precedes the injunction against homicide that God gives to Noah: "Whoever sheds the blood of man, by man shall his blood be shed" (Gen. 9:6).

2. While most commentators (e.g., Rashi) have derived their prohibition against suicide from this source, at least one commentator, Ibn Ezra, made somewhat different arguments to the same conclusion. An article by the Israeli Supreme Court Justice Haim Cohn (1976) has discussed these issues.

tent, full wits, nondeficiency in behavior, and noninebriation (*Yorah Deah,* 345). There are also exceptions to the prohibition against suicide. According to the Talmud (*Sanhedrin,* 74a), one is obliged to accept death when the alternative is to be forced to commit adultery, murder, or idolatry. We should emphasize that this means allowing oneself to be killed under certain prescribed circumstances, not actively killing oneself.

But the Jewish law on suicide is only one narrow aspect of a far wider and more important idea: that God loves humankind without qualification and indeed created humans in his own image. God has thus given the Torah to humans as a guide for living rather than merely as a preparation for death: "Ye shall therefore keep my statutes, and mine ordinances, which if a man do, he shall live by them: I am the Lord" (Lev. 18:5). The same idea is constant throughout the Bible and the rabbinic writings.

We shall discuss five central areas of this emphasis on life, based on Jewish sacred literature: (1) creation, (2) obligations and achievements, (3) choice and freedom, (4) the relationship between body and soul, and (5) suffering, pain, and martyrdom.

The Jewish View of Creation

Greek mythology held the view that the world preceded the Olympian gods, who, though immortal, were subject to fate and natural laws and were not omnipotent. Hesiod offered a theogony beginning with the mating of Gaea (earth) and Uranus (heaven) and ending with Zeus. Certainly the gods, whether Olympian or more local, were neither benevolent nor all-knowing. They were often in conflict with each other, fundamentally selfish and capricious, and they had no great love for humans or the world.

The Hebrew Bible describes the Creator in a distinctly different way. God is the Creator of the entire universe and continues to be omnipotent over it. No other power can rival God. Furthermore, God created the world solely as an act of kindness and, in the highest expression of love and benevolence toward human beings, created them in the divine image. To destroy or damage any human being defaces the divine image, insults and diminishes the whole of God's creation, and reduces the divine plan of love in which the world was brought into being (Soloveitchik 1973).

To murder oneself or another is a grievous degradation of life. The individual does not belong to God in the sense of being a chattel, but she does not belong to herself either. The notion of ownership implicit in the way the Greeks belonged to the state does not fit here. Instead, the human being, as the epitome of divine creation, has obligations commensurate with her central exalted position in the universe. To commit suicide destroys that position and scars the divine love on which the universe exists.

Not only is the world a continuing expression of the infinite love of the Creator, but the creation of humans is an act of love as well (*Avot,* 3). The Hebrew Bible and Midrash regularly refer to the human as the child of God, as the firstborn, as the precious daughter and son, and the like. God carries his people as an eagle carries her young (Exod. 19:4). The Song of Songs depicts this relationship in most tender terms — as that of two lovers. It is striking that this book has been viewed by Rabbi Akiba as the most sacred of the Bible. This sense of love is expressed by some of the leaders of the Hasidic movement, such as the rabbi of Berditchev, whose affection for God — as well as his twitting of God — are well known (though hardly unique) in Jewish literature. The importance of faith and trust in God is the subject of the fourth chapter of Bachya Ibn Pakuda's *Duties of the Hearts,* an important rabbinic work of the eleventh century. Bachya Ibn Pakuda defined faith as the sure confidence that God will help the individual in pure kindness and devotion. This is not an empty-headed notion that everything is wonderful, but a firm conviction that God's kindness and wisdom are total and that God is aware of all things and cares about them.

The human role is to use those God-given talents to fulfill God's commandments, including the general commandment to improve the world (Gen. 1:28). Success in one's work is possible, and one must work hard, but ultimately a person is in God's hands.

The Jewish View of Obligation and Achievement

A second important stopper in Jewish thought to any urge toward self-destruction focuses on the idea that the Creator has placed certain well-defined obligations on humans, not as a Sisyphean burden (see chap. 6 below) but for the general purpose of affording each individual the means of coming close to God and living the most fulfilled kind of life. The demands that God has made on people are not beyond the human ability to fulfill, nor are they aimed at tricking people and keeping them subservient.

They are a set of instructions given to them for their own benefit, just as a loving parent would instruct small children. This makes the human purpose on earth clear, at least on a working level. People need only do their human best to fulfill the divine dictates; they need not be disappointed in their failures to reach self-determined levels of success in any endeavor, whether intellectual or corporeal (*Avot*, 2.21). No self-proclaimed measure of success exists, except in a self-punitive mind, because human beings' obligations are set for them by the Torah.

It is highly significant within this system that the obligations are always completely purposive. The meaning or value of certain laws (e.g., the red heifer) is not explained, yet no law is capricious or arbitrary. Each is important and each gives the human being a constant and profound obligation and purpose in life. Each moment and each human act can be rich with purpose.

Plato's *Apology* portrays Socrates as being in love with Athens and with wisdom. He takes great joy from what he depicts as Apollo's mandate to him to seek wisdom, and he pursues it among the people of Athens for decades. According to Xenophon, however, Socrates' *joie de vivre* fails in the face of his fear of old age. Perhaps more than any other figure in Greek philosophy, Socrates comes close to a life based on purposive obligation; yet there is nothing in his code to prevent suicide. His thought does not include the notion of a benevolent deity whom he can trust all the way to the end. As the sense of hopelessness and helplessness grows within him, Socrates sees self-destruction as the easiest way. Apollo has given Socrates no message to the contrary. Therefore, feeling that he will soon begin to decline in physical and mental strength and to diminish in value, Socrates takes the path to the hemlock: he conducts a defense (according to Xenophon) that is so irritating to the jury that they will be certain not only to convict him but to sentence him to death as well. By contrast, the rabbinic system is not obsessed with the mysteries of birth, life, and death. Rather, the Mishna declares that birth, life, death, and the final judgment all take place against humans' will (*Avot*, 4).

Doctrinal explanations of the meaning of these events are not terribly important. One must have faith that each of these events is brought about by God and that he, in his omniscience and omnibenevolence, has planned them well. A Midrash states that, among the first generations of human history, there was no old age in the world: all adults looked young. The biblical patriarch Abraham then prayed that signs of aging should appear on the elderly so that one could distinguish sons from their fathers (*Gen. Rabbah,* 58:9; 59:2; 65.9). God granted his prayer, and Abraham was the first to show marks of aging. This was seen as a sign that people should respect the elderly.

The example of heroism is thus not the warrior facing his enemies on the battlefield but rather the "woman of valor" *(eishet chayil)* in Proverbs 31, the woman who "laughs at the final day." She laughs not from a lack of understanding but from her deep faith in God's loving care. One further example of this view is the parable offered by Rabbi Elchonon Wasserman, one of the rabbinic giants of Eastern Europe between World War I and World War II. Facing imminent death at the hands of the Nazis, Rabbi Wasserman explained the events around him in a parable. Perhaps it is not too far-fetched to view this as a kind of rabbinic *Phaedo.*

Once a man who knew nothing at all about agriculture came to a farmer and asked to be taught about farming. The farmer took him to his field and asked him what he saw. "I see a beautiful piece of land, lush with grass, and pleasing to the eye." Then the visitor stood aghast while the farmer plowed under the grass and turned the beautiful green field into a mass of shallow brown ditches. "Why did you ruin the field?" he demanded.

"Be patient. You will see," said the farmer. Then the farmer showed his guest a sackful of plump kernels of wheat and said, "Tell me what you see." The visitor described the nutritious, inviting grain — and then once more watched in shock as the farmer ruined something beautiful. This time, he walked up and down the furrows and dropped kernels into the open ground wherever he went. Then he covered the kernels with clods of soil.

"Are you insane?" the man demanded. "First you destroyed the field and then you ruined the grain!"

"Be patient. You will see." Time went by and once more the farmer took his guest out to the field. Now they saw endless, straight rows of green stalks sprouting up from all the furrows. The visitor smiled broadly. "I apologize. Now I understand what you were doing. You made the field more beautiful than ever. The art of farming is truly marvelous."

"No," said the farmer. "We are not done. You must still be patient." More time went by and the stalks were fully grown. Then the farmer came with his sickle and chopped them down as his visitor watched open-mouthed, seeing how the orderly field became an ugly scene of destruction. The farmer bound the fallen stalks into bundles and decorated the field with them. Later, he took the bundles to another area where he beat and crushed them until they became a mass of straw and loose kernels. Then he separated the kernels from the chaff and piled them up in a huge hill. Always, he told his protesting visitor, "We are not done, you must be more patient."

Then the farmer came with his wagon and piled it high with grain, which he took to a mill. There, the beautiful grain was ground into formless, choking dust. The visitor complained again. "You have taken grain and transformed it into dirt!" Again, he was told to be patient. The farmer put the dust into sacks and took it back home. He took some dust and mixed it with water while his guest marveled at the foolishness of making "whitish mud." Then the farmer fashioned the "mud" into the shape of a loaf. The visitor saw the perfectly formed loaf and smiled broadly, but his happiness did not last. The farmer kindled a fire in an oven and put the loaf into it.

"Now I know you are insane. After all that work, you burn what you have made."

The farmer looked at him and laughed. "Have I not told you to be patient?" Finally the farmer opened the oven and took out a freshly baked bread — crisp and brown, with an aroma that made the visitor's mouth water.

"Come," the farmer said. He led his guest to the kitchen table where he cut the bread and offered his now pleased visitor a liberally buttered slice.

"Now," the farmer said, "now, you understand."

God is the Farmer and we are the fools who do not begin to understand His ways or the outcome of His plan. Only when the process is complete will we all know why all this had to be. Until then, we must be patient and have faith that everything — even when it seems destructive and painful — is part of the process that will produce goodness and beauty. (Sorasky 1982, 431)

The Jewish answer to Socrates' fear of old age is that man can only place himself in God's hands and must continue to do his best to obey God's purpose. Further, his existence is meaningful and significant to God.

Therefore, decisions about his life and death should come not from his own limited mind and his own limited knowledge, but from God alone.

The Jewish View of Choice and Freedom

A third major aspect of rabbinic thought concerns the concept of choice and freedom. Greek mythology is peppered with stories involving a Hobson's choice, that is, a situation that appears to require a choice but in which there are in fact no livable alternatives.

The riddle of the Sphinx and Oedipus's response to it were a major theme of Greek mythology. The monstrous Sphinx — part lion, part eagle, and part woman — accosted travelers and asked her famous riddle: "What goes on four legs in the morning, two legs at midday, and three legs in the evening?" Travelers could not answer the riddle, and the Sphinx devoured them. Oedipus presented the Sphinx with the correct answer. It is mankind who walks (crawls) on four legs in the morning of his life, two in his maturity, and three (with a cane) in his later years. Oedipus slew the Sphinx; however, in doing so he showed that he accepted the two bad choices offered him by the riddle. He could either surrender his life or accept the Sphinx's deterministic and highly pessimistic view of life as a cycle. In accepting this decremental view of aging, Oedipus expressed his agreement with the Sphinx's philosophy of self-destruction and proceeded to live it out, fulfilling the self-destructive curse.

Comparing Greek and biblical attitudes toward suicide is illuminating. To the Stoic, there was a choice about whether to continue one's life or end it. Suicide is thus considered a viable option worthy of the philosopher's careful consideration: it is not a criminal act as long as one's decision is based on reason and not emotion. Indeed, it is more appropriate for the philosopher than for the average citizen. In the rabbinic system there is no thought of a decision about suicide. Suicide is forbidden by the Torah and is not at all the act of a Talmudic scholar. Indeed, it is considered a criminal act that should be punished by a court, where possible. Still, the criminal-victim is seen as probably acting under at least a temporary insanity and may therefore require pity and compassion more than persecution.

In rabbinic thought, the choice between life and death is not one to mull over daily in the way that talk of suicide filled the letters of Seneca and other writings by classical philosophers. It was a choice made once: "See, I have put before you today life and death, blessing and curse, and you shall choose life so that you and your seed shall live" (Deut. 30:19). The choice is not whether or not to destroy one's life, but how best to live it. The Stoics saw fate as a powerful force capriciously controlling human destinies. Indeed, necessity was so strong that they sought to escape it. In particular, they sought to escape from the inevitability of death through the illusion of gaining control over death through suicide. Knowing that he could bring about death by slitting his wrists gave Seneca the "feeling of freedom in every vein." The option of bringing about death seemed to give the Stoic an illusion of control by which he could prevent death from striking him by chance.

The Mishna is not concerned with fate: it declares that real freedom always exists in the human realm, that is, the freedom to act righteously. The Mishna does not posit illusory freedom or choice in matters beyond human control. This is where the rabbis disagreed with the Stoics. Where the Stoics felt overwhelmed by necessity or fate in all things *except* the time and manner of their death, the rabbis argued that in such matters as death there was, in fact, no choice. "Against your will you are born, against your will you live, against your will you die. Against your will you shall in the future give account before the King of Kings" (*Avot*, 4.29).

The Stoics desperately sought a feeling of freedom that would offer them at least a temporary illusion of control. In contrast, the rabbis accepted that God controls these matters of life and death. Feeling no need to take these impossibly difficult decisions from the hands of the one omnipotent and benevolent Deity, the human being gains the freedom to devote his attention wholly to those tasks that are peculiarly his, that is, loving God and man and studying and fulfilling God's commandments. The Mishna goes on to offer its own statement on freedom. The Ten Commandments were carved *(harut)* on stone: "Read not *harut* [carved] but *herut* [freedom]. One is not free unless he devotes himself to study of the Torah" (*Avot*, 6.2). Freedom here means the freedom of the human spirit from fears and desires. When one's fears and desires run rampant, then one is dominated by them and there is no freedom. The Stoic sought freedom from the terror of death by choosing his own means of exit. In contrast, the rabbinic Jew acknowledged God's total power over birth, life, and death. In so doing he accepted the responsibility of his freedom to make important moral choices. Birth and death are events beyond human understanding; God alone will handle them. The individual is given freedom in terms of following the Torah.

The Stoic comparison of life to a banquet from which one may depart at will meets a striking antithesis in a second-century Mishnaic statement: "This world is like a portico before the world to come. Prepare yourself in the portico so that you may enter into the banquet hall" (*Avot*, 4.21-22). That is, prepare yourself in this world by living righteously so that you may merit the rewards of the next world. The two worlds are dissimilar in function: in this world, good deeds and repentance are appropriate and more beautiful than all the rewards of the next world; at the same time, the peace of spirit attainable in the next world is preferable to all of the joys of this world. Therefore, earthly life is not a banquet that must inevitably end. It is a time for work and preparation. The contrast with Stoic views carries on to a second point: one must not assume that the next world is some sort of refuge from this one (*Avot*, 4). There is still awareness, and one must come before the King of Kings for a final judgment that will be beyond anything earthly people can comprehend. Both earth and heaven are thus important, but each in its own way.

The Relationship between Body and Soul

From the rabbinic point of view, body and soul should function together harmoniously. Though the body supports the soul in their joint service of God, there is none of the Platonic sense that the body must die to liberate the soul. Body and soul are different but need not be in conflict.

Human beings must keep their bodies both physically and morally clean (Buchler 1922, 14-20). The story is told that once, when Hillel left the house of learning with his students, they asked where he was headed, and he replied that he was going to perform a religious duty: to bathe in the bathhouse. A king appoints someone to keep his statue clean. Therefore, humans, created in the divine image, must certainly keep their bodies clean (*Avot de Rabbi Nathan*, 2.33). Hillel described the soul as a guest in the body: the body should keep itself fit in order to offer hospitality to so distinguished a guest. To Hillel, the body was neither an evil to be repressed nor a bastion of heroism to be glorified by Olympic victories. For him, both physical and spiritual activities were part of the human fulfillment of obligation to God.

The Israeli scholar Ephraim Urbach has pointed to the fact that *nephesh*, the Hebrew word for soul, is used in a number of places in the Bible to refer to the whole human being. Urbach has supplied a number of references to support this view (e.g., Exod. 4:19; 1 Kings 19:10), and he specifically distinguished the term *nephesh* from the Greek word *psychē,* or *anima,* which connotes a disembodied soul (Urbach 1979, 214-15).

Suffering, Pain, and Martyrdom: A Jewish View

Jewish thinkers were as aware as anyone of the inescapable pains that life has presented to humans after they knowingly rejected the physical and spiritual beauty of Eden. One of the great Talmudic teachers of the twentieth century was at times so darkly depressed that he could not lecture for weeks.[3] There is an account of another great Talmudist (Berlin 1943) who was thrown into a state of terror while watching a sunset from the balcony of a hotel room. Still, there is never the feeling that human suffering was desired by a capricious divinity. The human is not a plaything but a deeply beloved child.

In this post-Edenic state, each human personality has his or her own strengths and weaknesses, and humans feel fear, struggle, and pain. The Talmud tells the poignant story of Rabbi Elazar (*Berachot,* 5b):

> R. Elazar fell ill and R. Johanan went to visit him. He noticed that he was lying in a dark room, and he bared his arm and light radiated from it. Thereupon he noticed that R. Elazar was weeping, and he said to him: "Why do you weep? Is it because you did not study enough Torah? Surely we have learned: The one who does much and the one who does little have the same merit, provided that the heart is directed to heaven. Is it perhaps lack of sustenance? Not everybody has the privilege to enjoy two tables. Is it perhaps because of the lack of children? This is the bone of my tenth son!" He replied to him: "I am weeping on account of your beauty that is going to rot in the earth." He said to him: "On that account you surely have a reason to weep," and they both wept. In the meanwhile he said to him, "Are your sufferings welcome to you?" He replied "Neither they nor their reward." He said to him: "Give me your hand," and he gave him his hand and he raised him.

3. Private communication from one of his disciples.

The Hebrew Bible refers often to human suffering. The Psalms deal with human sadness, and in the book of Ruth, Naomi openly declares that God has given her a bitter load. Nevertheless, whatever their hardships, however depressed their emotional state, suicide is not a viable answer. A Talmudic debate is often cited concerning the basic value of life itself:

> Our Rabbis taught: For two and a half years were Beth Shammai and Beth Hillel in dispute, the former asserting that it were better for man not to have been created than to have been created, and the latter maintaining that it is better for man to have been created than not to have been created. They finally took a vote and decided that it were better for man not to have been created than to have been created, but now that he has been created, let him investigate his past deeds or, as others say, let him examine his future actions. (*Eruvin,* 13b)

This passage has often been cited to illustrate the basic pessimism in the rabbinic view of life. However, even in the most pessimistic interpretation, suicide is not permitted. The rabbis themselves had a brighter view of this debate. They saw it as referring only to the wicked, who make poor use of their lives, whereas for the righteous, life is indeed a benefit (Tosafot on *Eruvin,* 13b). This view stands in marked contrast to the pessimism with regard to human creation expressed by Hesiod.

Let us examine the understanding of pain and suffering that appears in the traditional Jewish attitudes toward martyrdom. These attitudes were put to the acid test for the rabbis of the Roman period: they had to decide to what extent a Jew might break the law of the Torah if threatened with death by persecutors. They decided that one could break any law under threat of death, except for three: adultery, murder, and idolatry, or unless public disgrace to the Torah was involved (*Sanhedrin,* 74a). Thus, under the severe persecutions of the Roman Era, there were many cases in which people were punished or put to death for trying to uphold the law. Death per se was never a desired solution, however, nor was martyrdom sought for its own sake. For example, the Romans tortured Rabbi Akiba cruelly when they found him teaching the Torah during the period of persecution that followed the Bar Kochba War (135 CE). As the story is told in the Babylonian Talmud (*Berachot,* 61b), a Roman officer saw Rabbi Akiba smiling and asked him why. Rabbi Akiba responded that he was in great agony and he knew that he would soon die.

He was only happy that, in his last moment, he could still sanctify God's name by reciting the Shema: "Hear Oh Israel, the Lord our God is one." Rabbi Akiba did not seek martyrdom and felt no beatific joy in his pain; rather, he continued to express his faith in God.

This story remained the model for Jewish martyrs facing marauding crusaders and other Jew-hating mobs through the Middle Ages. It is better to live and not to seek martyrdom; but if one must die, then let it be in the best possible way. It is significant that the Jews typically preferred peace and quiet to a martyr's death. Moreover, within their limited means, they often fought back. They were to avoid death, if possible. One chronicle reports the story of a young Talmudic student in the Middle Ages, who, when faced with torture, suddenly grabbed the sword from his torturer and killed him (Haberman, 1946, 74). A second case is reported in which Rabbi Simon Ben Abraham slew some Jewish children when they were in danger of forced baptism. A second rabbi called him a murderer and said that he should be punished with a horrible death. Then the persecutors began to skin the survivors and pour sand into their bodies. Suddenly, the torture was halted, and the victims survived, except for those whom the rabbi had killed. Clearly, the rabbi's killing of the children was not condoned (*Daat Zekenim* on Gen. 9).

The question of self-defense also arose. Some groups of people allowed themselves to be slaughtered by Seleucid soldiers rather than desecrate the Sabbath by defending themselves. This was a new problem, and the Jews had to decide how to handle it. According to the Talmud, the religious leaders proclaimed that Jews not only must defend themselves if attacked on the Sabbath but also *must attack* if the situation seemed to require offensive action (*Eruvin*, 45a; *Shulchan Aruch; Orach Chaim*, 329.6, 7). This has remained standard in Jewish law.

Exceptions to the Rule: Jewish Suicides

Despite these injunctions, a number of suicides are reported in Jewish writings. There are only six suicides in the entire Hebrew Bible and none in the Pentateuch. Chronologically, they are as follows: the self-stabbing of Abimelech (Judg. 9:54); the crushing of Samson (Judg. 16:30); the self-stabbing of Saul (1 Sam. 31:14; 2 Sam. 1:6; 1 Chron. 10:4) and his armor-bearer (1 Sam. 31:15; 1 Chron. 10:5); the hanging of Ahitophel (2 Sam. 17:23);

and the burning of Zimri (1 Kings 16:18). Significantly, the Hebrew Bible also portrays some cases of suicide prevention, which involved individuals who expressed suicidal wishes but were helped by God's therapeutic intervention (e.g., Elijah, Jonah, Job, and Jeremiah).

Other suicides have been reported in nonrabbinic writings of the Second Temple period as well. In the apocryphal book of 1 Maccabees, for example, Eleazar sacrifices himself by darting beneath the elephant of an enemy general and running his sword into it (1 Macc. 6:46). In the book of 2 Maccabees, two acts of suicide are recorded: first, that of Ptolemy, and second, that of Ragesh (Razis). Ptolemy, an advocate of the Judeans at the Syrian Court of King Antiochus Eupator, poisons himself after being accused of treason (2 Macc. 10:12). Ragesh first attempts unsuccessfully to die on his sword rather than fall into the hands of the Syrians (2 Macc. 14:41-42). He subsequently succeeds in disemboweling himself after throwing himself from a wall (2 Macc. 14:43-46). The historian Flavius Josephus also mentions a number of suicides in his work *Wars of the Jews*, including the mass suicides at Jotapata in 69 CE and Masada in 73.

No Talmudic passage can be taken as praising suicide or glorifying heroism in the Greek sense, nor is there an obsession with death as the solution to life's problems or with the issue of control. Nevertheless, according to the Talmud, suicide can be permissible and even preferred in select instances in which a person is faced with forced apostasy or tortures that might be more horrifying than death.

The great scholar Rabbi Hanina ben Teradion, who was burned to death by his Roman persecutors with a Torah scroll wrapped around him, would not even open his mouth so as to breathe in the flames and die more quickly: "Let him who gave me my soul take it away but no one should injure himself." In other words, he refused to advance his own death actively.[4] The Roman executioner, impressed by the personal greatness of Rabbi Hanina and the terrible awe of the moment, wanted to be joined to him (*Tosefot Avodah Zarah*, 18a; *Maharsha*). He offered to end Hanina's torture by removing the wet sponges from around his heart, which had artificially prolonged his life. Rabbi Hanina approved this, and he assured the executioner of a portion in the world to come.[5] The executioner then

---

4. This refusal, while highly commendable, cannot be expected from most people in such extreme circumstances.

5. Rabbinic law has never interpreted this story as encouraging active or assisted sui-

removed the sponges, and, knowing that he himself would now be severely punished by the Romans, he leaped into the fire. Both were assigned a place in the world to come (*Avodah Zarah,* 18a; *Sifre* and *Yalkut Shimoni* on Deut. 32:4).[6]

The story of the 400 boys and girls who leaped into the sea rather than be sent to lives of prostitution in Rome is comparable (*Gittin,* 57b). There is a similar story in *Lamentations Rabbah,* 1.45, where the basic principle is that if "they feared lest idol worshippers force them to sin by means of unbearable tortures, then it is commanded to destroy oneself" (*Tosafot, Avodah Zarah,* 18a; *Gittin,* 57b; see also Rabbi Jacob Emden, *Hagahot*). At such a point it may be more desirable to sanctify God's holy name by suicide than to sin. Again, this is not an approbation of suicide per se, nor an obsession with issues of control, as in many of the Greek suicides. Human life remains an object of great importance. We should note that the young people in *Gittin* 57 and the elders in the parallel story in *Lamentations Rabbah* asked for a rabbinic opinion before leaping into the sea, so that they would not lose their share in the world to come. Gittin also describes the suicide of Hannah after the martyrdom of her seven sons, and *Avodah Zarah* 18b recounts the suicide of Beruria, the wife of Rabbi Meier.[7] Other Talmudic suicides include the Hasmonean princess who was loved by her former slave, Herod (*Baba Batra,* 3b), a Roman officer who saved the life of Rabban Gamlieh (*Taanit,* 29a), and the suicides of a father and mother af-

---

cide. The reader should note that Rabbi Hanina refused his disciples' advice to open his mouth to take in the fire. Rabbi Hanina's allowing the executioner to remove the sponges from around his heart can be seen instead as a refusal to continue measures that artificially prolonged his torture.

6. A. J. Droge and J. D. Tabor (1992, 102) have suggested a parallel between Rabbi Hanina's position that God is the one who takes away life and the statements of Plato and Cicero that one is not to depart except at the bidding of the gods. However, there is no indication whatsoever that Hanina saw his torture as a divine bidding, nor did he have any love of death per se, or concern with personal control. He was faced with unbearable pain, unlike the relatively minor annoyance of Zeno's broken toe. Similarly, the pagan executioner was not awarded a place in the world to come because he committed suicide but because he participated in the awe of Hanina's final moment and performed an act of great compassion. The essential difference between the Jewish and Greek positions is this: Judaism was basically attracted to life rather than to death, even when external circumstances may make one's life unbearable. By contrast, Greek thought was basically attracted to death, even when life is quite bearable (see also Orbach, Millstein, Har-Even, Apter, Tiano, and Elizur 1991).

7. An alternative version portrays Hannah as "falling" rather than "jumping" off a roof (*Lamentations Rabbah,* 1.50).

ter the father threw their son from the roof for receiving food from a guest without permission (*Hullin,* 94a). Another suicide involved a student whose name was falsely besmirched by a prostitute (*Berachot,* 23a). The Talmud (*Semachot,* chaps. 2 and 5) also relates two incidents of childhood suicide, the first involving the son of Gornos of Lydda, who ran away from school, and the second, that of a child in Bnei B'rak, who broke a bottle on the Sabbath. Each child killed himself after his father threatened to punish him; neither was ruled an intentional suicide.

Two more suicides are mentioned in the *Midrash Rabbah.* The first (*Ecclesiastes Rabbah* 10:7) describes a pagan eunuch of the emperor of Rome who attempted to embarrass Rabbi Akiba. When the eunuch was shamed in return, he killed himself. The second (*Genesis Rabbah* 65:22) describes the suicide of Jakum of Tzeroth who, after taunting Rabbi Joseph Meshitha, inflicted as self-punishment the four modes of execution typically sentenced by the courts: he stoned, burned, strangled, and decapitated himself.

There are a number of significant suicides in later Jewish history as well, including five hundred Jews at York in the twelfth century, hundreds in Verdun, France, in 1326, and many more in response to the Spanish Inquisition. While it is not our intention to create a laundry list here, there have been periods of external persecutions throughout Jewish history that have put Jews in the position of choosing apostasy or suicide (Haberman 1946). Durkheim's aforementioned observation on the comparatively higher rate of suicide among Jews in late nineteenth-century Bavaria and the suicides among Jews in Central and Eastern Europe in the 1930s and during World War II are also clearly connected to external forces. The importance of the theme of suicide in modern Yiddish literature has been explored in a work by Janet Hadda (1988), who has focused largely on suicidogenic family themes. Famous Jewish suicides in modern times include that of Otto Weininger, the self-hating Jewish intellectual who in 1903 shot himself in Ludwig van Beethoven's apartment; Ernst Toller, a playwright and revolutionary who killed himself in New York in 1939 in despair after the fall of Madrid to Francisco Franco; and Samuel Zygelbojm, who in 1943 committed suicide in London to protest the indifference of Polish, British, and other authorities to reports of the Holocaust and the savage destruction of the Warsaw Ghetto. According to some accounts, Sigmund Freud, who was suffering from a painful and incurable illness, also took his own life.

It is obviously incorrect, then, to claim that there are no suicides in biblical and later Jewish history. Individual suicides have occurred despite the injunctions against them. Nevertheless, suicide is strongly prohibited in biblical and later Jewish thought, and when it has appeared within the culture, it may represent individual idiosyncrasies, impossible external situations, or profound Greco-Roman influences. The basic Jewish preference for life over death as expressed in the Hebrew Bible has never changed, nor has suicide ever been idealized as an end in itself.

When suicidal forces have emerged, they have typically represented an alien influence on Jewish life. For example, the family dynamic pinpointed by Hadda (passionate women, passive men) follows more of a Greek than a biblical family pattern. The thinking of Weininger represented Hellenic polarities of thought with regard to sexuality and to life in general (see chaps. 4 and 7 below).

Jotapata and Masada: Two Speeches on Suicide

There are glaring differences in Josephus's accounts between the mass Jewish suicide at Jotapata and the one at Masada. The story of the defense of Masada against the Romans and the mass suicide of its Jewish defenders in 73 CE has gained a new celebrity in our day, spurred on by the findings of Israeli archaeologist Yigael Yadin. The fortress of Masada was the only Jewish outpost not yet conquered by the Romans by that time, and it was defended by 900 Sicarii nationalists led by Eliezer Ben Yair.

Masada has become a symbol of bravery in modern Israel and around the world. Curiously, it is never once mentioned in rabbinic literature, and for years it was known only through the account of Josephus, a Jewish historian in Rome. Any mention of suicide is conspicuously absent in *Yosippon,* a later Hebrew account of the Jewish revolt, which portrays the defenders fighting against the Romans to the death (Ben Gurion, *Sefer Yosippon,* chap. 87). Numerous scholarly articles have debated the meaning and the veracity of Josephus's account. The story is useful for our purposes because it offers some insight into Josephus's own views on suicide. While Josephus obviously had his own agenda, one thing is clear: he viewed suicide as completely alien to Jewish intellect, spirit, and law. By now, the speech of Eliezer Ben Yair to his followers at Masada (at least the version in Josephus's account) ranks as one of the famous orations of antiquity. No less important for understanding Josephus's approach is an earlier speech of his own.

At an earlier point in the Roman-Jewish War, Josephus was the commander of the Jewish garrison at the town of Jotapata in Galilee. As Josephus described it, he saw little chance of holding out against the powerful Roman army of Vespasian, and he urged his people to surrender. However, those defenders would not give up, and they held out against the Romans for some weeks. Finally the city fell, and Josephus fled to a cave, where he found forty of his soldiers already in hiding. Soon the Romans also found the cave and demanded their surrender. The Jewish soldiers favored a mass suicide, but Josephus strongly disagreed (*Wars of the Jews*, 3.514-16). In his speech, he sought to dissuade the other fighters from suicide: he offered a traditional Jewish set of arguments that were opposed to Greco-Roman philosophical thinking on several points. First, in contrast to the Socratic/Platonic view, body and soul are the best of friends, and they should remain together. Second, it may be glorious to die in battle if it is for freedom, but it is not glorious to die at one's own hand. Third, suicide is an act not of bravery but of the utmost cowardice and foolishness. Self-murder is contrary to natural instinct; even more, it is impiety to God, who is angry when he sees his gift of life treated with contempt. God entrusts the body to the soul for safe-keeping.

Josephus was the only survivor of that group of soldiers in the cave, so we have no second account by which to verify the authenticity of his speech — or whether he even gave it at all. For our purposes, however, what is important is that Josephus had the chance to write the speech that he would have, at least, liked to have given; indeed, he may have given it in any event. And the speech represents a good pious sermon that a rabbi might have been proud of, a strong tirade against suicide.[8]

Josephus's subsequent portrayal of Eliezer Ben Yair's speech at Masada (*Wars of the Jews*, 7:598-603) presents a very different view of suicide. Again, scholars have debated whether Ben Yair ever gave the speech at all — or, if he did, what he actually said. It is quite likely that Josephus followed the practice accepted by classical historians since Thucydides of reporting not a verbatim account of an oration but rather an account of what

8. Droge and Tabor (1992, 94) have followed a different line of interpretation, deriving Josephus's argument against voluntary death in his Jotapata speech from Plato's discussion in the *Phaedo* of when to choose death.

could have (or perhaps even should have) been said. In Ben Yair's speech at Masada, Josephus, who hated the Sicarii, may well have put into Ben Yair's mouth ideas that Josephus himself deplored. The speech contains several parts. In the first part (7:600-601), Ben Yair argues that God had given the Sicarii freedom to choose their own kind of death. He says that the revolt against the Roman Empire has failed because God had sentenced the Jewish race to extinction; therefore, let the defenders of Masada take their own lives. Many of Ben Yair's arguments seem more suitable to Greek than to Jewish thinking: for example, the idea that humans display personal freedom in its highest form by choosing how and when to die. Furthermore, as for the Greeks, life has no meaning because God has forsaken his people.

When his followers did not respond enthusiastically to this call for a mass suicide, Ben Yair tried a second, even more explicitly Greek argument: "We should not fear death, because it is not death, but life which is the calamity. Death gives freedom to the soul which then returns to a wonderful abode where it dwells with God. Death is much like sleep" (7:601-2). At this point one may wonder where Ben Yair studied his Plato (*Phaedo,* 68d) or his Seneca (*Ep.,* 24). It is hardly likely that a Judean nationalist revolutionary such as Ben Yair knew much of Plato or Stoicism; but Josephus probably did, and he has put into Ben Yair's mouth a most extreme dualism between body and soul in an argument for suicide. He then portrays Ben Yair to be citing as a good example the Indian Brahmins, who bring on their own deaths with great pleasure and courage in their desire for death and immortality (7:602). It is noteworthy that Josephus portrays Ben Yair as using examples from a clearly non-Jewish philosophy to support his argument for suicide.

Next, Ben Yair's harangue enters a third stage. His references to freedom, the imprisonment of the soul, and the Brahmins have so far made no impression on his followers who, although misled, are still loyal Jews. He now turns to the great suffering of the Jews during the war, the immense trauma of the destruction of Jerusalem, and he reaches a peak of intensity when he depicts a man watching his wife and children being carried off by heartless enemies (7:602-3). Here, at last, Ben Yair speaks to the heart of the Jew about his love for his homeland and his family. The listeners respond with deep emotion to his plea, and they go forward with a mass suicide. Josephus thus shows that the Jew was essentially a good family person, even though some few had been duped by the wicked Sicarii, who were the foes of both everything Jewish and of the benefits of Roman civilization.

A comparison of the Jotapata and Masada speeches reveals more about Josephus's agenda than one can get from a concentration on either speech alone. It also reveals a dramatic contrast between Jewish and Greek attitudes toward suicide. Josephus was obviously interested in portraying himself positively and Ben Yair negatively, and he went about this in several ways. (1) He portrays Ben Yair as both anti-Jewish and anti-Roman: anti-Roman in that he refused to surrender to Rome; anti-Jewish in that he argued for suicide on anti-Jewish grounds. He cites Indian rather than explicitly Greco-Roman philosophers in support of these views, so that he would in no way be appealing to the Romans. Josephus also emphasizes throughout the story that the Sicarii fought bravely. It was not their lack of courage but their lack of Jewishness and/or *Romanitas* that brought about their fall.[9] (2) By contrast, Josephus portrays himself as loyal both to Judaism and to Rome. He had found favor with Rome by arguing for capitulation and accommodation rather than for pointless resistance. At the same time, Josephus was also a good Jew who had strongly defended his people's abhorrence of suicide. Josephus may have hoped that his rebuttal of the Stoics' doctrine of suicide would serve to increase his stature in Roman eyes, because the Stoics had declined in popularity among the Flavian emperors of the time (69-96 CE).

To return to our original point, many Jewish suicides may have been carried out for Greco-Roman reasons. Suicide is completely alien to Jewish intellect, spirit, and law; it is portrayed as a damnable act of fools, cultists, and traitors. For Josephus, the mass suicides at both Jotapata and Masada were carried out for largely non-Jewish — indeed, for Greco-Roman — reasons and were not to be used as models or examples of Jewish behavior.

Christianity

Christianity is called the daughter religion of Judaism and is based partially on the same Hebrew Bible. One would thus expect it to demonstrate the same life-centeredness, belief in a loving God, and general repugnance toward suicide. And in a sense it does, especially in its more modern forms. At the same time, Christianity grew up within the Greco-Roman world in

---

9. Droge and Tabor (1992, 94), by contrast, have argued that Josephus was attempting to portray both Ben Yair and himself as "philosophically" astute.

which Judaism lived, and its leaders were influenced by the Platonic ambivalence toward life and death and even by the Stoic elevation of suicide disguised as a kind of martyrdom.

Suicides and Martyrs in the Early Church

Only one suicide occurs in the Christian New Testament: Judas Iscariot hangs himself from the branch of an olive tree after his betrayal of Jesus (Matt. 27:3-5). Significantly, there is no condemnation of his suicide in the New Testament or in the writings of the early church fathers. On the one hand, martyrdom was a fact of life for the early Christians, who felt a kind of apocalyptic intensity and excitement that would be difficult for mainstream Western churches of the twentieth and twenty-first centuries to comprehend. Some early Christian writers — Mark is a good example — spent more time discussing exorcism, faith healing, miracles, and the end of days, and less time on ethics than do most modern theologians or biblical scholars. But we should also remember that Christianity in its first years grew up among pagan cults and was greatly influenced by Jewish pietistic, apocalyptic, and ascetic groups such as the Essenes, and that it soon absorbed influential strains of Greek thought as well. Consequently, a part of Christianity blended intense eschatological excitement with the chronic depression of Greek philosophy.

A number of Christian thinkers have seen Jesus' death as voluntary. How could it be otherwise if he was both divine and human? Tertullian, for example, held that when he was on the cross, Jesus Christ gave up the ghost freely and of his own volition before death by crucifixion overcame him (*To the Martyrs,* 4). Origen supported this point of view *(Exhortation to Martyrdom).* Even Augustine agreed on the voluntary aspects of the death of Jesus: "His soul did not leave His body constrained, but because He would and where He would and how He would" (*The Trinity,* 4).

Centuries later, Thomas Aquinas argued very much the same way in his discussion of whether Jesus was slain by another or by himself (*Summa Theologica,* 3.47.1). Aquinas began by offering three "objections" to the idea that Jesus was slain by another. First, he offers a quotation from the Gospel of John: "No man takes my life from me, but I lay it down of myself [my own initiative]" (John 10:18). Second, he cites Augustine: "Those who were crucified were tormented with a lingering death." This did not happen in the case of Jesus, because, "crying out, with a loud voice, he yielded up the spirit" (Matt. 27:50).[10] Third, Aquinas again cites Augustine's view that Jesus willed his soul to leave his body. At the same time, Aquinas points to a seemingly contradictory passage (Luke 18:33): "After they have scourged him, they will put him to death."

Aquinas attempts to resolve this seeming contradiction by distinguishing between direct and indirect causes. Jesus' persecutors were a *direct* cause of his death; however, Jesus was himself an *indirect* cause of his death because he did not prevent it: "Therefore, since Christ's soul did not repel the injury inflicted on His body but willed His corporeal nature to succumb to such injury, He is said to have laid down His life, or to have died voluntarily" (*Summa*, 3.47.1).[11]

The New Testament itself focuses on the mystery and passion of the sacrificial death of Jesus as part of a divine plan to save mankind: "For God so loved the world that He gave His only begotten son, that whoever believes in Him should not perish but have eternal life" (John 3:16). Furthermore, this act is seen as representing the epitome of martyrdom: "Greater love has no one than this, that one lay down his life for his friends" (John 15:13). Love and sacrifice are thus closely intertwined throughout the New Testament: "We know love by this, that he laid down his life for us and we ought to lay down our lives for the brethren" (1 John 3:16).

There is also a theme of ascetic withdrawal, which deemphasizes attachments in this world and concentrates on the superiority of the next. Several quotes bear this out:

> Do not love the world nor the things in the world. If anyone loves the world, the love of the Father is not in him. (1 John 2:15)

> If anyone comes to me and does not hate his own father and mother and wife and children and brothers and sisters, yes, and even his own life, he cannot be my disciple. (Luke 14:26)[12]

10. It is reasonable to assume that Jesus' short survival on the cross may have been occasioned by a weakened physical condition.

11. Droge and Tabor (1992, 21, 46) have pointed to the similarity between the deaths of Jesus and of Socrates. Socrates drank the poison voluntarily, in response to some necessity sent by the gods, in addition to having received the death penalty. The depiction of the death of Jesus in the Gospels is similar. For example, the author of the Fourth Gospel records Jesus as saying, "No one takes my life from me, but I lay it down of my own accord" (John 10:18).

12. Augustine anticipated the suicidal implications of this phrase but denied that it

He that hates his life in this world, shall keep it unto life eternal. (John 12:25)

Jesus' last utterance on the cross (Matt. 27:46; Mark 15:34), "Eli, Eli, Lama Sabachtani," that is, "My God, my God, why hast thou forsaken me?" expresses a feeling of abandonment atypical of the suicide-preventive narratives in the Hebrew Bible and among God-fearing Jews at the time of Jesus.

St. Paul's epistle to the Philippians is explicit in its almost Platonic praise of death over life. "For to me to live is Christ and to die is gain" (Phil. 1:21) reflects a certain perturbation as Paul considers both life and death, unsure as to which would be the better way to serve. Clearly, though, the true "commonwealth," or *politeuma* (Phil. 3:20), is in heaven, and Paul plays down the seeming materialism of Judaism as opposed to the spiritual mystery of Christianity. In the Epistle to the Philippians, Paul says that Jesus will "transform our lowly body that it may be conformed to his glorious body" (3:21), and Paul will stay at his appointed post, though he longs to depart: "For I am hard pressed between the two, having a desire to depart and be with Christ, which is far better. Nevertheless to remain in the flesh is more needful for you" (Phil. 1:23-24).[13]

Paul's strongly expressed dichotomy between body and soul, as well as his preference for the next world over this one, is reflected even more clearly in 2 Corinthians: "Therefore, we are always confident knowing that while we are at home in the body we are absent from the Lord. . . . We are confident, yes, well pleased rather to be absent from the body and to be present with the Lord" (2 Cor. 5:6-8). Humans are thus thought to be closer to Jesus Christ in that next world when they have shed the diversions of the flesh. This is much closer to the Platonic vision than to the rabbinic one, which values life in both this world and the next.[14]

Martyrdom was a major issue in the early church. Generally speak-

---

could be used to justify the self-homicide on the part of the Donatists (Donne, *Biathanatos,* 3.4.6).

13. Droge and Tabor (1992, 122) have argued that Paul "lusts after death." Although he finally rejects the "gain" of death, it is clearly death that he prefers.

14. On this point, we disagree with Droge and Tabor. They have suggested a tolerance for a certain kind of suicide among Jews, Christians, Greeks, and Romans. We contrast the antisuicidal strain in Judaism with the fascination with death apparent in the Greco-Roman world. The other-worldliness of the New Testament seems more Greco-Roman than Judaeo-Christian.

ing, the Romans were little interested in anyone's religious beliefs, but the Christians seemed to be political troublemakers, if not saboteurs and rebels. The belief in a man-god was understandable enough in an empire that deified its own rulers; but the Romans could readily feel suspicious about a cult that met secretly (in the catacombs, for example), proselytized among women and slaves, and rejected the worship of the divine caesars and the empire itself. Moreover, in the beginning at least, the Christians were associated with the Judeans (most of Jesus' earliest followers were Jews), who had their own foreign beliefs and ways of life and who had often revolted against their Roman overlords. By the late first century, the Roman government had begun to believe that force should be used to make Christians behave like good Romans, particularly in showing a patriotic respect to the government, including offering sacrifices to the emperor. A correspondence between the Emperor Trajan and Pliny, his governor in Bithynia, discusses the "Christian problem" (Pliny, *Letters,* Bk. 10).

Many Christians responded by refusing to compromise their faith in any way: they gave up their lives as *martyrs* (the Greek term for "witnesses") for their faith. Martyrdom was often the only choice for the Christian; yet, beyond the acceptance of martyrdom as unavoidable, early Christians often showed a desire — even an active pursuit — of death. One of the earliest martyrs was Ignatius of Antioch, who was fed to the beasts in the arena in Rome in about 107 CE. Little is known of his life, but he left some thoughts on religion and martyrdom in a series of letters he wrote while a prisoner on the way from Antioch to Rome. Many of his ideas show the influence of classical Hellenism.

Martyrdom was already a central theme in Christianity at the time of Ignatius. He begged his influential friends in Rome not to intervene to save him. He could be "an intelligible utterance of God, but if your affections are only concerned with poor human life, then I become a mere meaningless cry once more" (*Epistle to the Romans,* 1). This Christian martyr actively sought death, for only through death could his life be more than a meaningless cry. Ignatius seemed to feel an urgent need to prove his nothingness: "Pray leave me to be a meal for the beasts, for it is they who can provide my way to God . . . ground fine by the lion's teeth to make pure bread for Christ. . . . [L]et them not leave the smallest scrap of my flesh" (Ignatius, *Epistles,* 4). Ignatius called himself a useless burden who desired to be demolished and devoured to the last particle, "so that I need not be a burden to anyone after I fall asleep." His desire for martyrdom was active and uncompromising: "I am yearning for death with all the passion of a lover" (Ignatius, *Epistles*, 9). Ignatius separated himself, as did the later ascetics, from any interest in physical life: "In me there is left no desire for mundane things, but only a murmur of living water that whispers within me, 'come to the Father'. . . . I want no more of what men call life."

Ignatius here clearly displays the Greeks' pervasive and absorbing interest in death. However, he believed that, through Christian devotion, he could overcome death. By touching the resurrected Christ, the disciples "came by their contempt for death and proved themselves superior to it" (Ignatius, *Epistle to the Smyrneans*, 3). "His death . . . is the very mystery which has moved us to become believers and endure tribulation to prove ourselves pupils of Jesus Christ" (Ignatius, *Epistle to the Magnesians*, 8). Furthermore, the Greek dichotomy between soul and body that is so foreign to Judaism now appears in Christian terms: "When there is no trace of my body left for the world to see, then I shall truly be Christ's Disciple" (*Epistle to the Romans*, 4). The accomplishments of this world mean nothing to Ignatius: "Suffer me to attain light pure and undefiled, for only when I come thither shall I be truly a man." Perhaps the most striking passages in these letters are those in which he depicts his need for total self-obliteration: "How good it is to be sinking down below the world's horizon." In Ignatius's way of thinking, a person is lowly and insignificant until, by dying, he rises above death.

To Ignatius, martyrdom seemed to offer the hope of meaning in a life that otherwise has no inherent worth. There was thus a pressure to offer up one's life both because of the Christians' uncomfortable political status in the Roman Empire and also because of the themes of death and martyrdom so central in the New Testament. Still, as much as Ignatius might have longed for martyrdom, he seemed more to wish not to avoid it rather than to seek it as actively as many others did.

Christians were still being persecuted in the middle of the third century, when Bishop Cyprian of Carthage was executed for his faith by Roman officials. However, by that time the church was larger, and its adherents more militant. Martyrdom was no longer unusual, and many staunchly devout Christians went to their deaths in front of huge arena crowds, or, more privately, in prisons. Cyprian's letters and essays reflect the mood of a new age and also the personality differences between him and Ignatius. Many of his letters deal with events during the persecutions under the Emperor Decius. Cyprian was a great believer in martyrdom;

ironically, though, he was strongly criticized for absenting himself from Carthage for some time to avoid arrest.

Several themes appear repeatedly in Cyprian's writings. First, he discussed how much the world hated the Christians. There was, of course, much ill feeling between Christians and pagans in the third century. For Cyprian, however, the theme of hatred appeared to be a theological concept. He quoted Luke 6:22: "Blessed are ye when men shall hate you." Cyprian went on: "[I]f the world hates you, remember that it hated me before you. You can neither desire martyrdom till you have first hated the world, nor attain to God's reward unless you have loved Christ. And who loves Christ does not love the world." There had to be antagonism between Christ and the world; likewise, there could be only hatred between Christian and pagan. Second, Jesus' crucifixion brought salvation to the world. However, his act of self-sacrifice and suffering was so immense that it must now be "a great matter to imitate him who in dying convicted the world" (Cyprian, *On the Glory of Martyrdom*, 29). "[W]hat He exhorts man to suffer, He Himself first suffered for us" (Cyprian, *Letters*, 55.3). The crucifixion had set the example of the highest possible moment toward which humans had to strive, since the world of the body is evil and should be scorned: "Consider what glory it is to set aside the lusts of life. . . . What then is martyrdom, the end of sins, the limit of dangers" (*On the Glory of Martyrdom*, 54). Moreover, "[d]eath makes life more complete, death rather leads to glory."

Pontius, a friend and biographer of Cyprian, indicated in his work *A Life and Passion of Cyprian* that he, too, was elated by a passion for "the consummation of martyrdom" (Pontius, 7). Therefore, one must not condemn the cruel executioners; rather, one must "pray for the salvation of those that persecute him" (Pontius, 9); one "must forgive and forgive and again frequently forgive" (Pontius, 10). It was the general wish of the Christians who witnessed Cyprian's execution "that the entire congregation should suffer at once in the fellowship of a like glory" (Pontius, 18): "Much and excessively do I exalt his [Cyprian's] glory; but still more do I grieve that I remained behind."

Clearly, a passionate desire for martyrdom invigorated Christianity during these years of persecution. This is not to say that all Christian thinkers of this period were suicidal. Lactantius, in his description of the last great persecution early in the fourth century, gave full honor to the martyrs (*Divine Institutes*, 89, 90), but he castigated the persecutors, whom he saw as enemies rather than as helpers who brought glory to the martyrs. The era of persecution ended when Emperor Constantine accepted Christianity. Martyrdom was replaced by ascetic monasticism, which became the major beneficiary of Christianity's eschatological energies.

St. Augustine and After

Despite his insistence on the voluntary aspects of the death of Jesus, St. Augustine (354-438) strongly condemned suicide in the *City of God* as "a detestable crime and a damnable sin" (1.27). He based this prohibition on his interpretation of Deuteronomy 5:17: "Thou shalt not kill" (1:20).[15] He considered even the suicides of Judas Iscariot and of the Roman matron Lucretia to be evil, and he portrayed Jesus as urging flight from persecution rather than self-murder (1.17, 19, 22). One must not commit suicide out of magnanimity, because of physical violation of chastity, or to avoid future sin. Augustine declared his preference for the saintly Job over the suicidal Cato (1.24).

Augustine's attitudes toward suicide were tested in his controversies with the heretical Circumcelliones and Donatists. Augustine first argued that the Donatists tended to engage in waves of martyr suicides, often seeking to provoke and even invite their own persecution. After the battle of Bagai in 347, the two rebel leaders, Donatus of Bagai and Marculus, were arrested and died. According to the Donatist account, the two were executed: Donatus was thrown down a well, and Marculus was thrown from a rock. St. Optatus suggested that the Donatists caused their own downfall, and Augustine went even further: he questioned whether they were thrown down or actually threw themselves down. He declared that such self-precipitation was a common practice among the Donatists, which they attempted to justify by the example of Razis, as narrated in 2 Maccabees 14 (Willis 1950).

Both Optatus and Augustine condemned the dominant Donatist passion for quasi-martyrdom by suicide. Whole companies threw themselves from rocks (they despised hanging, since the traitor Judas had killed

---

15. The Hebrew phrase *lo tirtsach* (Exod. 20:13; Deut. 5:17) is more accurately translated as "thou shalt not murder" than "thou shalt not kill," and is so interpreted in rabbinic literature.

himself that way). But the Donatists did not kill themselves if they could persuade the authorities to do it. One device was to attack magistrates on the road. Sometimes they stopped ordinary travelers and invited them to kill them, sometimes even threatening those travelers with murder if they did not comply. Yet, despite his condemnation of suicide, Augustine wrote to a Roman soldier stationed at a frontier outpost that he should not defend himself against barbarians lest it give rise to sinful intentions in his heart (Augustine, *Epistles,* 185.2.7).

Christian thinking on suicide after Augustine reflected the political and legal changes from the Roman Empire to medieval Christendom. With the post-Constantinian success of Christianity, martyrdom, or dying for the faith, was no longer an issue within the old Roman Empire (though it remained so for Christian missionaries who sought to convert pagan tribesmen outside the boundaries of Christian civilization). The second Council of Orleans (533) produced the church's first official disapproval of suicide by denying funeral rites to suicides who were accused of crimes.[16] The Council of Braga (563) extended this ban to all suicides. In 590, the Council of Antisidor forbade the church to accept offerings for the souls of suicides (see also Donne 1608; Sullivan 1984).

Aquinas comes out strongly against suicide in his *Summa Theologica.* Despite his argument that Jesus was the voluntary indirect cause of his own death (*Summa,* 3.47.1), Aquinas attempts to demolish pagan arguments for suicide. He reiterates Augustine's argument from *City of God* (1.20) that associates suicide with murder (2.2.64.5). Aquinas then adds three arguments of his own. First, suicide is unnatural: everyone bears an instinctive charity toward himself and should thus desire to do himself no harm. Suicide, being both unnatural and uncharitable, is a mortal sin. Second, an individual is a member of a social unit. Thus, Aquinas echoes the Aristotelian argument that suicide is antisocial. Third, life is the gift of God: though it is given, it remains God's property; therefore, only God can pronounce the sentence of life and death: "I will kill and I will make to live" (Deut. 32:39).

Of all later Christian thinkers, John Donne (1572-1631) was unique in

---

16. The first anti-suicide legislation in canon law was actually passed at the Council of Arles in 452 CE. These measures were not directed against suicide in general but were simply a repetition of the earlier Roman economic legislation forbidding the suicide of slaves (see Fedden 1938, 115).

seeing the implications in the voluntary death of Christ for a Christian tolerance of suicide. For Donne, Christ's death was brave and voluntary: "[I]t is a heroic act of fortitude, if a man when an urgent occasion is presented, expose himself to a certain and assured death as he did" (*Biathanatos,* 3.4.5). Donne thus may be said to view the passion of Christ as a Greek altruistic suicide: he was a martyr who gave his life to redeem mankind. Many of the early Christian martyrs also seemed suicidal in nature: "And that Apollonia and others, who prevented the fury of the executioners, and cast themselves into the fire, did therein imitate this act of our Savior, of giving up his soul, before he was constrained to do it." This behavior certainly stands in marked contrast to that of the Jewish martyrs of faith, who tried to avoid death if at all possible and to live in a way that did not compromise their faith.

In summary, then, the Christian church slowly but surely formalized its opposition to suicide. This can be seen in the statements of Augustine, the church councils, and Aquinas. Nonetheless, Donne pointed to the potentially suicidal strain in the passion of Jesus Christ, which is the foundation of Christianity. One strand of Christian thought has emphasized the altruism of the story of Jesus while still opposing suicide. A second strand seems to bear much of the obsession with death inherent in early Greco-Roman heroism.

II. Individual Case Studies from
Greek Tragedy and Biblical Narratives

4. Cycle vs. Development: Narcissus vs. Jonah

Narcissus had played with her affections, treating her as he had previously treated other spirits of the waters and the woods, and his male admirers, too. Then one of those he had scorned raised up his hands to heaven and prayed: "May he himself fall in love with another as we have done with him! May he too be unable to gain his loved one!" Nemesis heard and granted his righteous prayer.

Ovid, *Metamorphoses*, 3.366-475

Now the word of the Lord came unto Jonah, the son of Amitai, saying, "Arise, go to Nineveh, that great city and proclaim against it: for their wickedness is come up before me." But Jonah rose up to flee unto Tarshish from the presence of the Lord. . . . So they took up Jonah, and cast him forth into the sea; and the sea ceased from its raging. . . . And the Lord had prepared a great fish to swallow up Jonah. . . . Then Jonah prayed unto the Lord his God out of the fish's belly . . . and the Lord spake unto the fish, and it vomited out Jonah upon the dry land.

Jonah 1–2

The Greek and Hebrew worlds offered widely divergent concepts of cycle and development, and these were linked closely to their attitudes toward life and death. The assumptions underlying the Greek and modern Western attitudes seem to be as follows: first, the course of life is filled with ir-reconcilable alternatives, a series of Hobson's choices; second, tragic-heroic man attempts to deal with this dilemma by hopelessly cycling through opposing alternatives; third, there is no way out of this trap, so the cycles become more helpless, hopeless, and suicidal.[1]

The assumptions underlying biblical and later Jewish thought are quite different: first, the world is not filled with irreconcilable conflicts; second, biblical and rabbinic man avoids the tragic-heroic trap; third, meaningful development is possible, and there is the potential to escape the dialectical-cyclical vacillation that leads nowhere. This sense of devel-opment is purposive, hopeful, and suicide-preventive.[2]

Sisyphus and the Conception of Cycle

Cyclical themes have appeared in literature from earliest antiquity, first in the concept of fertility cycles that were intertwined with the pagan beliefs in gods who die in autumn and return to life in spring (e.g., Thammuz, Osiris, Persephone). The notion of cycle pervaded Greek thought: a person rises up, only to be overcome by *hubris* (pride), and then is cast down into *nemesis* (retribution), the nadir of the cycle.

Historians have tended to see the story of nations in terms of a cycle:

1. Neuringer and Lettieri (1982, 31) have noted a relatively long history for the obser-vation that suicidal individuals display a narrow, highly focused, dichotomous, and fixed thinking style. Westcott (1885) first observed the suicidal situation as one in which the per-son perceives only two alternatives, of which the least odious is suicide. Cavan (1928) de-scribed the suicidal quality as a "fixity of ideas." The suicidal trap of wanting mutually exclu-sive opposites is expressed in Sylvia Plath's *The Bell Jar* (1986, 76). In this autobiographical novel of mental breakdown and suicide, the talented young poet Esther Greenwood says scornfully to her boyfriend: "If neurotic is wanting two mutually exclusive things at one and the same time, then I'm neurotic as hell. I'll be flying back and forth between one mutually exclusive thing and another for the rest of my days."

2. Curiously, it has become almost a truism of modern Western thought to view dia-lectical thinking, whether that of Hegel, Marx, or Jung, with admiration and Talmudic "hairsplitting" with disdain. Hairsplitting is seen as, at best, a clever but ultimately trivial at-tempt to avoid life's tragic irreconcilabilities. But biblical and rabbinic thought do not see the world as tragic. Furthermore, it is the very "hairsplitting" attacked by the Western world that offers an alternative to suicidally polarized thinking. Indeed, it offers the possibility of therapeutic development by avoiding irreconcilable extremes. Shneidman (1985, 179) has ar-gued for the suicidal implications of irreconcilable extremes in his essay on *Moby Dick*.

66

primitive peoples conquer established civilizations, become civilized themselves, and are, in their turn, conquered by other primitive, warlike invaders. Ibn Khaldun, Edward Gibbon, G. W. F. Hegel (with his construct of thesis, antithesis, and synthesis), and Arnold Toynbee — and we could add Karl Marx to the mix — have exhibited this trend of thought. The common element in all of the tragic cycles is that humans live in the face of an inevitable end. They are alone, and their activities are, in the long run, futile. The best they can hope for, the most admirable state, is that of the tragic hero, the individual who struggles against overwhelming odds with no real hope of effecting any change. This individual is Prometheus or the Man of La Mancha, with his "impossible dream." His efforts, as Aristotle points out in the *Poetics,* lead to misfortune and arouse pity; the very greatness of his heroism lies in its complete uselessness.

An important treatment of the idea of cycle appears in Albert Camus's great existentialist work *The Myth of Sisyphus* (1955). In one ancient Greek myth, Sisyphus, a clever fellow and by some accounts the father of the illegitimate and crafty Odysseus, was condemned, because of his various crimes and tricks against the gods, to push a boulder up to the top of a hill and over. But each time, just before he reached the top, the boulder would roll back down, and Sisyphus had to go back down the hill and start pushing it up all over again — surely an utterly futile existence.

For Camus, the tragic hero Sisyphus represents an existential model. The picture is horrifyingly stark and uncompromising: the hero must accept only that the world is totally absurd, and he must refuse any kind of consolation, hope, or reliable principles. Halfway measures are meaningless and unworthy. Everything or nothing must be explained, though, in truth, "any principle of explanation is useless" (75). "Between everywhere and forever there is no compromise" (61). Camus saw that the only true human achievement is the ability of the individual to struggle, even when he has realized and accepted that there is neither earthly achievement nor life after death. The overwhelming misery of Sisyphus's existence can be elevated only by the painful consciousness of ultimate futility that touched him each time he pushed the stone to the top of the slope and saw it roll back down again. In this moment of thought lies Sisyphus's tragic magnificence, his most meaningful and lucid insight into the human condition.

Since humans learn nothing new, the cycle must repeat itself. In fact, the tragic human, basing his sense of worth on his imperfect achievements, perhaps has as strong an urge toward failure as toward success. In the *Poetics,* Aristotle says that the arousal of fear and pity in the audience in response to the hero's suffering is a chief feature of drama. The grandeur of the lost cause arouses much attention and is a very attractive notion, however impractical it may be. There is no resolution to this pattern, and the individual must fail in her search for ultimate achievement. But she may try to maintain some illusion of mastery, by resorting to indifference (Camus 1955, 69) and the acceptance of the totality of absurdity. Sisyphus personifies Blaise Pascal's famous statement, "Man is but a reed, the weakest in Nature, but he is a thinking reed. . . . [H]e is great because he knows that he is miserable" (*Pensées* 1958, 6.347, 397).

The protagonist in the tragic cycle, as portrayed from the ancient Greek playwrights down to Camus, is also burdened by his grandiose need to avoid accepting any limitation on his power or freedom. The world seems alien and threatening, and only by means of his heroic achievements can the hero become worthy to surpass or transcend these limitations. Again, this effort can end only in failure. No amount of achievement can prevent the onset of nemesis. It is also noteworthy that Sisyphus pushes his burden alone. He has no companion, no fellow, no kin with him.[3] Camus writes: "There is only one truly serious philosophical problem and that is suicide. . . . The fundamental subject of *The Myth of Sisyphus* is this: it is legitimate and necessary to wonder whether life has a meaning; therefore, it is legitimate to meet the problem of suicide face to face" (11, 7).

Koheleth (Ecclesiastes) and the Concept of Development

The biblical book of Ecclesiastes (Koheleth, the preacher) rejects the pattern of the cycle that is inherent in *The Myth of Sisyphus.* Koheleth asks searching questions, as does Camus, but here the cycle is merely a problem with which to deal, not the all-determining basis of human existence. Koheleth's world is neither meaningless nor absurd, and in it humans may work, learn, and be happy. Let us look at Koheleth's rejection of the cycle design, which was an approach shared by later rabbinic thought. Koheleth does indeed speak of cycles early in the first chapter:

3. See Albert Camus, *The Myth of Sisyphus* (1955). Camus altered some of these ideas in his other works, for example, *The Plague* (1948).

> What profit has a man from all his labor in which he toils under
>   the sun?
> One generation passes away, and another generation comes;
>   but the earth abides forever.
> The sun also rises, and the sun goes down,
> And hastens to the place where it arose.
> The wind goes toward the south, and turns about to the north;
>   the wind whirls about continually, and comes again
>   on its circuit.
> All the rivers run into the sea, yet the sea is not full; to the place
> from which the rivers come, there they return again. (Eccles. 1:3-7)

This is the cycle of seasons: one might call it the ecological cycle. However, it is not a deterministic cycle of nations or of human lives, and it is not the product of some mystical fate. It is the same pattern that God established to reassure Noah after the great flood, a gracious gift to man and not a chafing burden. This pattern sets certain parameters for human activity and wisdom, but it does not foredoom the individual or greatly limit his ability to be useful, productive, or content. There is no indication that the preacher Koheleth sees this natural cycle as nefarious or threatening.

The famous third chapter, in contrast, seems to indicate a concept of development with regard to human affairs:

> To everything there is a season, a time for every purpose under
>   heaven:
> A time to be born, and a time to die;
> A time to plant, and a time to pluck what is planted;
> A time to kill, and a time to heal;
> A time to break down, and a time to build up;
> A time to weep, and a time to laugh;
> A time to mourn, and a time to dance;
> A time to cast away stones, and a time to gather stones;
> A time to embrace, and a time to refrain from embracing;
> A time to gain, and a time to lose;
> A time to keep, and a time to throw away;
> A time to tear, and a time to sew;
> A time to keep silence, and a time to speak;
> A time to love, and a time to hate;
> A time of war, and a time of peace. (Eccles. 3:1-8)

The above passage does not describe life as a cycle. Rather, it advises that there is a time for everything. Some situations may require planting, and other situations uprooting; there is a time to be born and a time to die. Indeed, many things that come from God are beyond human reach, but humans do not need to feel helpless or doomed. Recognizing mortal limitations and accepting divine omnipotence does not threaten the individual with annihilation.

Koheleth faces a dilemma, as does the Greek tragic hero; but the key question is not whether the individual should go on living in a world that has no use for him. Koheleth is not touched by suicidal doubts. Rather, since the world functions so well, he wonders what is left for humans to improve or create. "What profit has a man from all his labor in which he toils under the sun? . . . [T]here is nothing new under the sun. Is there anything of which it may be said, 'See this is new'? It has already been in ancient times before us" (Eccles. 1:3-10). This is not a mere academic exercise; it is a deeply troubling question. Yet, while an ultimate answer is not to be found, there is enough to do in the meantime, and Koheleth seeks to learn, to understand, and to do. "And I set my heart to seek and search out by wisdom concerning all that is done under heaven" (1:17). Wisdom can indeed increase both human sensitivity and human pain: "For in much wisdom is much grief" (1:18). But wisdom is still a good thing: "Then I saw that wisdom excels folly as light excels darkness" (2:13).

There is no suggestion here, as there is in Sophocles' *Oedipus*, that human wisdom's truest value lies in making people feel their misery (1.335). Misery is miserable, not sublime. Humans need not feel impelled toward a pitiable fate; they need not live in the rarefied yet horrifying pattern of tragic heroes, of Prometheus and Antigone. Humans can enjoy life, and God sees this as good. "There is nothing better for a man than that he should eat and drink, and that his soul should enjoy good in his labor. This also, I saw, was from the hand of God" (Eccles. 2:24).

In contrast to Sisyphus, Koheleth contends that a person should not live alone. Association with others can be frustrating, and yet, he says, "Live joyfully with the wife whom you love" (9:9). And he continues: "The three-fold cord is not quickly severed" (4:12). One cannot be totally egocentric. Koheleth opposes many aspects and implications of the cyclical-heroic view. Camus rejects a belief in God and any notion of human immortality; indeed, he saw in this rejection of God the basis of human freedom. Koheleth affirms that man is by nature morally free and able to reach some sort of accommodation with God. The problem is not God, nor the universe, nor humankind. Instead, there exists the practical question of what humans may do that will make a difference.

Camus sees Sisyphus's realization of his misery as his nirvana, the whole meaning of his being. Koheleth prizes wisdom but not as the sole value or as effective without the body. Koheleth is troubled by the very real dilemma of misery that is caused by factors beyond man's power. But this is not the only issue in life, and one need not completely despair if one cannot resolve it. In any case, some miseries are within human power to remedy. Koheleth does not depict the world as alternating starkly between the two poles of hubris and nemesis, success and failure, all or nothing. The question is not life versus suicide, "to be or not to be." Given that there is life and there is death, the question is how humans should react. There is no fencing with the illusion of a final answer. Rabbi Tarfon declared very succinctly centuries later: "It is not thy duty to complete the work but neither mayest thou desist from it" (*Mishna Avot*, 2.16).[4]

The difference between these two points of view is graphically illustrated in the stories of Narcissus and Jonah, which offer contrasting models of individual development. The myth of Narcissus depicts a chilling tale of wasteful self-disintegration; by contrast, the book of Jonah offers a compelling analysis of the struggle toward self-integration and maturation.

Narcissus and Jonah

The Myth of Narcissus

The earliest sources of the myth of Narcissus have long since been lost. Our most complete account from antiquity is in the *Metamorphoses* of Ovid (ca. 43 BCE to 17 CE). Although physically beautiful, Narcissus leads a life full of precarious oscillation, and ultimately it ends in suicide. His story develops thus:

---

4. Rabbinic literature does, in fact, contain the notion that the world was not created in a perfect state and that man may and should improve it; for example, "Everything that was created in the first six days needs improvement" (*Pesikta Rabbati,* 23). See also J. D. Soloveitchik, *Halakhic Man* (1983).

1. A seer prophesies that the handsome Narcissus will live to a ripe old age, provided that he never knows himself (*Metamorphoses*, 3.347-59). Narcissus's life thus begins with a riddle that presents him with an insoluble conflict. He is filled with primordial guilt and fear. Narcissus must avoid self-knowledge or die.

2. Although many fall in love with Narcissus, he heartlessly rejects lovers of both sexes. His lack of inner knowledge is masked by a stubborn pride (hubris) in his own beauty (3.359-78). Among these lovers is Echo, who has no voice of her own and can only reflect back what Narcissus says (3.379-92).

3. One of those whom Narcissus has scorned raises his hands to heaven and prays: "May he, himself, fall in love with another, as we have done with him; may he, too, be unable to gain his loved one!" (3.405-6).

4. Nemesis, hearing this prayer, causes Narcissus to seek shelter from the sun near a pool and to fall in love with his own reflection in it. At first, Narcissus unsuccessfully tries to embrace and kiss the beautiful boy who confronts him (3.414-54).

5. Subsequently, he recognizes himself and lies gazing at his image for hours. Desiring to separate his soul from his body, he seeks a "joint death."

   "Alas! I am myself the boy I see. . . . I am on fire with love for my own self. My very plenty makes me poor. How I wish I could separate myself from my body! I have no quarrel with death, for in death I shall forget my pain: but I could wish that the object of my love might outlive me: as it is, both of us will perish together when this one life is destroyed" (3.463-75).

6. Grief is destroying him, yet he rejoices in the knowledge that his other self will remain true to him. Saying "alas" (which Echo repeats), Narcissus pines away unto death, mourning the boy he loves in vain.

   His last words as he gazed into the familiar waters were "Woe is me for the boy I loved in vain!" and the farewell, "Farewell!" said Echo too. He laid down his weary head on the green grass, and death closed the eyes which so admired their owner's beauty. (3.497-502)

Conon's account of the myth ends with Narcissus plunging a dagger into his breast (*Narrations,* 24).

The Book of Jonah

Consider, by contrast, the biblical book of Jonah. Jonah is confused and conflicted several times during the narrative. In fact, he expresses suicidal ideas on several occasions, but he does not commit suicide. Here is an outline of his story:

1. Jonah is ordered by God to go warn Nineveh of its wickedness. Jonah attempts to avoid God by running away to Tarshish (Jonah 1:1-3).

2. God sends a great wind after him, endangering his ship. When asked his identity by his shipmaster, Jonah admits to being the cause of the storm. He then asks his shipmates to throw him into the sea so as to spare themselves: "And he said to them, 'Pick me up and throw me into the sea; then the sea will become calm for you. For I know that this great tempest is because of me'" (1:12).

3. They do so, and while the ship is thus saved, Jonah is also saved — by a great fish sent by God. While Jonah is in the belly of the fish, he prays to God. After three days, the fish vomits Jonah out safely onto dry land:

   > Then Jonah prayed to the Lord his God from the fish's belly. . . . "For You cast me into the depth, into the heart of the seas, and the floods surrounded me; all Your billows and Your waves passed over me. Then I said: 'I have been cast out of Your sight'; yet I will look again toward Your holy temple. . . . I will pay what I have vowed. Salvation is of the Lord." So the Lord spoke to the fish, and it vomited Jonah onto dry land. (Jonah 2)

4. Once again, God commands Jonah to go to Nineveh. This time Jonah goes and gives the people of Nineveh God's message. They repent and are saved (3:1-10). Jonah is angry, however, and desires to die: "But it displeased Jonah exceedingly, and he became angry. . . . 'Therefore now, O Lord, please take my life from me; for it is better for me to die than to live!'" (4:1-3).

5. Jonah leaves the city to sit on its outskirts. There he is shielded by a

gourd plant that God makes to grow up over him. "And the Lord God prepared a plant and made it come up over Jonah, that it might be a shade for his head to deliver him from his misery. So Jonah was very grateful for the plant" (4:6).

6. God then destroys the plant with a worm, exposing Jonah to the sun. Jonah again expresses the wish to die: "[A]nd the sun beat on Jonah's head, so that he grew faint. Then he wished death for himself, and said, 'It is better for me to die than to live'" (4:7-8).

7. God again intervenes, asking Jonah, "Is it right for you to be angry about the plant?" When Jonah replies, "It is right for me to be angry, even to death," God uses the opportunity to explain the meaning of divine mercy:

> "You have had pity on the plant for which you have not labored, nor made it grow, which came up in a night and perished in a night. And should I not pity Nineveh, that great city, in which are more than one hundred twenty thousand persons who cannot discern between their right hand and their left hand — and also much livestock?" (4:9-11)

The method God uses to impart this teaching is a deeply important part of the lesson. Rather than rebuke Jonah directly and impatiently as would seem fitting at this point, God uses a parable about a plant. This kind of intervention avoids wounding Jonah and enables him to meet God halfway, a clear step in his development (4:9-11).

A Comparison

The ideas of cycle and development appear quite vividly in the life stories of Narcissus and Jonah. The myth of Narcissus has been used in classic psychoanalytic thinking to refer to an individual who is totally self-absorbed, one who is *narcissistic* rather than object-invested (Freud 1914; Hartmann 1964). But a close examination of this myth suggests a cycling between seemingly opposing alternatives.

Table 4.1 divides the narrative into three phases. In the first part of the narrative, Narcissus tends to be self-absorbed and filled with hubris, treating his lovers as mere extensions of himself. This trend becomes ac-

Table 4.1
Individual Development for Narcissus and Jonah

Narcissus

Act	*Move*	*Outcome*
Narcissus mirrors and abandons Echo.	C	Mirroring Narcissism
Narcissus idealizes and is absorbed by face in pond.	A	Idealizing Narcissism
Narcissus recognizes face in pond as his own. He idealizes his own mirror image and commits suicide.	A/C	Suicide

Jonah

Act	*Move*	*Outcome*
Jonah runs away in confusion from God's command to go to Nineveh. He asks to be thrown overboard, but God sends fish to save him from drowning.	A/C→B_1	Level One Regression and Suicide Prevention
Jonah becomes stronger. God causes fish to vomit Jonah out on dry land.	E_1	Level One Emergence
Jonah goes to Nineveh but later expresses disagreement with God.	D_1	Level One Dialogue
Jonah sits outside Nineveh in confusion and again expresses suicidal desire. God shields him from the sun with gourd plant.	A/C→B_2	Level Two Regression and Suicide Prevention
Jonah becomes stronger. God causes worm to eat plant.	E_2	Level Two Emergence
God teaches Jonah the message of mercy: to help others without being absorbed by them.	D_2	Level Two Dialogue

centuated in his relationship with Echo, who becomes a perfect mirror for Narcissus, reflecting everything Narcissus says. Self-absorbed and egoistic, in Durkheim's terms, Narcissus is insufficiently connected with his environment (a C position of detached individuation in Figure 1.2), but he is not yet suicidal. Then a rejected suitor prays that Narcissus himself will experience unrequited love. Nemesis answers this prayer, seducing Narcissus with a false sanctuary: a beautifully clear pond to provide shelter from the heat. Nemesis uses the pool to cause Narcissus to fall hopelessly in love for the first time. Narcissus is infatuated with the face in the pond, not realizing that it is his own reflection. Narcissus is now other-absorbed, or altruistic in Durkheim's terms, insufficiently differentiated from his environment (an A position of deindividuated attachment, in Figure 1.2).[5]

Now, however, Narcissus recognizes that the face in the pond is his.[6] Narcissus is not self-invested but empty of self, striving to grasp his missing self, which has now been projected onto the outside world. Such a psychotic juxtaposition splits Narcissus apart (A/C, Figure 1.2): he takes his own life, either passively or actively (depending on the version). As Ovid puts his emotion: "How I wish I could separate myself from my body." This is schizophrenia. In Durkheim's terms, Narcissus is anomic, experiencing confusion about the boundaries between himself and the outside world.[7]

Narcissus kills himself or allows himself to die because he is unable to successfully resolve his individuation–attachment dilemma: he is

5. Kohut has termed these two phases "mirroring" and "idealizing" narcissistic configurations. For Kohut (1971), unlike Freud, narcissism is defined not by the target of the instinctual investment (i.e., whether it is the subject himself or other people) but by the "nature or quality of the instinctual charge" (26). Therefore, Kohut sees an idealizing configuration whereby one invests his energy in the "omnipotent other" as narcissistic, as is the withdrawal of psychic energy inward into the "grandiose self" (i.e., the mirroring configuration). The intent behind the idealizing position is as inherently self-serving (you are perfect, but I am part of you) as is that behind the mirroring position (I am perfect). Narcissus cycles between Kohut's mirroring and idealizing narcissistic configurations; but he is still not actively suicidal.

6. The theme of the double, or *Doppelgänger,* has been very popular in European literature. It typically involves the attempts of a hero to reunite with his missing double, often a reflection (see Rank 1971). In Kohut's terms, the mirror has become the ideal.

7. In Shneidman and Farberow's (1957) terms, Narcissus represents an example of "suicidal logic," or the inability to integrate one's personal self (I_s) and one's social self (I_o). For such persons, one can be obtained only at the expense of the other.

trapped along the AC axis. He cycles between hubris (C) and nemesis (A). First, he is individuated at the expense of attachment (i.e., the egoistic, or C position); then he is attached at the expense of individuation (i.e., the altruistic, or A position). Finally, overwhelmed by his conflicts on both of these issues (i.e., the anomic, or A/C position), he kills himself.

In the story of Jonah, the idea of cycle is missing. Jonah is presented with a difficult dilemma at the beginning of the story. Nineveh is a symbol of evil to him, and once he has preached God's message, he thinks that it should not be spared through God's mercy. At the same time, Jonah does not want to defy God. Jonah rejects the Hobson's choice between the altruistic (A) and egoistic (C) pitfalls of Narcissus (see Table 4.1).

When Jonah tells his shipmates to throw him overboard during the storm, the story could end in his virtual suicide. But it does not. Like a protective parent, God intervenes by securing Jonah in the stomach of a great fish (position B_1 in Table 4.1). As he becomes stronger, Jonah prays to God, and the fish spits Jonah out on dry land (E_1). Finally, Jonah agrees to take God's message to the people of Nineveh (D_1). He avoids antithetical thinking between individuation and attachment: he sees these life forces not as mutually exclusive opposites requiring dialectical resolution and suicide. God provides the stopper to allow Jonah to develop in a way that integrates individuation and attachment.

But Jonah's journey is not complete. He does not yet fully grasp God's higher purpose, and thus he becomes angry when the people of Nineveh repent and are saved. He is still in opposition to God (the A/C conflict), though at a higher stage of development. He runs away again, this time settling outside the walls of Nineveh, where he once more expresses his wish to die. God again intervenes by providing a second stopper or protective wall for Jonah: this time it is a gourd plant to shield Jonah from the sun (position B_2). God removes the wall a second time by having a worm destroy the gourd (E_2). Jonah once more expresses suicidal thoughts, but God again intervenes: this time he engages Jonah in a mature dialogue about the meaning of repentance, and he ends Jonah's confusion about integrating individuation and attachment (*Yalkut Shimoni*).

The suicide-preventive element in this story is the covenantal stopper that allows Jonah to regress out of a polarized dichotomy between individuation and attachment. Under God's protection, Jonah is able to grow and avoid the conflictual logic that leads to the demise of Narcissus.

The Suicide of Otto Weininger

The tragic end of the self-hating Jewish intellectual Otto Weininger exemplifies the threat of suicide to one who was torn between individuation and attachment. Weininger shot himself to death in 1903 at the age of twenty-three in the very apartment where Beethoven had died some seventy-six years earlier. Weininger became famous posthumously for his brilliant but erratic book *Sex and Character* (1903), which is noteworthy for its Jewish self-hatred, its misogyny, and its strongly Platonic elevation of logic and ideal form.

In this work Weininger argued that woman does not act from principle, because she has no continuity. Woman does not need logical support for her mental process; man feels the obligation to keep the logical standard that he has set up for himself, but woman resents any attempt to require that her thoughts be logical. She may be regarded as "logically insane" (149). Weininger equates women and Jews with the lack of any genuine self-being or integrity of self-definition. Woman believes in others; she has a center of gravity, but it is outside her own being. The Jew believes in nothing, either inside or outside himself (320-21).

Weininger projected his own inadequacies on women and Jews. Later, Nazi ideologues cited his ideas to elevate Aryanism and masculine strength. Weininger's ravings reveal much about his emotional condition. He regarded attachment and individuation as contradictory, a conflict that he expressed directly in letters regarding his own life. In one of his most poignant confessions, he says:

> That is the worst; not being able to love when one is loved and knows one is loved, with hatred toward that bitter feeling of a desire to love deep down in the heart. This petrification, this barrenness! An olive tree on the hardest granite! My soul cannot free itself and enter into that of another who loves me. (Weininger, *Condemnation*, 1902)

Weininger, though ethnically a Jew, followed the pathological pattern of the Greek Narcissus. He rejected those who would love him, and his soul remained aloof and barren. It is as though he perceived loving as weakness, yet he felt frozen and alone as a result. This conflict is potentially suicidal in itself. The psychiatrist David Abrahamsen (1946) has added, however, that Weininger did not simply reject the advances of others; sometimes he accepted them. The very acceptance of life gave birth to his loneliness and rejection of life. Abrahamsen puts it this way:

> He [Weininger] seems to have sought to establish relations with others, to join with the crowd. Yet to think he enjoyed being in the crowd would be a mistake. When he was part of a group, he was with the others only superficially. He wanted to belong to them, to share with them in youthful activity, so strong was his longing for life. And yet he was freezing within, alone. His earnest desire for life evolves into hatred and fear of it. The stronger the longing, the stronger the fear. The division within him appeared in many contradictory and irreconcilable attitudes in the form of ambivalency and splitting. This affective ambivalency became gradually apparent in his attitudes toward women and toward Jews. (Abrahamsen, 1946, 21-22).

Weininger was a prime example of an anomic personality (A/C). He was simultaneously drawn to and repelled by the irreconcilable alternatives of individuation and attachment,[8] of life and death.[9] He was not simply conflicted between individuation and attachment; he was conflicted within each of these drives as well. He craved attachment, yet feared it. He needed individuation, yet he feared it as well. Suicide became his only way out.

---

8. Kalman Kaplan (1988, 1990b, 1998b) has developed an Individuation Attachment Questionnaire (IAQ) to assess individuation and attachment. The IAQ assumes an inherent ambiguity in our traditional definitions of near and far and attempts to separate out the often fine distinctions found in relationship to these dynamics. For example, agreement with the statement "It is important for me to take other people's needs into account" may indicate a *need for attachment.* At the same time, agreement with the statement "It is important for me to meet others' expectations of me" may indicate a *fear of individuation.* Likewise, agreement with the statement "Other people's judgment of me seldom determines how I feel about myself" may indicate a *need for individuation,* while agreement with the statement "A person does not need involvement with others to be fulfilled" may indicate a *fear of attachment.* Weininger's personality indicates high needs and high fears on both individuation and attachment, hence his suicidal conflict.

9. Israel Orbach and his colleagues (1983) have developed instruments for separately assessing attraction and repulsion with regard to both life and death. This procedure generates four measures: attraction to life, repulsion from life, attraction to death, and repulsion from death.

5. Suicide in Greek Tragedy

> But now prostrate beneath so great a woe, not tasting food nor drink, he sits among the sword-slain beasts, motionless where he sank. And plainly he meditates some baleful deed. For so portend his words and lamentations. . . . Some scheme let me devise which may prove to my aged sire that I, his son, at least by nature am no coward, for 'tis base for a man to crave long life who endures never-varying misery.
>
> Sophocles, *Ajax,* 317-28, 471-75[1]

Leading figures, usually heroic ones, in the fifth-century dramas of Sophocles and Euripides often saw no way but suicide to free themselves from what they perceived as no-win life situations. These plays were familiar to educated Greeks and Romans of antiquity and were frequently quoted in the writings of the time.

An immensely important aspect of the Greek literary tradition is that the hero has basic flaws that drive him to destruction. He devotes himself to winning honor, and it is disgraceful for him to do less than strive to be a champion. So strong a drive may easily involve violence, harshness, or uncontrollable temper. Achieving heroism is more important than life itself, and this goal often demands the sacrifice of one's own life. The tragic hero is also typically trapped in a Hobson's choice. No mat-

---

1. This quotation and all subsequent quotations from Greek tragedies come from W. J. Oates and E. O'Neill Jr., *The Complete Greek Drama* (1938).

ter what he does, the Greek hero moves inexorably toward his doom. There is no stopper. Prophets in Greek drama often use what should be freeing knowledge to taunt or lead the hero to self-destruction through a series of vague riddles that present information in a concealed or inaccessible way.

The great tragedy of Oedipus exemplifies all these patterns. The characters feel trapped between the need to save Thebes and the need to protect or pacify Oedipus, who finally, in the truest heroic manner, sacrifices himself to save the city of Thebes. He accepts the classic Hobson's choice, the cyclical riddle of the Sphinx with all its destructive implications, and he finds no stopper in a grim and hostile world. Sophocles expresses this sense of hopelessness powerfully in *Antigone*. Greatness in human life brings doom, and a doomed human cannot even accurately distinguish good from bad. The house of Oedipus is utterly without hope: there is no possibility of a cure or of a prayer to a concerned deity to extricate the family from its fate. Creon is told this very thing by the chorus at the end of *Antigone:* "Pray thou no more, for mortals have no escape from destined woe" (1336). Finally, the riddles of Tiresias only confuse and antagonize Oedipus, who has been a good and devoted king of Thebes. Why do the Greeks use the riddle form rather than the form of the biblical parable, such as the one Nathan presents to David (2 Sam. 12)? Perhaps the riddle enables Tiresias to keep control of the situation: he gains his security by presenting himself as an indispensable source of knowledge. In any case, he gives Oedipus no clear information by which the latter may improve his situation; in fact, Tiresias makes matters worse.

Characters in Greek tragedy are trapped in no-win cyclical situations that are not entirely of their own making.[2] There is no way out of the cycle, nor is there much chance of seeing the alternatives clearly. Their prophets, such as Tiresias, speak in riddles that are meant to be misleading and unhelpful. Indeed, prophecy in Greek tragedy is completely deterministic: *Consequence Y will occur no matter which antecedent X_1 or X_2 the tragic hero*

---

2. Aristotle offered what has been regarded as the classic definition of tragedy "as an imitation of an action that is serious, complete, and of a certain magnitude; in language embellished with each kind of artistic ornament, the several kinds being found in separate parts of the play; in the form of action, not of narrative, through pity and fear effecting the proper purgation of these and similar emotions" (*Poetics,* chap. 6). The tragic hero is "a man who is highly renowned and prosperous, but one who is not preeminently virtuous and just, whose misfortune, however, is brought upon him not by vice and depravity but by some error of judgment or frailty" (*Poetics,* chap. 13).

attempts. Oedipus has no saving answers to the riddle of the Sphinx, for there are none. Answering "correctly" or "incorrectly" will lead to the same self-destruction of the house of Labdacus. There is neither hope nor prayer. The deities themselves, as products of the natural world, are both too powerless and too preoccupied with their own affairs to intervene (Kaufmann 1972, chap. 2). The entire tragic context is a breeding ground for suicide. An excellent study by M. D. Faber (1970) has noted sixteen suicides and self-mutilations in the twenty-six extant plays of Sophocles and Euripides. There is a seventeenth: Jocasta in Euripides's *Phoenissae.* [3] However, many of these suicides, especially those in Euripides, fall into a pattern of ritual murder, in which the person does not actually raise a hand against himself.

In these dramas, character after character is led to a suicidal end. Faber has used Durkheim's three categories of suicide to argue that the suicides in Sophocles tend to be primarily egoistic (initially outward destructive tendencies that are turned inward), while those in Euripides tend to be primarily altruistic (basically inward destructive tendencies that are sometimes disguised as outwardly heroic or martyrlike acts). Some cases in the plays of both playwrights may fall into Durkheim's anomic type (Table 5.1).

Sophocles

Oedipus Rex

Suicide is a major theme in four of Sophocles' seven surviving plays: *Oedipus Rex, Antigone, Ajax,* and *The Trachinae. Oedipus Rex* contains one egoistic suicide (Jocasta) and one anomic self-mutilation (Oedipus himself).

Oedipus Rex begins with the priest of Zeus telling King Oedipus of the ravages of the plague on the city of Thebes. Creon announces that the plague is due to the unavenged murder of Laius and describes the circum-

3. Only one possible act of self-destruction occurs in the seven surviving plays of Aeschylus, the third great Greek tragedian. It is the death of Eteocles in *Seven Against Thebes* (692-715). However, it is not definitively a suicide; it is more like a reckless disdain for life per se, and thus we will not treat it as such in this chapter. We will treat it later, when we pursue in greater detail the curse of Oedipus.

Table 5.1
Self-Destruction in Greek Tragedy

Character	Gender	Source	Method	Type
Oedipus	M	Oedipus Rex (Sophocles)	Self-blinding	Anomic
Jocasta	F	Oedipus Rex (Sophocles)	Hanging	Egoistic
Antigone	F	Antigone (Sophocles)	Hanging	Anomic
Haemon	M	Antigone (Sophocles)	Stabbing	Egoistic
Eurydice	F	Antigone (Sophocles)	Stabbing	Egoistic
Ajax	M	Ajax (Sophocles)	Stabbing	Egoistic
Deianeira	F	The Trachinae (Sophocles)	Stabbing	Anomic
Heracles	M	The Trachinae (Sophocles)	Burning	Egoistic
Phaedra	F	Hippolytus (Euripides)	Stabbing	Anomic
Menoeceus	M	The Phoenissae (Euripides)	Jumping	Altruistic
Jocasta	F	The Phoenissae (Euripides)	Stabbing	Altruistic
Evadne	F	The Suppliants (Euripides)	Burning	Anomic
Iphigenia	F	Iphigenia in Aulis (Euripides)	Hanging	Altruistic
Macaria	F	The Heracleidae (Euripides)	Stabbing	Altruistic
Polyxena	F	Hecuba (Euripides)	Stabbing	Altruistic
Alcestis	F	Alcestis (Euripides)	Unspecified	Altruistic
Hermione	F	Andromache (Euripides)	Attempted Stabbing	Anomic

stances surrounding that unresolved crime. Oedipus volunteers to reopen the search for the murderer of Laius, cursing the killer to a life of misery and solitude. Oedipus seems obsessed with past family connections that, at least on a conscious level, are not his. There is no stopper to lighten the heroic burden of excessive responsibility that Oedipus takes on.

The unfolding of the terrible secret continues in earnest. Oedipus summons Tiresias, the blind oracle, who, like the seer in the legend of Narcissus, speaks in unfathomable riddles and points to the dangers of self-knowledge: "Alas, how dreadful to have wisdom where it profits not the wise!" (316-17). He tries to leave, but Oedipus will not permit it. Tiresias speaks again, but the riddles are so maddening that even when he finally and bluntly accuses Oedipus of being the killer, Oedipus does not understand him. Oedipus becomes furious, accusing both Tiresias and Creon of lying and plotting against him; but at the same time, he wants to know more. Tiresias again resorts to riddles, reminding Oedipus of his prowess in deciphering the riddle of the Sphinx.

This same pattern continues through the play. Oedipus becomes more and more obsessed with the need to get at what the audience knows will be a most unwelcome truth. Oedipus calls in one reluctant party after another, and he gives them all the same Hobson's choice of revealing to him the awful truth about his past or incurring his wrath by withholding information. Still, Oedipus insists on charging full speed ahead to attain the knowledge that will prove to be his undoing, first with Jocasta, then with a messenger, and finally with the herdsman. Again, like the seer in the Narcissus story, Jocasta tries to stop Oedipus in his search for both the murderer and self-knowledge: "For the gods' sake, if thou hast any care for thine own life, forbear this search! My anguish is enough" (1060-61). She further warns: "Ill-fated one! Mayest thou never come to know who thou art" (1069).[4] Finally, the herdsman begs him to stop; but Oedipus offers the herdsman the same Hobson's choice on penalty of death: "Thou art lost if I have to question thee again" (1166). Oedipus forces the herdsman to reveal the last piece in the horrible puzzle, and he finally sees his position clearly: he has murdered his father, Laius, himself, and he has married Jocasta, his mother. He is now determined to kill Jocasta, believing that it was through her that he was cursed from his birth on: "Oh, oh! All brought to pass — all true! Thou light, may I now look my last on thee — I who have been found accursed in birth, accursed in wedlock, accursed in the shedding of blood!" (1182-85).

Oedipus rushes into the palace, where he finds that Jocasta has hanged herself. He then puts out his own eyes.

> For he tore from her raiment the golden brooches wherewith she was
> decked, and lifted them and smote full on his own eye-balls, uttering

---

4. This constant discouragement of Oedipus's and Narcissus's search for self-knowledge seems to contradict the "know thyself" dictum of the Delphic oracle. The Delphic dictum does not, in fact, command a search for self-knowledge; it actually exhorts humans to be aware of their loneliness and powerlessness before the gods.

words like these: "No more shall ye behold such horrors as I was suffering and working! Long enough have ye looked on those whom ye ought never to have seen, failed in knowledge of those whom I yearned to know — henceforth ye shall be dark!" (1265-70)

When the full truth is first revealed, Jocasta's first impulse is to call out the name of the long-dead Laius and then to blame Oedipus. Laius is at fault for fathering Oedipus, and Oedipus is to blame for murdering his father and causing her such misery. Only after this egoistic reaction does she hang herself (Durkheim's position C). The suicide is filled with anger toward Laius and Oedipus, both of whom have brought her such pain, isolation, and shame.

Oedipus's self-blinding follows this same basic pattern. Upon learning the truth, his first impulse is apparently to commit homicide (against Jocasta), not suicide. She has become not his wife but the ultimately betraying and abandoning mother, and he wants to kill her: "To and fro he went, asking us to give him a sword — asking where he should find the wife who was no wife, but a mother whose womb had borne alike himself and his children" (1255-57). Only when he sees that Jocasta is dead does he turn his aggressive impulses inward. It is significant that he puts out his eyes with the golden brooches from her dress rather than with his own sword. He is finally paying his debt to the devouring earth-mother. Self-blinding — even more than suicide — may serve to shield Oedipus from an overwhelming world. If he cannot see the world, he can diminish his contact with it. Further, his eyes have proved to be his undoing: "Why was I to see, when sight could show me nothing sweet?" (1335). Self-blinding also protects Oedipus from a feared reunion with his accursed parents in the place of the dead (1370-75). Oedipus's lethal combination of disengagement and enmeshment fits Durkheim's anomic (position A/C) pattern of self-destruction.

Antigone

Sophocles' *Antigone* contains three suicides, those of Antigone, Haemon, and Eurydice. Antigone, the daughter of Oedipus and Jocasta, has long been viewed in Western thought as a sterling example of a highly individuated and idealistic woman who ably senses the conflict between the higher moral law and the wickedness of an earthly ruler.[5] When faced with Creon's decree that her brother Polyneices should remain unburied, she invokes the authority of the law of the gods and buries him. However, closer scrutiny reveals a far more complex character. She has overidentified with her family of origin and with the opinion of the community at large; she is also obsessed with death. Antigone's idealism masks the driving force of her life: the fulfillment of the curse of the house of Labdacus with which the play begins.[6] Her hopelessness is so profound that it can only lead to self-destruction.

This theme echoes throughout the play. After she has been condemned by Creon to be buried alive, Antigone repeats her depressive obsession:

> Thou hast touched on my bitterest thought, — awaking the ever-new lament for my sire and for all the doom given to us, the famed house of Labdacus. Alas for the horror of the mother's bed! Alas for the wretched mother's slumber at the side of her own son, — and my sire! From what manner of parents did I take my miserable being! And to them I go thus, accursed, unwed, to share their home. Alas, my brother, ill-starred in thy marriage, in thy death thou hast undone my life!
> (859-71)

But Antigone has already expressed her thoughts of a noble death, and this theme develops as the play proceeds. Antigone now sees death as preferable to life, as freedom from life's miseries.

> Die I must, — I knew that well (how should I not?) — even without thy edicts. But if I am to die before my time, I count that as a gain: for

---

5. Indeed, this point of view was invoked by the prosecution at the Nuremberg trials as an argument that German citizens were obligated to disobey Hitler's racist and genocidal laws.

6. Faber (1970, 84) has made exactly this same point about Antigone: "Is it possible that Antigone, who is often singled out as the most individualistic of Greek heroines, is, in reality, one of the least individualistic? For I believe that what we have here is a person whose own integration into the family unit and whose deep preoccupation with the opinion of the community at large have prevented her from achieving the autonomy, the sense of individual worth, which is usually accorded her?" Indeed, it is remarkable that Western thought has idealized Antigone and ignored the pathological curse of the house of Labdacus that underlies her heroism. Clearly, Sophocles himself did recognize it.

when anyone lives as I do, compassed about with evils, can such a one find ought but gain in death? (458-62)[7]

Slightly later she declares: "Be of good cheer, thou livest; but my life hath long been given to death, that so I may serve the dead" (560-61).

Antigone links her death with the fulfillment of the curse on her family: "From what manner of parents did I take my miserable being! And to them I go thus, accursed, unwed, to share their home" (869). She seems to strive to fulfill the curse on the house of Labdacus by bringing about her own death without offspring. She goes "living to the vaults of death" to join her dead brother (916-20). Antigone even uses the image of being wed to Acheron, the "Lord of the Dark Lake" (808-14).

That this preoccupation is not just resignation regarding her sentence can be seen by her expression of a greater, even an incestuous allegiance to her dead family of origin than to the living, even at the very beginning of the play. She sees marriage through the metaphor of death. She defies Creon's order to leave Polyneices unburied: "I know that I please where I am most bound to please" (89). She sees herself as lying with her brother in love: "I shall rest, a loved one with him whom I have loved, sinless in my crime" (74). An even more definitive example of this overallegiance to her family of origin at the expense of present relationships is her striking statement that she would not feel compelled to bury a husband or child as she would a brother. The former are replaceable, but the latter is not:

> Never, had I been a mother of children, or if a husband had been mouldering in death, would I have taken this task upon me in the city's despite. What law, ye ask is my warrant for that word? The husband lost, another might have been found, and child from another, to replace the firstborn: but, father and mother hidden with Hades, no brother's life could ever bloom for me again. (909-18)

Antigone also seems thoroughly indifferent to Haemon, her fiancé: she remains strangely silent in the face of Creon's attacks on him. Indeed, most manuscripts give her sister Ismene line 572: "Haemon beloved! How thy fa-

---

7. See also Philippians 1:21: "For me to live is Christ and to die is gain," as well as the related discussion in chap. 3.

ther wrongs thee."[8] Antigone is unable to relate to anyone. She rejects her sister Ismene roughly: she seems to go out of her way to insist that the deed be made public, while Ismene wishes to keep it quiet. Furthermore, Antigone is exceptionally insolent in her confrontation with Creon. Yet she later laments that she will die alone, forlorn, and friendless.

She expresses her embeddedness with her family of origin further in her method of suicide, which mimics that of her mother: "We described her [Jocasta] hanging by the neck . . . [w]hile he was embracing her with arms thrown around her waist" (1220-23). In her vacillation between enmeshment and isolation, and her confusion between self and other, Antigone proceeds to an anomic suicide (the A/C position).

Haemon, son of Creon and the fiancé of Antigone, enters midway through the play (628-30), "grieving for the doom of his promised bride Antigone." What develops is an accelerating step-by-step struggle between father and son. Creon questions whether Haemon will remain loyal to him, given Creon's sentencing of Antigone: "Art thou come in rage against thy father? Or have I thy good will?" (635). Haemon's first response is quite mild: he submits to his father's authority. To be sure, Haemon then skillfully attempts to present his own deeply felt views and defends Antigone forcefully, far more forcefully than she defended him. Creon responds by invoking the authority of age over youth; at this point the quarrel intensifies until Haemon openly threatens suicide.

The leader of the chorus warns Creon of Haemon's suicidal state, but Creon chooses to ignore it for too long. When he at last relents, it is too late. Haemon's emotions reach a peak when Creon interrupts his son's mourning for the dead Antigone. Creon's attempts at intervention are useless at this point and, in all likelihood, seem to Haemon to be another effort by his father to reestablish control. Haemon reacts violently: he tries to stab his father. When he fails at this, he turns his murderous wrath inward and falls on his own sword:

> But his father, when he saw him, cried aloud with a dread cry and went in, and called to him with a voice of wailing. . . . But the boy glared at him with fierce eyes, spat in his face, and, without a word of answer,

8. The noted translator Elizabeth Wyckoff has said that this line is Ismene's in almost all manuscripts. The only traditional evidence for giving this line to Antigone is that the Aldine edition (1502) and Turnebus (1553) gave it to her (1960, 227-28).

drew his cross-hilted sword: — as his father rushed forth in flight, he missed his aim; — then, hapless one, wroth with himself, he straight-away leaned with all his weight against the sword, and drove it, half its length, into his side. (1225-39)

Haemon's suicide is egoistic (position C). He feels controlled by his father, and his resultant rage, like that of Oedipus, he first projects outward against his father before he inverts it. Once again, there is the horrible image of marrying in death. "Corpse enfolding corpse he lies, he hath won his nuptial rites, poor youth, not here, yet in the halls of Death" (1240-41).

The final suicide in Sophocles' *Antigone* is that of Eurydice, the wife of Creon and the mother of Haemon. She enters late in the play and has only one speech (1183-90). She has heard of the family disaster and asks the messenger to repeat the story. Upon hearing of Haemon's suicide, Eurydice silently returns to her house. Her silence justifiably arouses concern from both the leader of the chorus and the messenger. Then the messenger reports that Eurydice, too, has killed herself:

Sire, thou hast come, me thinks, as one whose hands are not empty, but who hath store laid up besides; thou bearest yonder burden with thee; and thou art soon to look upon the woes within thy house. . . . Thy queen hath died, true mother of yon corpse — ah, hapless lady! — by blows newly dealt. (1279-87)

The messenger's further description reveals Eurydice's rage toward her husband, blaming him not only for the death of Haemon but also for the death of her other son, Megareus, as well. This hostility is characteristic of egoistic suicides (position C).

There, at the altar, self-stabbed with a keen knife, she suffered her darkening eyes to close, when she had wailed for the noble fate of Megareus who died before, and then for his fate who lies there, — and when, with her last breath, she had invoked evil fortunes upon thee, the slayer of thy sons. (1297-1300)

Ajax

A prime example of Sophoclean egoistic suicide is the Greek warrior Ajax in the play bearing his name. Ajax has gone mad with jealousy because Achilles' armor has been given to Odysseus; so, in a frenzied state, he tries to murder Odysseus. The goddess Athena prevents him from doing so by deflecting his anger so that he slaughters a herd of sheep instead. The text makes clear that Athena not only wants to restrain Ajax but to humiliate him deeply as well, and to mock him in his madness in front of Odysseus. Ajax's hubris has provoked Athena's anger:

> Then boastfully and witlessly he answered, "Father, with heaven's help a mere man of nought might win victory, but I, albeit without their aid, trust to achieve a victor's glory." . . . By such words and such thoughts too great for man did he provoke Athena's pitiless wrath. (759-77)

The very intensity of Athena's wrath sets the stage for Ajax's subsequent suicide. As his rage passes, it is replaced by a potentially self-destructive depression, which is not uncommon among egoistic suicides:

> Yet hope we: for ceased is the lightning's flash: His rage dies down like a fierce southwind. But now, grown sane, new misery is his, for on woes self-wrought he gazes aghast, wherein no hand but his own had share; and with anguish his soul is afflicted. (256-62)

His defenses are overcome, and he cries for the first time, refusing food or drink. Ajax first contemplates murdering Odysseus, and then himself. Ajax's suicidal aims are even more clearly articulated in his ruminations about his lost honor in the eyes of his father. An honorable suicide may be his only solution:

> With what face shall I appear before my father Telamon? How will *he* find heart to look on me, stripped of my championship in war that mighty crown of fame that once was his? No, that I dare not. . . . Some scheme let me devise which may prove to my aged sire that I, his son, at least by nature am no coward, for 'tis base for a man to crave long life who endures never-varying misery. (463-67, 471-75)

The egoistic nature of Ajax's suicide is already hinted at in his initial incli-
nation toward homicide (also shown by Oedipus and Haemon), in his rejection of tears as cowardly, and in his excessive concern with honor in his
relationship with his father. In his final talk with his young son, Ajax reveals
his own sadly erroneous views of human development. The childhood
years are sweet in their innocence, before a man must prove his manliness
in facing life's tragic tribulations. The pattern that Ajax prescribes for his
son appears to describe his own childhood. Ajax himself was broken to his
father's "stern rugged code" and plucked early from his mother's embraces.
This premature rupturing of Ajax's bond with his mother has impelled him
toward an egoistic suicide (position C). The need for his mother's attention
appears in Ajax's daydream of her grief at his death: "She, woeful woman,
when she hears these tidings will wail out a large dirge through all the town"
(848-49). Immediately after this refrain, Ajax falls on his sword and dies.

Ajax's friends do not know how to deal with his problem. He certainly does not disguise his suicidal intent, yet those around him allow him
to go off by himself, which is clearly not recommended for suicide prevention. In fact, Ajax's brother, Teucer, is the only one to take a step toward
suicide prevention: he sends a messenger from the Greek chieftains order-
ing that Ajax not be left alone. The messenger arrives too late, but the
commonsense suicide-preventive message is clear: Do not leave a suicidally depressed person alone!

The behavior of Odysseus, the rival of Ajax, is quite sensible
throughout this play, an unusual pattern among characters in classical
drama. At the beginning of the play, Odysseus is appropriately afraid to
confront the crazed Ajax when Athena proposes to summon him. But later
it is the same Odysseus who pleads with Agamemnon for the burial of
Ajax's corpse. Agamemnon finds this incomprehensible, given Odysseus's
previous hatred of Ajax. Odysseus responds maturely. Although it is the
sign of a wise man to adjust to changing situations, Agamemnon sees it
differently: he accuses Odysseus of instability and impulsiveness.

> *Odysseus:* Then listen: For the gods' sake, venture not thus ruthlessly
>   to cast forth this man unburied.
> *Agamemnon:* Thou, Odysseus, champion *him* thus against *me?*
> *Odysseus:* Yes; but I hated him while hate was honorable.
> *Agamemnon:* Shouldst thou not also trample on him when
>   dead? . . .

> *Odysseus:* This man was once my foe, yet was he noble. . . .
> *Agamemnon:* Unstable of impulse are such men as thou.
> *Odysseus:* Many are friends now and hereafter foes. (1332-59)

The Trachiniae

Two suicides occur in *The Trachiniae:* the anomic self-stabbing of Deianeira, the unhappy wife of Heracles, and Heracles' own egoistic self-burning. In her first speech, Deianeira expresses great conflict between her gratitude toward Heracles for fighting for her hand and delivering her from dangers and her anger at his prolonged absence from her after their marriage. She feels abandoned and resentful toward him but seems able to express these feelings only through excessive concern. Deianeira goes on to chide her son, Hyllus, for not having looked for his father.

Her uncertainty toward Heracles surfaces in her hesitance to accept what should be the good news of Heracles' safety — and indeed, his triumph. Even after she comes to believe this news, her joy is short-lived, rapidly followed by a desire to know why he was away so long and by her great misgivings about the future. These fears are natural to one raised with the Greek understanding of cycle: "Yea, have I not the fullest reason to rejoice at these tidings of my lord's happy fortune? To such fortune, such joy must needs respond. And yet a prudent mind can see room for misgiving, lest he who prospers should one day suffer reverse" (300-304).

Deianeira's misgivings are borne out as she learns the truth about the love affair of Heracles and Iole, whom Deianeira has already befriended and welcomed into her house. It is the pursuit of this love that has kept Heracles away so long. Deianeira's unrealistic and idealized self-expectations seem to prevent her from openly expressing a well-justified anger and hurt (Faber 1970, 56). Rather, she seems bewildered and hapless, and she goes so far as to excuse Heracles and Iole, at least on the conscious level: she will not say a harsh word about either of them.

At the same time, however, Deianeira struggles with an inner fury that threatens to break out of control, though she cannot accept her own anger. Finally, she decides to send Heracles a robe that she had dipped in the blood of the centaur Nessus many years earlier, after he was mortally wounded by Heracles' poisoned arrow. As he lay dying, Nessus had instructed Deianeira to take some of the blood from around the wound and to use it as a charm on her husband — so that he would never look at another woman.

Nessus's response contains a riddle in the style of Tiresias. Might he not have meant that Heracles will die before he looks at another woman? Deianeira seems to ignore the hints of danger in the gift: she treats it only as a love potion, though she has hinted at a far more sinister intent slightly earlier. On the one hand, Deianeira cannot accept responsibility for having done any wrong, even when she is accused of this by her son, Hyllus; on the other, she walks away rather than defending herself because she knows or fears that at some level she has done something wrong. It is this smallness, timidity, and excessive concern with others' opinion of her that distinguishes her from a more actively aggressive figure such as Medea. These characteristics were no doubt accentuated by the total failure of her father to protect her from the sexual advances of the river god Achelous. Indeed, her treasured Heracles saved her from that ravishment as well.

This embedded, altruistic quality surfaces along with egoistic anger turned inward, Deianeira's vacillation and confusion about the boundaries between self and other are typical of an anomic (position A/C) suicide. At this point Deianeira resolves to take her own life: "Howbeit, I am resolved that, if he is to fall, at the same time I also shall be swept from life; for no woman could bear to live with an evil name, if she rejoices that her nature is not evil" (718-20). She cannot go on living with a feeling of being seen as less altruistic than she has always seemed to herself. She offers no expression of sympathy or remorse toward her husband.

One can only wonder how Deianeira could have been so naive all along, unless she purposely aimed her naiveté at providing an acceptable way to express her murderous hostility toward Heracles. Both the anger and embeddedness in Deianeira's suicide are evident in the fact that she stabs herself in her own marriage bed, presumably the same bed Heracles intends to share with Iole.

"Ah, bridal bed and bridal chamber mine, farewell now and forever; never more shall ye receive me to rest upon this couch." She said no more, but with a vehement hand loosed her robe, where the gold-wrought brooch lay above her breast, baring all her left side and arm .... [S]he had driven a two-edged sword through her side to the heart. (925-35)

Deianeira is not a larger-than-life tragic figure like Medea or Antigone. She is in many ways a repressed, somewhat average homebody confronted with an unfaithful husband. Deianeira is not crazy at base, yet she is made mad by events and by a structure that does not allow her to express normal anger in a healthy way. Rather, she bottles up her anger until it explodes, first against Heracles and then against herself.

The second suicide in this play is that of Heracles, who seems to be an unsympathetic brute. Because he is racked with pain from the burning robe, his first reaction — like that of Oedipus, Haemon, and Ajax — is the urge to kill Deianeira, not himself. Only after Heracles learns from Hyllus that Deianeira has already killed herself does he ask Hyllus to assist him in committing suicide, because he is now too incapacitated to complete the act.

> Thither, then, thou must carry me up with thine own hands, aided by what friends thou wilt; thou shalt lop many a branch from the deep-rooted oak, and hew many a faggot also from the sturdy stock of the wild-olive: thou shalt lay my body thereupon, and kindle it with flaming pine-torch. (1193-96)

This direct turnabout from homicide to suicide has the earmarks of yet another egoistic suicide: aggression first turned outward and then rotated 180 degrees inward. The extremely egoistic (position C) and controlling quality of Heracles is portrayed in even starker relief by his almost incredible command to Hyllus to marry Iole, whom Hyllus holds responsible for the death of his mother, Deianeira. Heracles nearly drives his own son to suicide.

The illness and dysfunction in the classical Greek family is never more apparent than in this complicated and brilliant play by Sophocles. First, the quite average Deianeira is driven to suicide; second, Hyllus blames his mother, Deianeira, for Heracles' death; next he blames Iole for his mother's death; and finally, his dying father, Heracles, orders Hyllus to marry Iole despite Hyllus's warning of his own suicide. Thus we can see that average people, too, can be pathologized by such an unhealthy structure.

Euripides

Suicides in the plays of Euripides are very different from those of Sophocles' characters. Many seem like ritual deaths or martyrdoms in which the victims submit passively to group demands. These are mostly altruistic people with insufficient boundaries in relationship to the outside world; some are anomic, with confused boundaries. Suicides occur in seven of Euripides' nineteen extant plays: *Hippolytus, The Phoenissae, The Suppliants, Iphigenia in Aulis, The Heracleidae, Alcestis,* and *Hecuba.* An eighth play, *Andromache,* portrays an attempted suicide.

Hippolytus

In *Hippolytus,* Phaedra, the wife of King Theseus of Athens, is caught in a miserable family situation, and at the same time she has unrealistic expectations of herself. By Aphrodite's design, she falls madly in love with her stepson, Hippolytus. Though she resists her passion, with great misery to herself, her servant betrays her secret to Hippolytus. Phaedra then hangs herself, leaving behind a note that falsely accuses Hippolytus of raping her. Theseus believes the note and pronounces a curse of death on his son. The curse is soon fulfilled, and the truth of Hippolytus's innocence is revealed too late. According to this play, the gods are selfish and cruel, utterly without compassion toward humans. Aphrodite plots to destroy Hippolytus for living in chastity: she has filled his stepmother, Phaedra, with passion for him, and has turned the heart of his father against him.

Phaedra mixes an exaggerated sense of honor and guilt with a tendency toward self-punishment: "My hands are pure, but on my soul there rests stain" (317). She must hide her passion to save her honor: "Alas for thee! My sorrows, shouldst thou learn them would recoil on thee" (327) — even if it means suicide: "[O]ut of shame I am planning an honorable escape" (331). The nurse accuses her of trying to be better than the gods: "O cease, my darling child, from evil thoughts, let wanton pride be gone, for this is naught else, this wish to rival gods in perfectness" (474-75). There is no stopper in Phaedra's rush toward suicide. She is too overwrought to remain silent, Aphrodite works against her, and her nurse betrays her by spilling the secret of her passion to Hippolytus.

When discretion and good sense fail, death seems to be the only cure: "And last when I could not succeed in mastering love hereby, me thought it best to die; and none can gainsay my purpose" (397). As she expresses it with finality, "I know only one way, one cure for these my woes, and that is instant death" (599).

Phaedra's punitive conscience is accompanied by low self-esteem engendered by her fears of misogyny and her unhappiness and helplessness at being a woman. This view is echoed by the chorus and by Hippolytus, who delivers a particularly sharp attack on women. Women are vile and filthy: "I can never satisfy my hate for women, no! Not even though some say this is ever my theme, for of a truth they always are evil. So either let some one prove them chaste, or let me still trample on them forever" (665-67).

Phaedra suffers under the burden of a family background that rivals that of Oedipus. Her mother had slept with a white bull, her sister had been raped by Dionysus, and she herself is the "third to suffer" (337-40): "That 'love' has been our curse from time long past" (343). She fears most that her passion for Hippolytus will become known and that she will be seen as a traitor to her husband and children. She would rather die: "This it is that calls on me to die, kind friends, that so I may ne'er be found to have disgraced my lord, or the children I have borne" (426-27). Phaedra struggles to free herself and her children from her family pattern, but she is too enmeshed to succeed and destroys both herself and Hippolytus.

In his last breath, Hippolytus also laments that he is bound by a miserable family past that cannot be expiated: there is neither repentance nor forgiveness. The gods remain unhelpful to the end. Hippolytus is special to Artemis, but she cannot help him in his final pains. She leaves before his death, the sight of which would be a pollution to her: "And now farewell! 'Tis not for me to gaze upon the dead, or pollute my sight with death scenes, and e'en now I see thee nigh that evil" (1432-33).

Phaedra lives in a world in which her gods and her family have been at best uncaring, in which her individuality and womanhood are despised, and in which error cannot be corrected. Caught in a conflict between Aphrodite and Artemis, she sees no way out but suicide. Phaedra destroys herself because, much like Sophocles' Antigone, she is embedded in a miserable situation. At the same time, she has an unrealistic expectation of herself. Vacillating between the altruistic and egoistic positions leads Phaedra to an anomic suicide (position A/C). All of Euripides' suicides are either anomic or altruistic, not egoistic.

The Phoenissae

In *The Phoenissae,* Euripides treats the story of Oedipus's family quite differently from the way Sophocles does in his trilogy.[9] Euripides portrays Antigone as a bright-eyed Gidget who is eager to sneak a look at the attacking army. Jocasta is still living, and Oedipus sits shut up in a house in Thebes, feeling miserable about himself and his misfortunes and cursing his sons, who have put him there. There are two altruistic suicides in *The Phoenissae* — Menoeceus, Creon's son, and Jocasta.[10]

The seer Tiresias informs the Thebans in his usual taunting way that the city can be saved from the invaders only by the death of a young unmarried man to repay the earth for the slaying of Ares' dragon. This is the very essence of a Hobson's choice: an apparent pressure to destroy either one's own life or that of one's city. Menoeceus pretends to let Creon persuade him to flee the city, but he secretly goes to the appropriate site and stabs himself. Menoeceus genuinely believes that he must give precedence to the city over his own private needs and indeed his own life, so he offers his life as a gift, and his suicide is thus altruistic (position A):

> Now I go to make the city a present of my life, no mean offering, to rid this kingdom of its affliction. For if each were to take and expend all the good within his power, contributing it to his country's weal, our states would experience fewer troubles and would for the future prosper. (1013-16)

The second suicide, Jocasta, has failed to reconcile her two sons, Eteocles and Polyneices, with each other. They are greedy and ambitious, and Oedipus himself is predictably pessimistic. Jocasta is certain that one will kill the other in a duel, and she warns Antigone: "Daughter, thy brothers are in danger of their life" (1268). Jocasta then links her sons' imminent deaths with her own: "If I can forestall the onset of my sons, I may yet live; but if they be dead, I will lay me down and die with them"

9. This play is named after the Phoenissae, a group of Phoenician women who represent the point of view of outsiders and who view the events occurring in Thebes from an uninvolved point of view.

10. Megareus, the other son of Creon, was one of the Theban champions who defended a gate of the city in Aeschylus's *Seven Against Thebes.* In *The Phoenissae,* Euripides calls him Menoeceus and presents another version of his death.

(1281-82). She kills herself after discovering that her sons have indeed killed each other:

> So both at once breathed out their life of sorrow. But when their mother saw this sad mischance, in her o'er mastering grief she snatched from a corpse its sword and wrought an awful deed, driving the steel right through her throat, and there she lies dead with the dead she loved so well, her arms thrown around them both. (1465-69)

The suicide of Sophocles' Jocasta is egoistic: it emerges from introjected anger. Euripides' Jocasta, on the other hand, is altruistic and kills herself from "o'er mastering grief." She has never freed herself from her oppressive family mythology (position A). As Creon says: "Ah! woe is thee, Jocasta! What an end to life and marriage hast thou found the riddling of the Sphinx! But tell me how her two sons wrought the bloody deed, the struggle caused by the curse of Oedipus" (1350-52).

The gods bring about much of the human misery in *The Phoenissae*. Oedipus says: "For nature did not make me so void of understanding, that I should have devised these horrors against my own eyes and my children's life without the intervention of some god" (1611-13). Earlier he observes: "So today father, the god, whosoe'er this issue is, has gathered to a head the sum of suffering for our house" (1579-80).

Creon, Menoeceus, Antigone, and Jocasta all show genuine good character, but the gods are narcissistic, and thus the human beings are stuck. Both suicides in *The Phoenissae* are caused by a lack of knowledge of a better way to live. The Greek world offers no stoppers and no outlets for a person like Menoeceus: it puts him in an irresolvable Hobson's choice. It offers neither end nor resolution to the curses of dragons and sphinxes that destroy the family of Oedipus.

The Suppliants

Euripides' *The Suppliants* treats the story of Oedipus's children from a different angle. Here the families of the seven champions who fought against Thebes come to seek help from Athens and Theseus, its king. *The Suppliants* depicts the different mentalities of Theseus and Evadne: Theseus is open, flexible, confident, and at the same time serious; Evadne is uncommunicative, flighty, and lacking confidence both in herself and in the world around her. She is without a stopper, and ultimately she becomes an anomic suicide (an A/C position).

While many Euripidean characters are heavily embedded in their life patterns, Theseus is a clear-thinking, balanced man who sizes up situations well, can recognize flaws in his own character, and can treat others empathetically and considerately. His optimism is unusual among Euripidean characters: "For there are [those] who say there is more bad than good in human nature, to the which I hold a contrary view, that good o'er bad predominates in man, for if it were not so, we should not exist" (197-98). He displays a religious faith that is both serious and realistic without being morbid. Although Theseus appears to accept the prevalent Greek idea of mother earth, he is not overly burdened by it, perhaps because he sees the gods as benign. Euripides portrays the gods, especially Athena, as friendly and encouraging to Theseus. Are the gods good to Theseus because he has a positive approach to living, or is his approach to living positive because the gods are good to him? In any case, Theseus stands in marked contrast to Evadne, the wife of the champion Caponius.

Evadne is not caught up in an inescapable destructive environment. Rather, her largely personal problems impel her to jump into the funeral pyre of her husband. Morbid and depressed, she is "resolved not to save her life, or to prove untrue to her husband" (1028). She seeks some recognition or notice, especially from her father, and will "leap from this rack in honor's cause" (1015). She tries to hide her purpose from her father, but she clearly also wants attention. She resorts to riddles: "It would but anger thee to hear what I intend, and so I fain would keep thee ignorant, my father" (1050). She adds: "Thou wouldst not wisely judge my purpose" (1053). Yet, at the very same time, Evadne, like Sophocles' Antigone, wants her deed to be a model for all Argos.

Evadne's final challenge to Iphis, her father, before she leaps onto her husband's funeral pyre, is worth examining: "'Tis all one; thou shalt never catch me in thy grasp, lo! I cast me down, no joy to thee, but to myself and to my husband blazing on the pyre with me" (1070-71). Indeed, it seems less important for her to burn with her husband than that he burn with her. The father then commences a long soliloquy on his own troubles in old age (1080-1113), showing little concern for Evadne herself. Perhaps her father's indifference is the root of Evadne's anomic behavior and her suicide as she vacillates erratically between a desire for symbiosis and fear of any human contact (position A/C).

Iphigenia in Aulis

Iphigenia, daughter of Agamemnon, is an altruistic suicide in Durkheim's terms. She accepts willingly, almost gladly, a seer's order that she must be sacrificed before her father's army will be able to sail for Troy. This is ritual murder, not suicide in the contemporary use of the word; however, in this play there is no real distinction. The play's characters are encumbered with the same problem as so many other characters of Hellenic drama — the general cheapness of human life in the heroic view of man.

There is the usual foreboding of calamity. Agamemnon declares this very clearly at the beginning of the play. Hubris will be followed by nemesis, and every human is born to grief. Agamemnon laments: "Woe's me for mortal men! None have been happy yet" (162-63). All must go as the fates will. Again, in Agamemnon's words: "Woe, woe is me, unhappy, caught by fate, outwitted by the cunning of the gods" (442-45). Nevertheless, Agamemnon still feels compelled to kill Iphigenia, even when Menelaus relents in his demands for her sacrifice.

Indeed, Iphigenia herself seems to avoid any active attempt to evade her death. She grasps for a freedom that she does not have by trying to make her death seem voluntary instead of obligatory: "I have chosen death: it is my own free choice. I have put cowardice away from me. Honor is mine now. O mother, say I am right" (1375-77). Iphigenia is a dependent young girl who attempts to ingratiate herself with her father by offending her mother: "O mother, blame me not! Let me go first, [a]nd put my arms about my father's neck" (633-34). Yet the theme of abandonment is constant: "Mother, my father has gone, [l]eft me, betrayed and alone" (1317-20).

Iphigenia is at first horrified at the suggestion of her sacrifice. However, she finally accepts her situation bravely, as suits a woman from a heroic family. In addition, she wishes to defend her father against what she perceives as the anger of her mother toward him: "Oh, hate him not — my father, and your husband" (1453). Agamemnon, weak and indecisive, will not commit himself to any course of action that will preserve his daughter's life. The success of the expedition to Troy, his own prestige, and his fear of an attack on his own city seem more important to him.

These problems seem serious enough, but the biggest difficulty again is that classical Greek society offers no stopper, no way out. What is Iphigenia to do? Who is to explain to her that this situation is another Sphinx riddle that offers only a road to obliteration? It seems normal to Iphigenia that she should die in a heroic attempt to help the army and thereby salve her father's feelings, win his approval, and fulfill her family's tradition. This negation of self shows Iphigenia's suicide to be altruistic (position A). She is unable to free herself from the group pressure around her.

The Heracleidae

The Heracleidae begins after the death of Heracles. Afterwards, his family seeks refuge in Athens from his old enemy, King Eurystheus of Argos, who wishes to kill them. Demophon of Athens is willing to help the fugitives, but an oracle pronounces that a girl of noble descent must be sacrificed to the goddess Persephone in order for him to defeat the Argives. Once again the characters are faced with a Hobson's choice: the safety of the family versus an individual life. Heracles' daughter Macaria learns of the trouble from Iolaus, her father's old friend, and she seems to take total responsibility for her brothers while neglecting herself. Iolaus takes advantage of this self-sacrificing streak in Macaria to pressure her, not very subtly, to resolve the state's perplexity by offering herself as the victim. Macaria takes the bait, revealing a willingness to let herself be sacrificed for others. Death is welcome to her as long as it is glorious and she has freely chosen it.

Iolaus is greatly moved by Macaria's altruistic gesture, praising her as a true daughter of Heracles. He suggests a fairer method, a lottery involving Macaria and her sisters, but Macaria will have none of this. Her sacrifice for others has no meaning if it is imposed through a lottery, nor does she seem to want to avoid the sacrifice through winning the lottery: "My death shall no chance lot decide, there is no graciousness in that peace, old friend. But if ye accept and will avail you of my readiness, freely do I offer my life for those, and without constraint" (541-43). She wishes to protect her sisters, but it is also possible that an altruistic suicidal urge underlies this dramatic gesture in the name of others (position A). She echoes Seneca in saying that one fulfills one's purpose in life most fully by the way one leaves it: "For I, by loving not my life too well have found a treasure very fair, a glorious means to leave it" (532-33). This wins the approval of those around her: "Who can speak more noble words or do more noble deeds henceforth for ever?" (534-35) Again: "Daughter, thou art his own true child, no other man's but Heracles; that godlike soul" (539).

She travels the high road of heroism as her fathers did before her. Through her self-sacrifice, Macaria likewise fulfills the way of her father, Heracles. Perhaps more important, she seeks his approval, but she must do it freely: "Stand by and veil my body with my robe, for I will go even to the dreadful doom of sacrifice, seeing whose daughter I avow myself" (563-64). This seems to be the epitome of altruistic suicide: she must die to fulfill her father's glory, but she must have the heroic sense that she has chosen it freely.

Hecuba

Polyxena, prisoner of the Greek conquerors after the fall of Troy and the last surviving daughter of Queen Hecuba, is another altruistic suicide. Her sense of noblesse oblige makes it impossible for her to escape the ritual death demanded of her. The play commences with the Greek fleet ready to return home after sacking Troy. The ghost of Achilles appears and demands that a virgin be sacrificed on his tomb before the fleet can sail. Primal terrors horrify the protagonists: "O'er the summit of his tomb appeared Achilles' phantom, and for his guerdon he would have one of the luckless maids of Troy" (97). The ghost demands: "Whither away so fast, ye Danai, leaving my tomb without its prize" (114). At the very moment of Polyxena's sacrifice, Achilles' son raises the knife and invites his dead sire to come drink the black blood of a pure virgin.

Euripides' characters seem laden with a sort of primal guilt simply because they exist. For them, the pristine simple world of nature is not to be reworked or improved by man's labors or even by his mere existence. Its virginity is not to be disturbed. Man can expiate the innate foulness of his existence only by returning something in its virgin state to the monstrous and hellish earth that demands its due. What better sacrifice than a young virgin who will now be devoted only to earth and to no one else?

This overwhelming sense of primal guilt adds to the daily pressures of life in captivity to push Polyxena to her death. First, there is her sense of ruin and outrage: "For my own life, its ruin and its outrage, never a tear I shed; nay death is become to me a happier lot than life" (210-11). The duty of the hero is to act heroically; indeed, she prefers death to unheroic behavior. Rather than rebuke her executioners for murdering her, she forgives them, Like Iphigenia and Macaria, she seeks to create the illusion of control over her own death: "Of my free will I die; let none lay hand on me; for bravely will I yield my neck" (559-62). The Greeks are impressed with the bravery of their Trojan captive, and they unbind her. Polyxena then voluntarily tears open her robe, sinks to her knee, and bares her breast. Her heroic sense of noblesse oblige leads her on to altruistic suicide: "Young prince, if 'tis my breast thou'dst strike, lo! here it is, strike home! or if at my neck thy sword thou'lt aim, behold! that neck is bared" (563-65).

From Polyxena's point of view, this becomes altruistic suicide, or martyrdom (position A). She needs to feel that she is dying freely because she cannot confront her captors with their injustice.[11] From the point of view of the Greeks, her ritual sacrifice is a necessary evil, part of the Hobson's choice with which they confronted themselves. Achilles' son is emotionally torn about the necessity of killing a girl so heroic and brave, "half glad, half sorry in his pity for the maid, cleft with the steel the channels of her breath" (560). He almost seems to wish that he would not have to kill Polyxena, but there is no stopper, no way out.

Alcestis

In one of Euripides' most puzzling plays, King Admetus of Thessaly is told that the fates demand his death unless he can find someone who is willing to die in his place. His aged parents sharply refuse his request, but Alcestis, his young and beautiful wife, offers herself. Both general and personal motives seem to be prompting Alcestis in her decision.

The demands of the gods of the underworld are inexorable and horrifying; not even the Olympian gods can overrule them. In the opening scene, the god (Death) meets Apollo in a deadly serious debate for the life of Alcestis. Humans do not really have a right to enjoy their life on the

---

11. Contrast the altruistic Greek heroine with Rabbi Akiba, who at the moment of death recited the Shema: ("Hear O Israel, the Lord is our God, the Lord is one"). Akiba reconfirmed his faith in God and in life and did not need to seek illusory control by pretending to die willingly.

earth: who they are or what they have accomplished mean nothing. In the end, the netherworld makes demands, and all of this means that one of the characters must die. Alcestis is the one who will satisfy Death's claims. Man's situation is, in its deepest sense, cheerless and hopeless. He may be met at any moment by the cruel demands of mysterious forces that show him neither mercy nor understanding. Alcestis accepts this view: "But these things are a god's doing and are thus" (297-98). It is perhaps more natural for an intelligent, concerned woman like Alcestis to accept these demands than for a selfish and hypocritical coward such as Admetus.

On the personal level, Alcestis's motives for substituting her life for Admetus's are quite complex: she is not a heroic or epic figure, nor does she speak of her debt to heroic ancestors. Rather, she is a lady of the noblest kind. When the day of her death arrives, she bathes, dresses in her best finery, and prays to the goddess of the earth to watch over her children. She seeks to comfort each servant in the house individually as they weep sorrowfully over her. Like so many Greek heroines, she bewails the loss of intimacy in her marriage bed. She puts Admetus first, even before her own life, and seems unable to fulfill herself unless she gives her unworthy husband her entire existence.

On the other hand, Admetus's only concern about his wife's sacrificial death is the fact that he will be abandoned. Alcestis's puzzling response to Admetus seems to reveal another aspect of her psyche: "But, torn from you, I would not live with fatherless children, nor have I hoarded up those gifts of youth in which I found delight" (283-85). This statement makes no sense on the surface. Why are the children better off losing Alcestis than losing Admetus? Alcestis appears to be one of those women who must always cover up for a miserably inferior husband. She feels totally responsible for him and can never consider looking at her situation in any other way, whether it kills her with one blow, as here, or makes her life miserable for many years, day by day. Perhaps she fears showing her own weakness or dealing decisively with an unrewarding marriage. Perhaps she is simply disillusioned, and she is leaving the field and abandoning a totally dependent husband.

The choice here is not the classic Hobson's dilemma of Greek drama. Other protagonists who are offered a chance to die in Admetus's place have refused. This is not the heroism that proves so destructive to Ajax or the house of Atreus. Instead, it is a false sense of responsibility rooted in Alcestis's over-idealized conception of herself and an insufficient differentiation from her environment. She is clearly an altruistic martyr-suicide (position A).

Andromache

The complex plot of Euripides' *Andromache* includes one surrender to be murdered (Andromache) and one attempted anomic suicide (Hermione), both unsuccessful. Andromache, the widow of the Trojan hero Hector, is now a slave concubine of Neoptolemus, son of Achilles. While Neoptolemus is away at Delphi, his jealous wife, Hermione, and her father, Menelaus, threaten to kill Andromache's son unless Andromache surrenders herself to them to be put to death in his stead. When she does so, Menelaus announces that both will be killed. They are saved only by the timely arrival of old Peleus, father of Achilles. As much a coward as a bully, Menelaus withdraws, leaving his prisoners to Peleus. At her father's departure, Hermione goes into a panic. She is deeply afraid of what her husband (Neoptolemus) will say when he hears about her plotting; he might send her away in scandal. This leads her to thoughts of suicide, for now her deeds will make her abominable in the eyes of all men. Only the quick action of her servants restrains her from hanging herself and later stabbing herself.

The suicide attempt by Hermione is anomic (position A/C): it is initiated by Menelaus's cowardly abandonment of her, in conjunction with her overdependence on him. In that family, clearly, troubled relationships have been passed down from one generation to the next. Yet Hermione's suicide seems to be prevented by her returning home to her father's house, with its seeming protection. Orestes enters her life to rescue her from her immediate difficulty. The arrival of a father figure twice saves characters in this play: first, Peleus arrives to save Andromache and her son from Menelaus and Hermione; second, as despicable as Menelaus himself may be, his home proves to be a suicide-preventive haven for Hermione.

Summary

The world of the Greek drama offers no protection to an individual confronted with a Hobson's choice. The gods are uninvolved and capricious, and they do not intervene to limit the effects of a suicidal cycle. All the narratives resemble the myth of Narcissus in that they involve fixation and os-cillation (the AC axis). Characters obtain individuation at the expense of attachment, and attachment at the expense of individuation. Suicide is the all-too-frequent result.

6. Suicide and Suicide Prevention in Biblical Narratives

But he [Elijah] himself went a day's journey into the wilderness, and came and sat down under a broom tree; and he requested for himself that he might die, and said, "It is enough; now O Lord, take away my life; for I am not better than my fathers." And he lay down and slept under a broom tree; and behold, an angel touched him, and said unto him, "Arise and eat." . . . And he arose, and did eat and drink, and went on the strength of that meal forty days and forty nights unto Horeb the mount of God.

1 Kings 19:4-8

The relative infrequency of suicide in the Hebrew Bible is striking when compared to Greek narratives. The entire Tanach presents only six cases (Ahitophel, Zimri, Abimelech, Samson, Saul, and Saul's armor-bearer). More significant for our theme are several additional figures who express a wish to die or to kill themselves yet do not carry it through (e.g., Elijah, Moses, David, Job, and Jonah). There seem to be two major reasons for this. First, the basic biblical thought pattern rejects the pressing necessity of constantly making Hobson's choices (the A-C choices in Figure 1.2). Second, in trying situations, God acts as a positive parent or therapist protecting his confused children and providing the necessary stopper to support the individual in her time of need (see Figure 1.3).

Not all the biblical suicides conform to Shneidman's definition of suicide as "a conscious act of self-induced annihilation." L. D. Hankoff (1979, 6) has suggested that the six suicides have the following characteris-

Table 6.1
Suicide in the Hebrew Bible

Character	Gender	Source	Method	Type
Ahitophel	M	2 Sam. 17:23	Strangled	Egoistic
Zimri	M	1 Kings 16:18	Burning	Egoistic
Ahimelech	M	Judges 9:54	Sword	Egoistic
Samson	M	Judges 16:30	Crushing	Covenantal
Saul	M	1 Sam. 31:4; 2 Sam. 1:6; 1 Chron. 10:4	Sword	Covenantal
Saul's Armor-Bearer	M	1 Sam. 31:5; 1 Chron. 10:5	Sword	Altruistic

tics in common: "All of the self-destructive behaviors were plausible, having clear-cut precipitants or situations which offered the reader an understandable explanation for the self-destruction. All were males in a state of physical stress or apt to be in mortal danger at the hands of enemies very shortly, and in the midst of a turbulent, rapidly moving situation. All but one, Saul's armor-bearer, were prominent people whose positions of leadership were seriously damaged or threatened."

Durkheim's typology can be applied once again to these suicides. Three of the six suicides (Ahitophel, Zimri, and Abimelech) seem egoistic, one (Saul's armor-bearer) is altruistic, and none are anomic. Two (Samson and Saul) can be termed "covenantal" (see Table 6.1).

The Bible is not obsessed with the sense of heroism so endemic to the Greek world; nor is there the Greek dualism between body and soul. The biblical God is a strong and nurturing parent, not a capricious deity. The highest goal of humans is thus to be obedient to God's will rather than to liberate the soul from the body. Freedom is a movement toward something rather than merely away from something. Humans do not have to earn love through fame or achievement, for it comes unconditionally from God, nor is there the same sense of the tragic that exists in the Greek world. Humans are free to choose good over evil. There is no belief in doom, and there is always the possibility of prayer, repentance, atonement, and genuine change. A person's life is not warped beyond cure or without hope. Prophecy in the biblical world typically aims at social intervention. *Consequence Y will occur unless some antecedent X intervenes.* In the book of Jonah, the people of Nineveh will be destroyed — unless they repent. But it is the possibility of the saving antecedent X that gives the Hebrew Bible an inspiring therapeutic vision rather than a tragic one, and this possibility makes the prophet a concerned messenger of God rather than a taunting actuary. If the biblical prophet is successful in his endeavors, then his dire predictions will not come to pass.

Finally, biblical characters do not face the same Hobson's choices that Greek heroes do. They are not presented with riddling sphinxes and oracles that distort their sense of judgment. Even when they do seem to be mired in no-win situations, there is typically a stopper, an opportunity to return to their covenant to deepen their relationship with God. In short, the Bible is not a Greek tragedy.

Egoistic Suicide

Ahitophel, a counselor of King David, has joined Absalom's rebellion. But when he perceives that Absalom has been tricked into following a foolhardy plan that is certain to lead to David's victory, Ahitophel sets his house in order and strangles himself:

> And when Ahitophel saw that his counsel was not followed, he saddled his ass and arose, and got himself home unto the city; and set his house in order, and strangled himself; and he died and was buried in the sepulcher of his father (2 Sam. 17:23).

Several reasons, all egoistic, have probably prompted Ahitophel's suicide. First, he now fears that Absalom's attempt to overthrow David is doomed and that he will die a traitor's death. Second, and less likely, is Ahitophel's disgust at Absalom's conduct in setting aside his counsel, which has wounded Ahitophel's pride and disappointed his ambition. Third, David's curse may have prompted Ahitophel to hang himself (*Makkot*, 4a). Finally, rabbinic writers have also argued that, since Ahitophel is a suicide, his family inherits his estate. If he were to be executed as a rebel, his possessions would be forfeited to the king. Ahitophel thus seems to be an egoistic suicide (position C) and is listed in the Mishna (*Sanhedrin*, 10:2) as among those who have forfeited their share in the world to come.

The wicked Zimri is an egoistic suicide (position C) with no redeeming qualities. King Elah of Israel passes his days drinking in his palace while his warriors battle the Philistines. Zimri, a high-ranking officer, takes advantage of this situation, assassinates Elah, and mounts the throne. His reign, however, lasts only seven days. As soon as the news of King Elah's murder reaches the army on the battlefield, they pronounce General Omri to be king and lay siege to the palace. When Zimri sees that he is unable to hold out against the siege, he sets fire to the palace and perishes in the flames: "And it came to pass, when Zimri saw that the city was taken that he went into the castle of the king's house, and burnt the king's house over him with fire, and he died" (1 Kings 16:18).

Abimelech's suicide is, strictly speaking, an assisted suicide. After carving out a principality for himself in Israel by means of various brutalities, he is mortally wounded by a millstone that a woman throws from a fortress he is besieging. Realizing that he is dying, Abimelech asks his armorbearer to finish him off so that it will not be said that a woman has killed him. This act of hubris qualifies him as an egoistic suicide (position C).

> And a certain woman cast an upper millstone upon Abimelech's head, and broke his skull. Then he called quickly to the young man, his armor-bearer, and said to him: "Draw your sword and kill me, lest men say of me, 'A woman killed him.'" So his young man thrust him through, and he died. (Judg. 9:53-57)

Covenantal Suicide

Samson, the great defender and leader of the Israelites, had been blinded and publicly mocked by the Philistines. Faced with torture and death, he asked God for the strength to take as many Philistines with him as possible; when granted his request, he pulled down the central pillars of the temple of Dagon, killing thousands in one last blow:

> And Samson called to the Lord, saying, "O Lord God, remember me, I pray! Strengthen me, I pray, just this once." . . . And Samson took hold

of the two middle pillars which supported the temple, and braced himself against them, one on his right and the other on his left. Then Samson said, "Let me die with the Philistines!" And he pushed with all his might, and the temple fell on the lords and on all the people who were in it. (Judg. 16:28-30)

It is tempting to see Samson as the biblical equivalent of Sophocles' Ajax. Samson, like Ajax, has fallen from his previous state of leadership. Is he, too, using suicide to restore his lost image in the eyes of others? Closer examination indicates that Samson's suicide is not egoistic like that of Ajax: he is not alienated from his society but is very much a part of the people of Israel. His uncut hair is part of his Nazarite consecration to God, not a symbol of macho heroism. He loses his strength when he abandons his consecration by falling to the wiles of Delilah and having his hair cut. His death is not an attempt to restore his own lost honor at the expense of his people, but it comes about in his effort to strike a telling blow against the enemies of Israel.

Is Samson's suicide, therefore, altruistic and self-sacrificing? We must also reject this interpretation. Samson does not suffer from a failing sense of his own personality; rather, he calls on God to strengthen him in his final attempt to destroy the Philistines. His purpose is not self-annihilation but the carrying out of his divinely ordained mission to free Israel from the Philistines. Samson's suicide thus seems to be neither egoistic nor altruistic; rather, it may be labeled covenantal (position B) in the sense that it is in the service of the biblical God, with neither over-isolation (position C) nor over-integration (position A) in his boundaries with his society. Significantly, his final action in life leads to a long period of peace (Judg. 13).

A second covenantal suicide is that of King Saul. Rabbinic literature has regarded King Saul as a man of great stature, the anointed of the Lord. Yet his reign was marked by series of mistakes, ending with his own suicide during a losing battle against the Philistines on Mount Gilboa. Saul has seen three of his sons and many of his fighters slain, and he himself is severely wounded. Surrounded by enemies and not wishing to be taken prisoner and exposed to the mockery and brutality of the Philistines, King Saul entreats his armor-bearer to kill him. The latter refuses, and Saul falls on his own sword: "Then Saul said to his armor-bearer: 'Draw your sword, and thrust me through with it, lest these uncircumcised men come and thrust me through and abuse me.' But his armor-bearer would not, for he was greatly afraid. Therefore Saul took a sword, and fell on it" (1 Sam. 31:4).

The suicide of Saul has been taken by commentators in different ways. The Midrash Rabbah (on Gen. 9:5) has pointed to Saul as an example of a permissible suicide (see also *Midrash Rabbah*, 34:13 and *Shulchan Aruch, Yoreh Deah*, 345.3). One commentator has considered Saul as a special case because, before the final battle with the Philistines, he has received a message from the witch of Endor that he will die. Thus, by taking his own life, he is not defying Providence. Other commentators have viewed Saul as an example of a suicide who takes his own life in order to avoid greater profanation of the divine name. In this view, Saul fears that if he is captured alive by the Philistines, they will desecrate his body, either by torture or by forcing him to commit idolatrous acts. This interpretation means that suicide may be permissible if it is committed in order to prevent dishonor to God's name rather than for personal reasons. As such, Saul's suicide can be classified as covenantal rather than as either egoistic or altruistic.[1]

Two of Saul's earlier actions place him in conflict between excessive altruism and egoism (Kaplan and Schwartz 1990). King Saul provokes God's rejection of his kingship over Israel because, in his attack on Amalek, he fails to destroy all the livestock and also spares the life of King Agag (1 Sam. 15:7-9). God then reveals to Samuel that he has rejected Saul's kingship because Saul has not fulfilled the divine intention of completely obliterating the nefarious Amalek (1 Sam. 15:10-23). Here Saul is being overly altruistic (position A).

In the second case, Saul orders the murder of the priests of Nob: he accuses them of siding with the innocent and fleeing David, the newly anointed one of God (1 Sam. 22:13). Ahimelech, a priest of Nob, protests the innocence of the priests, but Saul orders his servants to kill them. When they refuse to kill "the priests of the Lord," Saul turns to the informer, Doeg the Edomite, who carries out the murderous job, killing not only the priests but all their livestock (1 Sam. 22:18-19). Eventually, God departs from Saul and will no longer answer him (1 Sam. 28:6). In this case, Saul is being overly egoistic (position C).

In neither situation does Saul's response fit the precipitating event, and God strongly disapproves of his actions. In fact, the two decisions can be seen as polarities along the counter-normative AC axis. First, Saul

---

1. See Herman van Praag (1986) on the depression of King Saul.

spares King Agag: this act is too altruistic (position A) and does not maintain a sufficiently impermeable defensive wall for Saul against that very dangerous and aggressive king. In the second case, he attacks the sanctified priests of God: this act is too egoistic (position C) and represents an overly impermeable wall against people who have not harmed him. Vacillating, he first *underreacts* against the real threat of the Amalekites and then *overreacts* against the innocent priests of Nob because they have helped David.

The rabbis of the Talmud have described a voice coming from heaven after the incident of Amalek, saying, "Be not overly righteous." After the Nob incident, the voice again comes, saying, "Be not overly wicked." The point is that one who pities the wicked will eventually be cruel when he should be merciful (*Babylonian Talmud, Yoma,* 22b; Rosenberg 1976).

Altruistic Suicide

The suicide of Saul's armor-bearer can be classified as altruistic because of his seeming lack of differentiation from Saul (position A): "And when his armor-bearer saw that Saul was dead, he also fell on his sword, and died with him" (1 Sam. 31:5). The biblical passage tells us that the armor-bearer first refuses to kill Saul and then falls on his own sword in response to Saul's suicide. An Amalekite comes to David and reports that he has assisted in Saul's suicide; for this, David orders him killed (2 Sam. 1:9-10, 13-16). Commentaries have seen David as behaving correctly in condemning the Amalekite to death, even though the Amalekite was simply following Saul's orders in assisting the latter to die (Ralbag on 2 Sam. 1:14).

There is no example of Durkheim's anomic suicide in the Hebrew Bible; the six suicides seem to be either egoistic, altruistic, or covenantal. The most sympathetic rabbinic treatment is given to the covenantal suicides (Samson and Saul). The harshest judgments are applied to suicides that seem clearly egoistic (Ahitophel, Zimri, and Abimelech).

Biblical Suicide Prevention

In contrast to the cycles of heroism and suicide so endemic to Greek narratives, the Hebrew Bible recounts a number of interventions that prevent situations of despair from becoming full-blown suicide attempts. The Jew-

Table 6.2
Suicide Prevention in the Hebrew Bible

Character	Gender	Source	Method Employed by God
Elijah	M	1 Kings 18–19	Protected Withdrawal and Nurturance
Moses	M	Numbers 11	Support and Practical Advice
David	M	Psalm 22	Renewal of Faith
Job	M	Job	Renewal of Relationship
Jeremiah	M	Jeremiah	Punishment of Evil
Rebecca	F	Genesis 27–28	Appropriate Matchmaking
Jonah	M	Jonah	Protected Withdrawal and Guidance

ish sacred literature clearly prefers living to suicide. The Bible portrays God as intervening, much as a good therapist might, to deflect the death wishes uttered by one biblical character or another. Two themes stand in marked contrast to Greek literature: first, the biblical characters are not typically under pressure to make a decision that will destroy them; second, God provides a stopper by offering the characters a chance to overcome their problems (Table 6.2).

Elijah

Elijah reaches a peak of triumph (1 Kings 18:41) when he gains a stunning moral and political victory over the priests of Baal in their confrontation on Mount Carmel. Even King Ahab supports Elijah, and now God has sent rain to end the long drought in Israel. However, Queen Jezebel, Ahab's Phoenician wife, remains recalcitrant. She threatens to kill Elijah, and he flees for his life to the desert of Be'er Sheva. There he sits alone under a bush and asks God to take away his life:

> But he himself went a day's journey into the wilderness, and came and
> sat down under a broom tree. And he prayed that he might die, and

said, "It is enough! Now, Lord, take my life, for I am no better than my fathers!" (1 Kings 19:4)

Does this express the same serious suicidal wish that we have become accustomed to seeing in Greek stories? Perhaps not. Were death Elijah's true objective, he might have let himself be killed by Jezebel. Instead, he flees to Judah, which is not under her rule, to seek safety. Nevertheless, Elijah is exhausted and deeply disappointed at the failure that has followed so soon after his moment of seeming victory. He falls into despair, questioning the very value of his own life. This is consistent with the Greek cyclical plunge from hubris into nemesis. By contrast, however, God treats his suicidal outburst as a call for help. God first provides rest for Elijah; then, unlike Sophocles' Ajax or Euripides' Phaedra, an angel of God twice provides him with food and drink, preparing him for the work that remains to be done (1 Kings 19:5-8):[2]

> Then as he lay and slept under a broom tree, suddenly an angel touched him, and said to him: "Arise and eat." . . . So he arose, and ate and drank; and he went on the strength of that food forty days and forty nights as far as Horeb, the mountain of God. (1 Kings 19:5-8)

This is the mountain where Moses had received the Torah from God. Elijah goes back to the roots (position B) of Israelite thought and prophecy in order to regenerate himself and overcome his despair and self-doubt (movement ahead on the BED axis). God provides the stopper that is missing in the Greek narratives by confronting Elijah in a mighty but loving theophany, discussing Elijah's problems with him, and providing him with guidance in carrying on. The potentially suicidal crisis overcome, God assigns Elijah several new tasks, including the job of training Elisha as his successor (1 Kings 19:9-14).

---

2. Showing consideration for others by giving them food shows up several times in the biblical account about Elijah. God sends Elijah food, carried by ravens, from the table of King Asa of Judah. It is Elijah whom God sends to announce the end of the frightful famine in Ahab's kingdom. Elijah also saves the woman of Zarephath and her son from starvation. After the excitement and exhaustion of the confrontation on Mt. Carmel, it is Elijah who reassures King Ahab and gets him to eat and drink. Finally, when Elijah comes to Elisha to anoint him as his successor, Elisha slaughters his two oxen to provide a feast for his family and friends to celebrate his new elevation (Radak on 1 Kings 18:4; 19:14).

Moses

Deeply disappointed about the complaints of the Israelites, Moses cries out to God that the responsibilities of leading the people are too great and that God should kill him:

> So Moses said to the LORD, "Why have You afflicted Your servant? And why have I not found favor in Your sight, that You have laid the burden of all these people on me? Did I conceive all these people? Did I beget them, that You should say to me, 'Carry them in your bosom, as a guardian carries a nursing child,' to the land which You swore to their fathers? Where am I to get meat to give to all these people? For they weep all over me, saying, 'Give us meat, that we may eat.' I am not able to bear all these people alone, because the burden is too heavy for me. If You treat me like this, please kill me here and now — if I have found favor in Your sight — and do not let me see my wretchedness!" (Num. 11:11-15)[3]

Moses is expressing his weariness and frustration with regard to going on alone (position C) with his burden (position A). His complaint to God may thus be seen as a message, a bargaining point, rather than as a serious desire for death. "If you do not help me with my burden, then go ahead and kill me." Nevertheless, suicides do occur in frustrating situations such as this, even when the original intent is not death. God, the divine therapist, does listen and intervenes with a stopper (position B), a positive and practical solution. Let Moses select seventy elders to help him lead the Israelites (Num. 11:16-19).

David

Feelings of despair, abandonment, and even suicidal thoughts are apparent in many of David's psalms, but the psalmist renews his faith in God and overcomes these feelings of heavy self-doubt. An example of this process can be seen in the famous Psalm 22. It begins in despair over the psalmist's perception of his complete and utter abandonment by God (position C).

---

3. The rabbinical commentator Rashi has suggested that Moses could not bear to see the punishment that he thought was coming to his people.

> My God, my God, why have You forsaken me
> Why are You so far from helping me, and from the words of my
>   groaning?
> O My God, I cry in the daytime, but
> You do not hear. . . . (Ps. 22:1-3)

Indeed, the first verse of this psalm is cited in the Gospel of Matthew as the last thing Jesus said as he was dying on the cross (Matt. 27:46).

Psalm 22 continues with the psalmist's return to the roots of his faith — to the earliest stages of trust (Erikson 1968). He overcomes the reproach of mockers and, like Elijah at Sinai, he recovers his faith and overcomes his despair (position B).

> But You are He who took me out of the womb;
> You made me trust while on
> my mother's breasts.
> I was cast upon You from birth,
> From my mother's womb You have been my God. (Ps. 22:9-11)

God provides the stopper. He has been the rock of the psalmist's faith since the primal experiences of birth and nursing. This basic trust that the psalmist has established with God is sufficient to overcome the writer's doubts and fears of abandonment:

> [N]or has He hidden His face from him;
> But when he cried to Him, He heard. (Ps. 22:24)

Job

The book of Job is, of course, an immense subject all by itself. A just man, Job is assailed by a series of awesome misfortunes — the loss of his wealth, his family, and his health (AC axis). He is deeply grieved by these events, but his existential faith in God and life is not destroyed. He searches for reassurance that God has not forsaken him. Pat answers will not do for Job, nor will a simple glorification of suffering. In his relationship with God, Job is strong, questioning, and unrelenting in his demands. He does not turn to suicide as an answer; instead, he drives his way through to a deepened affirmation of life.

Job does express what a modern suicidologist might interpret as a threat of suicide: "So that my soul chooseth strangling and death rather than these my bones. I loathe it; I shall not live always. Let me alone; for my days are vanity" (Job 7:15-16). Still, what Job is really interested in is a reaffirmation of his relationship with God.

Job maintains his innocence in his suffering (9:21), refusing to be silent (10:1), and again he expresses the weariness of his life while he calls on God for meaning: "My soul is weary of my life" (10:1). Even so, he again refuses to be silent: "I will say to God, 'Do not condemn me; show me why You contend with me'" (10:2). Job finds strength in his faith (position B): "Though He slay me, yet will I trust Him" (13:15). Indeed, he will continue to trust God no matter what God does to him. He asks only that God maintain an open relationship with him: "Then call, and I will answer; or let me speak, then You respond to me" (13:22). Beginning in Job 38, God does speak directly to Job, confirming the importance of their continuing relationship and God's care for his creation.

Jeremiah

A sense of grief and loss appears in certain passages of the book of Jeremiah and in the book of Lamentations, also ascribed to Jeremiah. In Jeremiah 20, the prophet speaks of his disappointment with life in the most uncompromising terms:

> Cursed be the day in which I was born!
> Let the day not be blessed in which my mother bore me!
> Let it not be blessed! . . .
> Why did I come forth from the womb
> To see labor and sorrow,
> That my days should be consumed with shame? (Jer. 20:14, 18)

These thoughts are the despairing words of a very sensitive man who is overwhelmed by the evil and suffering that he sees around him. Yet he is protected by his faith (position B), and there is no indication that he thinks of suicide, nor do the rabbinic commentators find any hint of suicide in his words. His belief that God will punish evil comes across clearly in an earlier passage (in chap. 20):

Sing to the Lord!
Praise the Lord!
For He has delivered the soul of the poor
From the hand of evil-doers. (Jer. 20:13)

Rebecca

After participating in the deception by which they have obtained Isaac's
blessing, Rebecca sends Jacob away to his Uncle Laban, so that he won't be
killed by an angry Esau (Gen. 27:42-45). Immediately afterward, Rebecca
tells Isaac that her life has been made miserable (position A) by Esau's
Hittite wives, and she worries that Jacob may marry similarly:

> And Rebecca said to Isaac, "I am weary of my life because of the
> daughters of Heth. If Jacob takes a wife of the daughters of Heth, like
> these who are the daughters of the land, what good shall my life be to
> me?" (Gen. 27:46)

Although this has been read as a "suicidal ideation" narrative, such
an interpretation is far overdrawn and matches neither the wording of the
text nor the best of scholarly opinion. Rebecca's words seem more like a
message to her husband: "Please fix this situation because I can't stand it!"
In any case, the tactic works, and Isaac involves God as a stopper in his
command that Jacob not marry one of the daughters of Canaan, who are
so offensive to Rebecca. Instead, let him marry a daughter of Laban, a kinsman (position B). Rebecca is presumably satisfied, and there is no more
mention of her "suicidal" musings (Gen. 28:1-4).

Summary

The Hebrew Bible contains many stories in which God intervenes in the
lives of characters who express some sort of death wish. He does not place
characters in a Hobson's choice situation in which they are compelled to
make a decision that will destroy them. Further, God plays the role of a
stopper, offering the characters a chance to overcome their problems. Thus
all these narratives resemble the story of Jonah: God offers individuals spe-

cial support (B) to prevent them from committing suicide. This is not a suicidal return to an "inanimate state," as Freud described it, but rather a protective intervention that allows individuals to understand that their lives are important to God and that he will help them seek fulfillment in their relationship with God and with the world.

III. Marriage and Family Case Studies from Greek Tragedy and Biblical Narratives

7. Couples: Polarization vs. Growth, Prometheus-Pandora vs. Adam-Eve

When he had made the lovely curse, the price for the blessing of fire, he brought her to a place where gods and men were gathered, and the girl was thrilled by all her pretty trappings, given by mighty Zeus' daughter with grey eyes. Amazement seized the mortal men and gods, to see the hopeless trap, deadly to man.

Hesiod, *Theogony*, 11.587-93

And the Lord God said: "It is not good that man should be alone; I will make a helper fit for him." . . . And Adam called his wife's name Eve, because she was the mother of all living. Also for Adam and his wife the Lord God made tunics of skin, and clothed them.

Gen. 2:18; 3:20-21

Couples in the Greek world oscillate between enmeshment and disengagement. Mothers show a fear of individuation (position A), while fathers manifest a fear of attachment (position C). By contrast, couples in the biblical narrative show greater balance or congruence between individuation and attachment (the BED axis). Although parents with problems in the areas of enmeshment and disengagement may not always be suicidal themselves, they are more likely to produce offspring who are. In his important book on family treatment of suicide, Joseph Richman (1986) has emphasized the suicidogenic implications of family symbiosis and separation issues. First, a child's efforts at individuation disrupt the family system and are seen by the family as a threat. Second, members of the family may see the formation of intimate attachments outside the family as threatening, as if there can be only one intimate attachment or one social group. The threat to the family is that of loss or separation. Finally, disturbances in the family communication system, an intolerance for crisis, and an accumulation of crisis situations all culminate in double-bind dilemmas in which suicide is perceived as the only possible solution.

Pathological and healthy couples are distinguished in Figures 7.1 and 7.2 (Kaplan 1990b). Figure 7.1 presents the pathological AC axis: position AA represents an enmeshed couple type, position CC a disengaged couple type, and position AC a rejection-intrusion couple type.[1]

Enmeshed couples (position AA) are afraid of autonomy but not of bonding: they are attached but not individuated. Conflict emerges when the parties in the couple become too remote from each other. Disengaged couples (position CC) are afraid of bonding but not of autonomy: they are individuated but not attached. Conflict emerges when the two people become too intimate (Kohut 1971; Minuchin 1974). In a rejection-intrusion couple (AC), one partner (C) is afraid of entrapment, while the other (A) is afraid of responsibility and abandonment. The A partner wants togetherness, while the C partner wants freedom (Napier 1978; Willi 1982). Couples on this clinical axis will show the same fixation as individuals, which we have described in Chapter 1 (figure 1.2), oscillating or cycling back and forth between enmeshed and disengaged positions, and being unable to move ahead to the next life stage.

Figure 7.2 portrays healthy couple development. Immature reciprocal couples (BB) are neither individuated nor attached: they fear both bonding and autonomy. Conflict emerges when the partners become too intimate with each other or too remote. Emerging reciprocal couples (EE) are semi-individuated and semi-attached. The partners do not fear either bonding or autonomy; nor do they need it. Their relationship is neither close nor distant. Mature couples (DD) are highly individuated and highly attached, needing both bonding and autonomy. They can enjoy both inti-

---

1. This summarizes the conceptual framework of a number of the most important marital and family theorists and therapists (e.g., Bowen 1960; Minuchin 1974; Stierlin 1974; and Wynne et al. 1958). D. M. Olson, D. M. Sprenkle, and C. S. Russell (1979) have worked with the same single dimension, although they have broken the scale into four points (disengaged, separated, connected, and enmeshed) rather than into three.

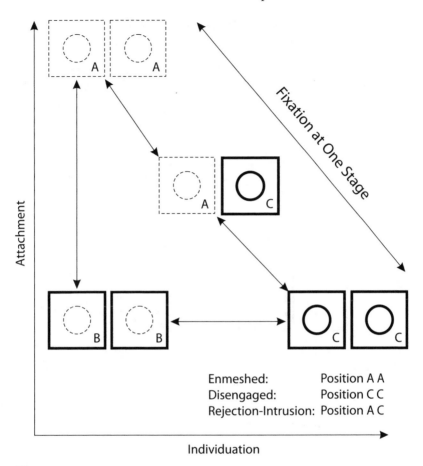

Enmeshed: Position A A
Disengaged: Position C C
Rejection-Intrusion: Position A C

Figure 7.1
The Couple Clinical Axis

macy and separation. Like individuals, couples on the developmental axis can fowardly regress from position DD at one life stage to position BB at the next. In other words, they must move temporarily backward in level to advance in stage (see figure 7.2).

Healthy couple growth involves the step-by-step replacement of interpersonal defenses or walls by healthy self-definition or boundaries. Weakening the walls before the boundaries are strong enough or leaving them up after the boundaries have formed leads to pathological outcomes. Let us use this model to study two early Greek and two early biblical "couples."

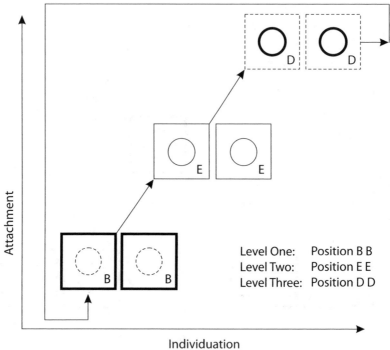

Figure 7.2
The Couple Developmental Axis

Greek Marital Patterns

Prometheus and Pandora are the closest thing we have to an early Greek "couple." Deucalion and Pyrrha are the couple who experience a great flood as told in Greek myth.

Prometheus and Pandora

The choice of Prometheus and Pandora requires some explanation, since they are not actually a couple at all. It is Prometheus's brother, Epimetheus, who is married to Pandora. Nevertheless, the leading male and female roles in this story are played by Prometheus and Pandora, even though there is no indication in the myth that they have ever met each other. This lack of a true original couple may in itself indicate the underlying feeling among the Greeks that male-female relationships are somewhat of an aberration.

The following events can be highlighted for our purposes:

1. Prometheus attempts to make humans autonomous by stealing fire and thus the mechanical arts from the gods. This enrages Zeus, who gets revenge by sending Pandora, a seductive but deceitful woman, to Epimetheus to be the "ruin of mankind" (Hesiod, *Works and Days*, 60-86).
2. Prometheus warns his brother Epimetheus against becoming entrapped by Pandora and tells him not to accept any presents from Zeus. Epimetheus forgets this warning (87-90).
3. Pandora opens the urn Zeus has given her, releasing every manner of pain and evil into the world, leaving only hope still locked up inside (90-96).
4. Prometheus is bound to a cliff at the edge of the world to punish him for helping humankind (Hesiod, *Theogony*, 616-20).
5. Pandora becomes the progenitress of all women: from her comes the deadly female race, who live with mortal men and bring them harm (591-94).

Because Epimetheus fails to carry out the job of achieving autonomy for humankind, Prometheus must intervene, but on the sly. He steals fire and the technical arts for man; these are the basis for human civilization (Plato, *Protagoras*, 320-22). A tragic figure, Prometheus must act in isolation (C) from the gods (see Figure 7.3).[2] At the same time, Prometheus unsuccessfully warns Epimetheus against becoming entrapped by Pandora (A), who releases evils such as sickness and old age into the world. This enmeshment is exacerbated by the suicidogenic hopelessness

2. It is clear that Prometheus does not descend to Zeus's level of villainy and that, despite suffering, he holds fast to his standard of morality and of right and wrong. His reaction may be the best possible one in the face of a narcissistic Zeus, but moral autonomy, though heroic, is not sufficient. There is no safe space for Prometheus in Zeus's world, and thus he is isolated on a cliff at the earth's farthest edge (position C). Prometheus is often used as a standard of heroism for Western humankind. Unfortunately, in the absence of covenant, the Promethean struggle often degenerates into pointless rebellion and even suicide.

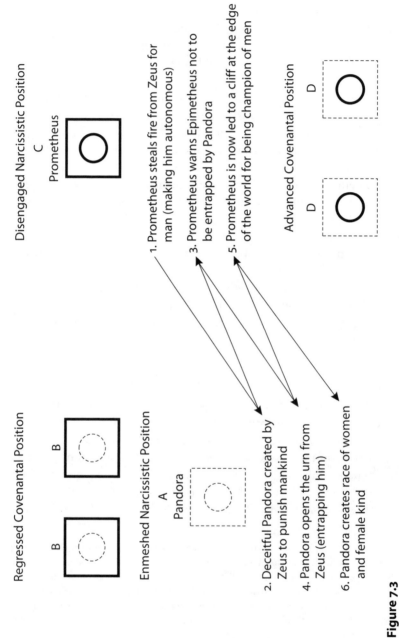

Regressed Covenantal Position

B | B

Enmeshed Narcissistic Position

A
Pandora

Disengaged Narcissistic Position

C
Prometheus

Advanced Covenantal Position

D | D

1. Prometheus steals fire from Zeus for man (making him autonomous)

3. Prometheus warns Epimetheus not to be entrapped by Pandora

5. Prometheus is now led to a cliff at the edge of the world for being champion of men

2. Deceitful Pandora created by Zeus to punish mankind

4. Pandora opens the urn from Zeus (entrapping him)

6. Pandora creates race of women and female kind

Figure 7.3
Prometheus and Pandora

of the situation: hope alone is still trapped in the jar of Epimetheus and unavailable to humans.

Epimetheus is thus a passive object between Prometheus and Pandora. Prometheus is wary and rejecting, warning Epimetheus against Pandora, while Pandora is controlling and entrapping, undoing Prometheus's hard-won autonomy with her jar of evils (AC).[3]

Zeus's acquiescence and even desire for this kind of narcissistic male-female relationship is shown by his role in the entire affair. His cruelty and pathological need for control set up the antagonism between Prometheus and Pandora. It is, after all, Zeus who withholds fire from humans, forcing Prometheus to steal it. It is Zeus who makes Pandora deceitful and sends her to entrap men. Finally, it is Zeus who attempts to maintain the respective narcissistic positions of man and woman by arranging their continuing enmity.

Deucalion and Pyrrha

This polarized pattern is further illustrated in the Greek story of the flood and of Deucalion and Pyrrha. As depicted by Apollodorus (1.7-2), the conflict is not between Deucalion and Pyrrha, who seem to be decent enough people, but between them and Zeus, who, out of personal pique, sends a great flood to destroy humankind. Zeus fails in this aim: a few people escape the flood by climbing onto high mountain peaks. Deucalion and Pyrrha survive by building a boat on the sly with help from Prometheus, who again rebels against Zeus. When the flood is over, Deucalion sacrifices to Zeus, who allows him to rebuild the human race. But Zeus has the last laugh, for humans are created from stones cast separately by Deucalion and Pyrrha: he makes the men, and she makes the women.

Ovid focused on Deucalion and Pyrrha, good people who are lonely for human company. They pray to Themis (not to Zeus, as in Apollodorus) and eventually puzzle out the instructions of the goddess to toss the bones of their "great mother" earth over their shoulders. Her "bones" are stones that repopulate the wet and empty world (Ovid, *Metamorphoses*, 1.381-98).

---

3. Curiously, the modern stereotype of the "devouring Jewish mother" fits Pandora better than it does Eve, and it certainly applies to Hera as described by Philip Slater (1968). The issue of how the modern Jewish mother came to be seen in ancient Greek rather than biblical terms is a complex one that deserves serious study.

The following points in the above narratives may be highlighted this way (Figure 7.4 represents this schematically):

1. Deucalion is the son of Prometheus; Pyrrha is the daughter of Pandora (and Epimetheus).
2. Zeus sends a flood to destroy the Bronze race of men without warning Deucalion and Pyrrha.
3. However, Prometheus warns Deucalion and advises the couple on how to build a boat.
4. Deucalion and Pyrrha are saved by the boat during the flood and are described as a happy couple. After the flood, when Deucalion and Pyrrha emerge from the boat, the former asks the gods (either Zeus or Themis, depending on the account) for a renewal of the human race.
5. Zeus responds and arranges to repopulate the world by having men spring from the stones thrown by Deucalion and women from the stones thrown by Pyrrha (rather than from their sexual union).

At first, Pyrrha and Deucalion seem to fall into the rejection-intrusion (AC) pattern of their respective parents, Pandora and Prometheus. Zeus sends a flood to destroy humanity. His narcissistic attempts to drown them drive the couple into an enmeshed (AA) collusion with him, while Prometheus's intervention pushes them to the opposite polarity, a disengaged (CC) collusion against Zeus. They escape the flood by building a boat, about which Zeus is ignorant. Their time together on the boat seems to tilt them off their narcissistic collusion, establishing the beginning of a developmentally healthy relationship (position BB). Ovid describes them as a happy couple. However, rather than allowing this relationship to mature, Zeus quickly repolarizes it, causing women to come from Pyrrha and men to come from Deucalion, reestablishing the narcissistic (AC) collusion.[4] Zeus seeks thereby to weaken the basis of family life and the continuity of generations so that people will never be able to develop secure, harmonious, and supportive family patterns.

4. To be sure, a subsequent account in Apollodorus does suggest a sexual union between Deucalion and Pyrrha. "Deucalion had children by Pyrrha, first Helen, . . . second Amphicyton, and third, a daughter, Protogenia" (Apollodorus, 1.7-3). Nevertheless, the account of separate parentage seems highly significant in a society as misogynistic as classical Greece. In this story women continue to be seen as "a race apart," cloning women after themselves.

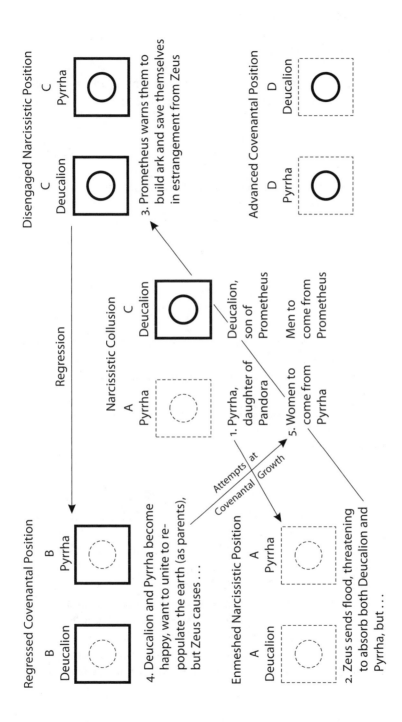

Figure 7.4 Deucalion and Pyrrha

Biblical Marital Patterns

Adam and Eve are the original biblical couple. Later, Noah and his wife live through the great flood and the subsequent renewal of life.

Adam and Eve

Adam and Eve differ from Prometheus and Pandora in that they are clearly a married couple. God's relationship with the first couple can be summarized by the following events immediately after creation:

1. God commands Adam not to eat of the tree of knowledge, or he will die (Gen. 2:16-17).
2. God creates Eve for Adam from his rib (2:18-22).
3. The serpent traps Eve into eating fruit from this tree; Eve entraps Adam (3:1-7).
4. Adam and Eve hide from God, and they unsuccessfully try to deny their act (3:8-10).
5. When they are caught and God confronts them, Adam blames Eve; Eve blames the serpent (3:11-12).
6. Instead of killing them, God makes clothes for them and exiles them from Eden (3:22-23).
7. In exile, they will come to know the pain and toil of earning a livelihood and raising children (3:17-20).

Adam and Eve are in a rejection-intrusion (AC) dilemma with each other. Beneath Eve's entrapment of Adam lies a fear that she alone will take the responsibility and consequences for her act (position A). Therefore, Figure 7.5 portrays her as being initially in the A position. Adam's blaming reflects his effort to place the entire responsibility on Eve and avoid any share of God's anger (position C). This pattern resembles the narcissistic collusion of Prometheus and Pandora, with Adam blaming and Eve entrapping. But the biblical God, unlike Zeus, will have none of it.

Indeed, some commentators have argued that the reason God exiles Adam and Eve from the garden is precisely his disapproval of this narcissistic pattern. For example, a midrash (*Gen. Rabbah,* 19:12) declares that the main reason that the man and woman are driven from the garden is

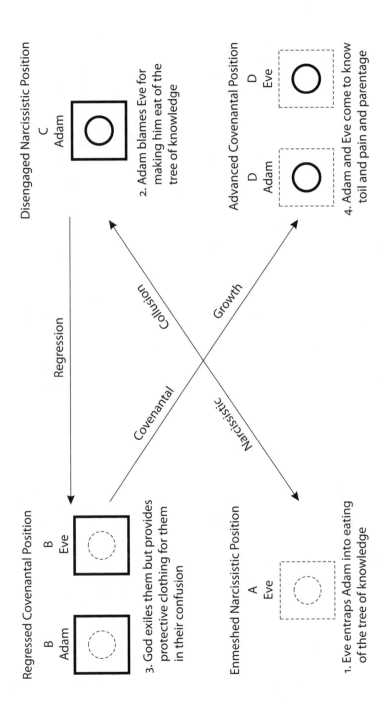

Figure 7.5 Adam and Eve

Regressed Covenantal Position

Disengaged Narcissistic Position

B Adam

B Eve

C Adam

3. God exiles them but provides protective clothing for them in their confusion

2. Adam blames Eve for making him eat of the tree of knowledge

Regression

Collusion

Growth

Covenantal

Narcissistic

Enmeshed Narcissistic Position

Advanced Covenantal Position

A Eve

D Adam

D Eve

1. Eve entraps Adam into eating of the tree of knowledge

4. Adam and Eve come to know toil and pain and parentage

that each one tries to blame someone else for his or her sins (also see Rashi, on Gen. 3:12). Similarly, Eve's trapping of Adam can be seen as an attempt on her part to avoid solitary death: "She [Eve] came to him and said, 'Do you think that I will die and another Eve will be created for you? Do you think that if I die you will survive me?'" (*Gen. Rabbah*, 20:8)

Despite his disapproval of their narcissistic pattern, God continues to care for Adam and Eve. He does not kill them, but instead provides them with clothing to protect them in their exile (an impermeable wall) and confusion (an inarticulated boundary). This allows them to regroup (position BB). They then begin to develop their marital relationship, and they learn to live with the labor and pain of life and parenthood (position EE). After the tragic events surrounding Cain's murder of Abel and his own banishment, Adam and Even have a third son, Seth (position DD).

In the Greek story, Pyrrha and Deucalion get along with each other, but Zeus is hostile to both. Zeus uses his power to try to destroy human development, whereas the God of Genesis opens an important dialogue with the couple, and he provides them with the protection of clothing in their exile. This enables Adam and Eve to renew their relationship with each other and with God despite their sin and their expulsion from the garden. With God's help, they slowly mature and finally achieve the successful joint parenthood of their third son, from whom humankind is descended.[5]

Noah and His Wife

A similar suicide-preventive, covenantal pattern emerges in the narrative of Noah and his wife. First, the Genesis 5 account shows how Noah (and his wife) descended from Adam and Eve. God then warns Noah of the impending flood and makes arrangements for his safety. We can highlight the following events in the story of Noah:

1. Noah and his wife are descendants of Adam and Eve (Gen. 5:1-32).
2. God sends a flood to destroy mankind (6:17).
3. God warns Noah and instructs him how to build an ark and to save two or more of each creature, male and female.

5. In one Midrashic version, Noah's wife is a descendant of Cain (*Gen. Rabbah*, 22).

And God said to Noah, "The end of all flesh has come before Me, for the earth is filled with violence through them; and behold, I will destroy them with the earth. . . . But I will establish My covenant with you; and you shall go into the ark — you, your sons, your wife, and your sons' wives with you. And of every living thing of all flesh, you shall bring two of every sort into the ark, to keep them alive with you; they shall be male and female. (6:13, 18-22)

4. After the flood, Noah and his wife and all the creatures, male and female, repopulate the earth according to God's design (8:15-19; 9:1).
5. God places a rainbow in the heavens as a sign of his covenant with humans, and also a sign that that there will not be another flood to destroy humans (9:12-17).

Figure 7.6 illustrates this process. First, God sends the flood because of humankind's wickedness. But, unlike the narcissistic Zeus, God does not try to destroy Noah and his wife; instead, he provides an ark to protect them from the flood (BB position). Moreover, God provides the plan for them to reemerge as grandparents (DD position). The continuing race of people (both men and women) comes from the union of Noah's sons and daughters-in-law. The rainbow symbolizes the ongoing covenant, even in the face of human sinfulness.[6]

This signal of faith stands in marked contrast to the suicidogenic hopelessness that pervades the conclusion of the Prometheus-Pandora myth. Pandora releases evils from the jar of Epimetheus into the world. Hope alone remains locked up, and humans are provoked into a quixotic quest to release it.

Implications for Suicide

These Greek couples seem pathologically fixated and tragic, while those in the biblical world have hope for development. The relationship between men and women in Greek narratives cycles endlessly between enmeshment and disengagement: men exhibit a fear of absorption and women a fear of abandonment. Men and women in the biblical narratives, by contrast, turn expectantly to God to overcome these fears.

6. See Rabbi A. I. Kook's *Musar Avicha* (34-39) for a comparable argument.

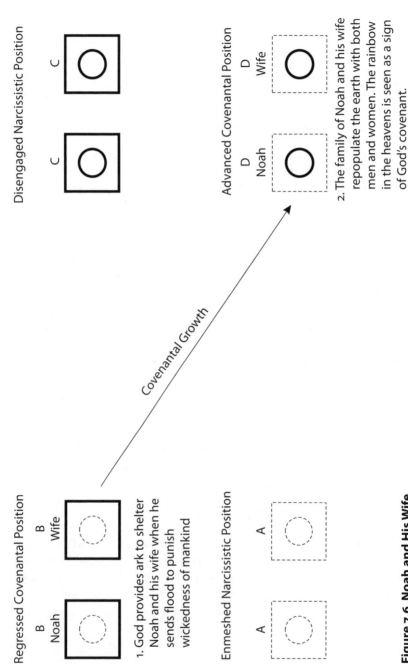

Figure 7.6 Noah and His Wife

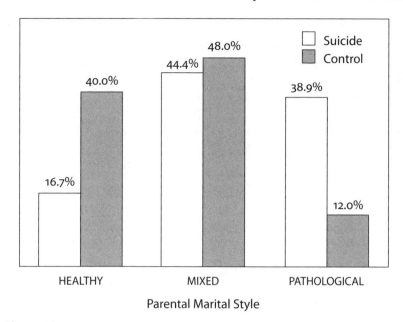

Figure 7.7
Marital Pathology and Completed Adolescent Suicide

A recent literature review (Kaplan and Maldaver 1990a; 1993) has pointed to the suicidal implications of this difference. A review of eighty-five research studies over the past twenty years has yielded the following results. Marriages on the clinical AC axis are generally more suicidogenic for their offspring than those on the developmental BED axis. Adolescent suicidal behavior (completions, attempts, or plans) occurs more frequently in the disengaged (CC) parental style, followed respectively by the immature reciprocal (BB) parental pattern, the enmeshed (AA) pattern, and the rejection-intrusion (AC) pattern. Our literature review has revealed no suicidal attempts or completions for the offspring of more mature reciprocal (EE or DD) parents.

Particularly striking results are apparent in an original empirical study by Kaplan and Maldaver (1990a; 1993). The parents of twenty-five adolescent suicides were compared to the parents of twenty-five comparable non-suicidal adolescents. As can be seen in Figure 7.7, only 16.7 percent of the adolescent suicides came from families with two healthy (BED axis) parents, while 44.4 percent came from a mixed parental pattern (one healthy BED-axis parent and one clinical AC-axis parent), and 38.9 percent came from two pathological (AC axis) parents. The non-suicidal families showed a dramatically different pattern. Forty percent of the control adolescents had two healthy (BED axis) parents, 48 percent had a mixed parental pattern (one BED and one AC parent), and only 12 percent had two pathological (AC axis) parents (Kaplan and Maldaver 1990b).[7] Approximately three times as many suicides came from pathological families, while three times as many non-suicides came from healthy families.[8]

7. The Chi-square statistic describing this interaction equals 5.16 and is significant at the .075 level.

8. An alternative, "backward" explanation is that experiencing the suicide of a child will make the parents more pathological. However, the research of M. D. S. Ainsworth (1972) has provided support for the "forward" interpretation, specifically, the importance of secure parenting, especially mothering, for a later resilient sense of self that is capable of withstanding life stressors (cf. Bowlby 1977; Main, Kaplan, and Cassidy 1985; Kaplan and Worth 1992-93; Kaplan and O'Connor 1993).

An interesting recent study of suicide in Yiddish literature (Hadda 1988) has pointed to a pervasive theme in relationships. Women are passionate and men passive, at least in suicidal relationships. This is more reflective of a Greek rejection-intrusion (AC) pattern than a biblical reciprocity (DD).

8. The Suicide-Promoting Structure of the Greek Family: Oedipus and Electra

From what manner of parents did I take my miserable being!
And to them I go thus, accursed, unwed, to share their home.

Sophocles, *Antigone*, 862-63

Ah! Hapless mother, what a love was thine! . . . Where will this
history end? That "love" has been our curse from the time long
past.

Euripides, *Hippolytus*, 337-43

Ah me! alas! and whither can I go? What share have I henceforth
in dance or marriage rite?

Euripides, *Electra*, 1198-99

Conflictual family structure is one of the greatest contributing factors to
the urge toward suicide in Greek thinking. Mothers are intrusive, not allowing their children any space for growth or autonomy; fathers are disengaged, with children feeling rejected and abandoned. The child's energies
become completely involved in attempting to solve the insoluble problem
of gaining the recognition and love of each parent (Orbach 1986; 1988). In
this system the child has no real right to live, and she is often burdened
with a deeply guilty feeling that she is not wanted. Suicide becomes a pre-
dictable result of this oppressive sense of worthlessness.

The child is caught in the destructive interplay between the two parents themselves. The wife feels abandoned and demeaned, while the husband often feels irrelevant and controlled. Each partner uses the child as an ally in the battle against the other. This pattern can be seen in the relationship of the first divine Greek family (Apollodorus, 1.1.1). Sky, the father, is unrooted and disengaged; Earth, the mother, is fixed but intrusive. Such a mix can be deeply destructive to children, can even make them homicidal or suicidal. The father provides no support, and the mother gives no space. This is the experience of insecure parenting that can lead to Oedipal problems.

> Grieved at the loss of the children who were thrown [by Sky] into Tartarus, Earth persuaded the Titans to attack their father and gave Cronus a steel sickle. . . . Cronus cut off his father's genitals and threw them into the sea. Having thus eliminated their father, the Titans brought back their brothers who had been hurled to Tartarus and gave the rule to Cronus. (Apollodorus, 1.1.4)

This vicious family pattern continues as Cronus swallows his own newborn children to avoid being supplanted by them — though Zeus, his youngest son, survives. Zeus overpowers Cronus with the collusion of Rhea, his mother, and becomes king; and he, in turn, devours Metis with an embryo still in her womb (Apollodorus, 1.1).

The sociologist Phillip Slater (1968) has demonstrated the constant presence of aggression between parents and children in Apollodorus: forty-seven cases between fathers and sons, twelve between mothers and sons, one between mother and daughter, and sixteen between fathers and daughters. These often lead to suicide or self-mutilation. Our selection of narratives in Table 8.1 first examines sons, and then daughters.

Greek Fathers and Sons

In the following stories, Greek fathers and sons are in a bitter rivalry, with sons seen as a threat and the fathers as a block. Sons must not threaten their fathers' position in any way, and it is perfectly legitimate for fathers to practice infant exposure. Cronus eats his children, and Zeus begets and abandons illegitimate children all over the earth. The son in this system

Table 8.1
Greek Parent-Child Narratives

	Fathers	*Mothers*
Sons	Laius — Oedipus	Medea — sons
	- - - - - - - - - -	- - - - - - - - - -
	Creon — Haemon	Jocasta — Oedipus
Daughters	Agamemnon — Iphigenia	Clytemnestra — Electra
	- - - - - - - - - -	- - - - - - - - - -
	Oedipus — Antigone	Hecuba — Polyxena

has no real right to live. Two relationships exemplify this pattern: (1) Laius and his son Oedipus and (2) Creon and his son Haemon.

Laius and Oedipus

Consider first the story of Oedipus, who unknowingly slays his father, Laius, becomes king of Thebes in his place, and marries his own mother, Jocasta. Two things are relevant for our present purposes: first, the nature of the relationship between Laius and Oedipus; second, the fact that Oedipus winds up mutilating himself.

The story of Oedipus begins with an oracle's warning to King Laius that there is danger to his throne in Thebes if his newborn son should reach man's estate. This warning leads Laius to hand his son over to a herdsman to be destroyed. The herdsman, after piercing the infant's feet, gives him to a fellow shepherd, who is a kind person and carries him to King Polybus of Corinth and his queen, who adopt him and call him Oedipus (meaning swollen feet).

Many years later, when Oedipus grows up, another oracle presents him with a riddle rather than an intelligible prophecy, and this leads him to destruction. The oracle prophesies that Oedipus will be the death of his father. Oedipus, who has known his adoptive father, Polybus (with whom he has a good relationship), as his only father, takes the oracle to mean that he will kill Polybus. Note the strange tone of the oracular pronouncement: Avoid the parent you love lest you hurt him. This is in stark contrast to the biblical commandment "Honor your father and mother." The oracle picks on the weakest link in the relationship between father and son, the point of primal suspicion and fear that must exist in some small amount in even the best of relationships. Furthermore, the oracle's prophecy brings about what it purports to warn against, the murder of Oedipus's biological father and the destruction of any chance that Oedipus has for fulfillment.

It happens that, as Oedipus is fleeing from Corinth to Thebes in order to avoid killing the man he believes to be his father, he encounters his real (biological) father, Laius, on a narrow road as the latter is heading to Delphi. In the ensuing quarrel that breaks out, Oedipus does indeed kill Laius — as well as his attendant. Shortly after that event, Oedipus saves Thebes from the Sphinx, a monster who is part woman, part lion, and part eagle, who has been devouring all those who cannot guess her riddle. In gratitude for their deliverance, the Thebans make Oedipus their king and give to him in marriage their queen — Laius's wife and Oedipus's mother, Jocasta.

An interesting side note here is the nature of the Sphinx's riddle: "What walks on four legs in the morning, two legs in the afternoon, and three legs in the evening?" Oedipus correctly answers that it is "man," and thus he destroys the Sphinx and saves Thebes. When he does give this answer, though, Oedipus is implicitly accepting a curvilinear or decremental view of aging, where the older adult is seen as an infant, and this may contribute to the blurring of the generational boundaries between himself and his mother-wife, Jocasta.

Let us now return to the oracle's warning to Oedipus that he would kill his father, which is in itself a riddle. The oracle has placed Oedipus in a no-win situation. It becomes impossible for him to maintain any kind of relationship with his father and derive the sense of security essential to his normal development. When Oedipus rebels, he is doomed. Precisely because he is so well intentioned, Oedipus is unable to face his parents in the next world, and he blinds himself with brooches from his mother's clothing. The immediate precipitant to his self-blinding is his mother's suicide. Despite his fury toward her, he is enmeshed with her.

Creon and Haemon

The relationship between Creon and Haemon in Sophocles' *Antigone* shows some of the same characteristics, except that here it is not an outside oracle but the father, Creon himself, who places his son in an impossible situation, a Hobson's choice. Will Haemon obey his father and consign his fiancée, Antigone, to her doom, or will he oppose his father in an attempt to save her? Creon sees Haemon's attempt to express his own point of view as disloyalty to the family agenda, and thus his first words are to question whether Haemon will remain loyal to him. Haemon responds mildly at first, submitting to his father's authority, but then he attempts to defend Antigone to his father. Creon responds: "Men of my age, are we indeed to be schooled by men of his?" (727-28). The exchange between father and son becomes quite bitter: Haemon demands that his father judge him by his merits rather than his years, and Creon responds by accusing Haemon of shamelessly feuding with his father. Creon emphasizes his control and power by introducing the notion of Haemon's death: "Thou canst never marry on this side of the grave." Haemon's response contains a clear suicidal threat: "Then she must die, and in her deeds, destroy another" (750-51). Creon calls his son's bluff, and Haemon raises the ante to suicide. When Creon interrupts Haemon's mourning for the now-dead Antigone, Haemon reacts violently: first, he tries unsuccessfully to kill his father, and then he kills himself.

Greek Mothers and Sons

Slater's studies of Greek mythological families have led him to focus on mother-son relationships as potentially more destructive than even those between father and son. The mother's low self-esteem intensifies her fear of being abandoned. She responds to her miseries by using her sons to hurt her husband, thus venting her rage on those who she feels keep her in her wretched state. But she will typically hurt her children as well. She expresses her guilt, anger, and self-hatred by creating disharmony and conflict within the family. She does this by "triangulating," allying with the son against the father. Sometimes this leads to the mother's murder of her son, sometimes to the son's self-destructiveness. An example of the first is Medea and her sons; an example of the second is Jocasta and Oedipus.

Medea and her Sons

The potential brutality of the mother is expressed in Euripides' magnificent drama *Medea*. The legend of Medea's aid to Jason and the Argonauts in their quest for the Golden Fleece is among the best known of ancient Hellenic tales, and it also forms the subject of the third-century epic poem *The Argonautica,* by Apollonius of Rhodes.

The action in Euripides' *Medea* begins some years later, when Jason rejects his wife Medea to marry a wealthy princess of Corinth. Medea is devastated: "And she [Medea] lies fasting, yielding her body to her grief, wasting away in tears" (24-26). She plots a terrible revenge, the murder of the new bride, as well as of the two sons she has had with Jason. As the plot develops, Medea expresses her misery at being a woman and her resentment toward both Jason and her sons: "Curse you and your father too, ye children, damned sons of a doomed woman! Ruin seize the whole family!" (112-14). She despises her role as a woman, since a man's role is so much more enviable. Both she and Jason demean the woman's role: "And yet they say we live secure at home, while they are at the wars, with their sorry reasoning, for I would gladly take my stand in battle array three times o'er, than once give birth" (244-51).

She cannot bear the thought of being rejected and abandoned by Jason or of being mocked by her enemies. Jason criticizes her for being illogical and impractical, and his disdain for women is clear. Men are truly superior, and women bring ruin: "Yea, men should have begotten children from some other source, no female race existing; thus would no evil ever have fallen on mankind" (573-75).

Medea hates Jason's disdain for her gender, but she is also disgusted with the role of a woman. She will not be a weak, feeble-spirited stay-at-home. What is horrible here is Medea's solution, which is self-destructive as well as frighteningly inhuman to others. It reveals much about the deep rage and hostility inherent in the typical Hellenic family. She feels she can respond most effectively by destroying everything.[1]

Medea sends Jason's bride a beautiful white dress and a golden crown as wedding gifts. However, she has treated them with poison, so that they burn the princess to an agonizing death when she puts them on. Medea then completes her revenge by murdering the two boys. In the final scene, Medea appears above the house in a chariot drawn by flying dragons; the bodies of her sons are with her. Jason pleads to be allowed to bury them. Medea torments and rebukes him cruelly (1354-60).

---

1. Erich Wellisch (1954) has used the term "Medea complex" in *Isaac and Oedipus* (1954); it was coined by Edward Stern (1948).

Medea is largely motivated by the feeling that Jason is abandoning her. If she cannot be with him any longer in marriage, she will still be united with him. She slays her sons to vex Jason and to gain his full attention. Jason may now hate her, but he can no longer scorn her as weak, powerless, and irrational. Medea proves herself cleverer, more macho, and more destructive than any warrior. At the same time that she punishes Jason for abandoning her, she repays her sons for making her a mother and contributing to her debasement. Medea does not acknowledge her sons as individuals with their own rights to live; she sees them simply as enmeshed extensions of herself. And she murders them to punish Jason.[2]

Jocasta and Oedipus

The mother in Greek mythological families is in constant conflict with her husband, and she uses her sons against her husband. Like Rhea, she can support them in overthrowing their father; or, like Medea, she can murder them to deprive her husband of an heir, fulfilling her own hatred of them at the same time. The royal couple of the gods, Zeus and Hera, presents a prime example of the second pattern. Hera, bitterly hostile toward Zeus, constantly plots the destruction of his numerous illegitimate children. According to some accounts, she bore him no children herself.

The passive role of Jocasta in Sophocles' *Oedipus Rex* can be seen as representing a pale reflection of this deep and hostile pattern on the part of the Greek mother-wife. This time it takes a self-destructive rather than a homicidal form. First, Jocasta hangs herself; then, immediately after coming upon his dead mother, Oedipus puts out his eyes with the golden brooches that she wears. Oedipus has been set up by the riddling oracle and placed in an insoluble dilemma: he has unknowingly married his biological mother. When he discovers this, Oedipus feels betrayed and wishes to murder her; but she has already killed herself, awakening Oedipus's sense of abandonment. He turns his anger inward and blinds himself, using an article of her clothing, saying that he does not wish to see his parents in the next world.

---

2. A poignant example in English literature of this expendable condition occurs in Thomas Hardy's *Jude the Obscure.* The scribbled suicide note left by three unwanted children says it all: "Done because we are too menny" (1974, 356).

The Oedipus Complex and Suicide

As described by Freud, the Oedipus complex represents an archetypal dilemma for the son within the family, and it is directly linked to suicidal pathology. The Oedipal son wishes to replace his father and have his mother for
himself: "King Oedipus, who slew his father Laius and wedded his mother
Jocasta, is nothing more or less than a wish-fulfillment, the fulfillment of the
wish of our childhood" (Freud 1954, 296). For this reason, the father rejects
his own son from the time of his very birth, and the son fails to develop a
sense of his own worth. He becomes bound to and dominated by his "earth"
mother and at best will have a standoffish relationship with his "sky" father.
Indeed, Greek father-son myths abound with instances of castration and incorporation (again, see Apollodorus, 1.1). In none of these stories does the
son feel even the most minimal acceptance from his father. The son either re-
volts against his father or acquiesces in his own destruction.

Split between enmeshed and disengaged states, the child is simply
torn apart and is likely to produce a persistent pattern of self-defeating and
self-destructive behaviors. The son becomes a pawn in the battle between
his parents, neither of whom sees the son as an individual with a right to
his independence and his own creativity. He lacks the approval, permission, and indeed the blessing of his parents to live his own life. Greek plays
constantly return to the theme of the curse on the house of Labdacus and
the curse of Oedipus on his own sons: "The glory of wealth and of pride,
with iron, not gold, in your hands, ye shall come, at the last, to divide"
(Aeschylus, *Seven Against Thebes*, 785-86). This is a curse that is horribly
fulfilled when his sons murder each other. What makes this especially
tragic is that Oedipus in many ways is a good and well-meaning man; but
he is one who is trapped by an all-enveloping suicidal doom. This situation
was keenly perceived by the Greek dramatists, who understood the tragic
drives underpinning their great society but felt helpless to provide any antidote or solution.

The link between the Oedipus complex and suicide is diagrammed
in Figure 8.1. The Greek husband-father is disengaged from (C) and deprecating toward his wife (MW), yet terrified of absorption by her.[3] He also

---

3. Bruno Bettelheim (1955, 115) has argued that one illustration of this male fear of absorption by the female is the theme of *vagina dentata* (castrating vagina with teeth) in primitive art.

fears displacement by his son (MS) and threatens to demean and castrate him.[4] The Greek wife-mother, in contrast, is enmeshed (A). She envies her husband (WM), yet she fears that he will abandon her. She also attempts to control and seduce her son (WS). This, of course, evokes the classic Oedipus complex of the son wanting to displace his father (SM = C) and possess his mother (SW = A). The son is thus anomic (A/C), driven to possess his mother and displace his father.[5] Anomic suicide is a serious risk unless something drastic changes in the situation (see Figure 8.1, top).[6]

According to classic psychoanalytic thinking, the father counters the son's threat of displacement by activating his own threat of castration. This serves to neutralize rather than resolve the son's desire to displace the father, resulting in a mutual standoffishness (SM = C, MS = C) in the father-son relationship (Figure 8.1, bottom). The husband-wife relationship, however, remains unchanged, with the husband still deprecating his wife (MW = C) and the wife still envying her husband (WM = A). The mother will still try to seduce her son (WS = A), but the son has given up his desire to possess his mother, now fearing incorporation by her (SW = C). He has displaced the fear of castration from his father to his mother. This ambivalent neutralization of the Oedipal dilemma leaves the son in the disengaged C position with both his father and his mother. The son, of course, remains at risk for suicide, now falling into Durkheim's egoistic suicidal type, which is so typical of the Sophoclean plays. He cannot genuinely attach to anyone.

Saddest, indeed, is the dependence on fear in achieving this neutralization. No fundamental resolution has occurred in the relationship of father and son. There is no sense that the father accepts his son's right to exist. The child is expendable! Still driven to displace his father, he is simply

---

4. In this diagram, the husband-father is designated by M (man) and the wife-mother by W (woman); the son is designated by S and the daughter by D.

5. Given this analysis, Olympiodorus's emphasis on Plato's curious suggestion of suicide as a remedy for a man possessing uncontrollable erotic passions for his mother (Taylor 1834) becomes more comprehensible.

6. Certain passages in the New Testament can be read as placing the family of Jesus in this rejection-intrusion (AC) pattern. Jesus' last words on the cross emphasize the theme of abandonment by the Father: "My God, My God, why hast thou forsaken me?" (Matt. 27:46). In another passage, Jesus seems to want to distance himself from his mother: he responds to his mother's request for wine during the wedding in Cana, "Woman, what do I have to do with you?" (John 2:4).

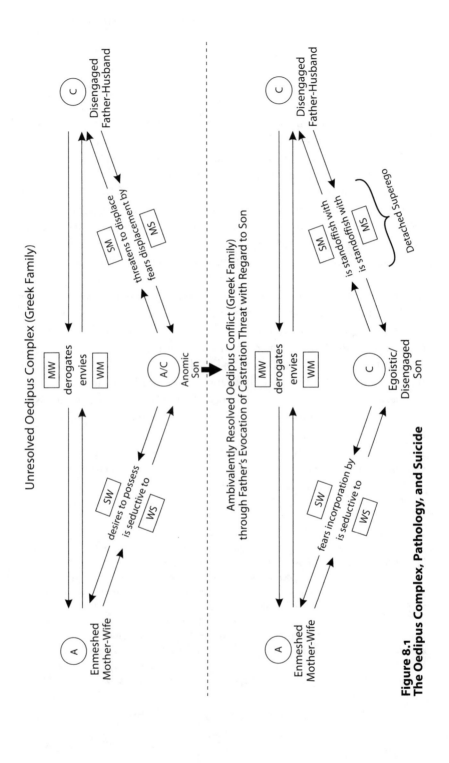

Figure 8.1
The Oedipus Complex, Pathology, and Suicide

inhibited in this desire by fear of punishment. As the superego is internalized in this process (Freud 1923a; 1923b; 1924), the son's moral identification with his father must have a detached and isolated quality, leaving him susceptible to egoistic (position C) suicide. Furthermore, this pathology, without outside intervention, is likely to reproduce itself from generation to generation. Escaping self-destruction, the disengaged (C) son will himself grow up to be a disengaged father. If he marries an intrusive (A) woman, they will pass on the unresolved Oedipal conflict, with its suicidal implications, to their sons.[7]

Greek Mothers and Daughters

Although the basic relationship between mother and daughter is very close in the Greek literary tradition, it is tainted by a potentially suicidal lack of genuine self-esteem. Woman is seen as the mysterious "other," closely associated with the devouring earth. This "otherness" is implied in the creation of Pandora as a curse to man, rather than as a suitable helper and a source of life. Woman's "alien" nature is perhaps most clearly expressed in taboos regarding the uncleanness of her menstrual blood. Taboos about menstruation lead to envy of the male (cf. Stephens 1962) and the daughter's willingness to abandon the mother and to look to her father. The Greek mother's only defense in this regard is to lower her daughter's self-esteem by eliciting even further shame about the latter's menstruating condition,

---

7. An example of this recurrence of narcissism across generations can be found in the family history of Otto Weininger, the suicide discussed in chap. 4. In a letter to Weininger's biographer, the psychiatrist Dr. David Abrahamsen, Weininger's sister Rosa described their parents' marriage:

> The married life of my parents was not peaceful. That was due to my father's strong personality, his sharp criticism, and his great demands upon his family. We children let Mother spoil us, we confided in her, but to us Father was the supreme judge. (Abrahamsen 1946, 213)

Abrahamsen went on to speculate:

> Undoubtedly the disharmony between his parents impressed young Otto deeply. Having a highly gifted but severe father and a mother of quite ordinary talents affected his sensitive mind. . . . Apparently Otto tried to identify himself with his father and developed hostility, unconscious though it may have been, toward his mother. (Abrahamsen 1946, 13)

to make it risky for the daughter fully to abandon the mother lest she herself wind up totally alone — without either mother or father. This is obviously a poor solution to the daughter's low self-esteem. Any attachment between Greek mother and daughter is permeated with a suicidal symbiotic quality, leaving the daughter unable to cope with life stresses. Psychoanalysis has understood this problem as the "Electra complex."

Clytemnestra and Electra

In his play *Electra*, Euripides depicts Electra, daughter of Agamemnon, as waiting for years, completely obsessed by plans for the return of her brother Orestes and their revenge on Clytemnestra for her murder of Agamemnon. Raised by both mother and father to see herself as debased in her womanhood, Electra is hostile both toward men and toward her mother, as well as toward her own lowly role. She is married to a farmer from a good family, "one of a noble nature" (262). Yet Electra treats him badly and boasts to strangers that she is still a virgin. Plotting to murder Clytemnestra, Electra sends a messenger to tell her that she has just given birth. When Clytemnestra arrives, Electra lets out her long-cherished hostility in a lengthy speech, accusing her mother of betraying and cuckolding Agamemnon.

Clytemnestra's response to Electra has some insight as to the preference of the daughter for her father over her mother: "Daughter, 'twas ever thy nature to love thy father. This too one finds; some sons cling to their father, others have deeper affection for their mother" (1102). Although Electra (with the help of Orestes) does murder her mother rather than herself, her reaction further displays her essential feeling of debasement as a woman: "Ah me! alas! and whither can I go? What share have I henceforth in dance or marriage rite? What husband will accept me as his bride?" (1198-1200).

Electra's sister, Iphigenia, significantly carries these same feelings of worthlessness into suicide. Agamemnon tricks Iphigenia into coming to the camp of the Greek army to be sacrificed to Artemis by pretending that she is to marry the great warrior Achilles (Euripides, *Iphigenia at Aulis*, 104-6). Clytemnestra soon discovers the truth about the "marriage"; still, she feels powerless and does nothing but bemoan her lot: "O, we are lost, my child and I. Lost, lost!" (886) Even before she knows of the plot,

Clytemnestra reveals her fear that her daughter will prefer her father to herself. Rather than show support when Iphigenia runs to embrace her father, she emphasizes the bitter triangular rivalry: "Go, go, my girl. You always loved your father more than the other children" (653-56). This line, of course, shares the same reproach as that previously cited from *Electra*. Clytemnestra is poignantly aware that both of her daughters prefer their lordly father to their ineffectual mother, and that they share her low self-esteem.

Hecuba and Polyxena

A second mother-daughter narrative involves the relationship between Hecuba and Polyxena that is described in Euripides' *Hecuba*. Hecuba, the brave widow of King Priam of Troy, is a captive of the Greeks. Her first speech reveals the depths of her own despair and distaste for life:

> Woe, woe is me! What champion have I? Sons, and city — where are they? Aged Creon is no more; no more my children now. Which way I am to go. . . . Ye have made an end, an utter end of me; life on earth has no more charm for me. (163-70)

When Odysseus informs them that Polyxena will be sacrificed to the ghost of Achilles, Hecuba's own emotional structure crumbles so badly that she cannot function as a mother. When Polyxena attempts to talk to her mother about her impending disaster, Hecuba seems unable to concentrate on anything but her own problems.[8] Polyxena says, "Unwedded I depart, never having tasted the married joys that were my due!" (416). Hecuba replies, "Tell them of all women I am most miserable" (424). Hecuba is without hope. Furthermore, she expresses this fatalism to her daughter: "Alas, my daughter! . . . Woe for the life! Ah, my daughter, a luckless mother's child" (179-85).

Faber (1970, 117) has offered a radical interpretation that Hecuba's own paralyzing depression and inability to show a full empathy pushes Polyxena toward suicide. For Faber, the Greeks actually offer Polyxena a

---

8. Hecuba lacks the religious perspective and the hope shown in the parable of Rabbi Wasserman (ch. 3).

means of escape, which she will not use, but rather expresses a preference for death over life:

> Alas, for thy cruel sufferings! My persecuted mother! Woe for thy life of grief! . . . Not more shall I thy daughter share thy bondage, hapless youth on hapless age attending! . . . For thee I weep with plaintive wail, mother doomed to a life of sorrow! For my own life, its ruin and its outrage, never a tear I shed; nay, death is becoming to me a happier lot than life. (200-216)

Greek Fathers and Daughters

The father-daughter relationship in the Greek family presents the final link in the chain of interlocking hostility and conflict within the nuclear family. The father carries uncertain feelings about his own manhood into the relationship and transmits ambivalent signals to his daughter. He demands that she idealize him as a male, but he simultaneously degrades her. If she does not idealize him, he threatens her with rejection and abandonment. At the same time, she is so debased that she is worthy of nothing other than rejection and abandonment. Both signals are apparent in Agamemnon's attitude toward his daughter Iphigenia.

Agamemnon and Iphigenia

Iphigenia, like many young girls, desperately wants her father's attention. She is literally willing to be sacrificed for her father's interests and seems to prefer him to her mother. Her self-esteem is so low that she leaps at the chance to be martyred in her father's name, and yet she allies herself with her father against her mother: "O mother, blame me not! Let me go first. And put my arms about my father's neck. Father, how glad it makes my heart to see you! It is so long since you have been away!" (Euripides, *Iphigenia in Aulis,* 631-37).

Agamemnon has no interest in his daughter, only in himself. His response to her upcoming sacrifice is totally self-involved: "O *my* wretched fate" (1135, italics added). Iphigenia pleads with her father for her life and recognition, revealing her feeling of powerlessness: "I have only tears. . . .

They are all my power. I clasp your knees, I am your suppliant now. I am your own child; my mother bore me to you. O kill me not untimely!" (1215-18). When he rejects her, she is unable to express her anger to him. Instead, she complains to Clytemnestra: "Mother, my father has gone, left me, betrayed and alone!" (1313-15). Finally, her basic behavioral pattern reasserts itself when she accepts her martyrdom and glorifies it as heroic altruism: "My death will save them, and my name will be blessed. She who freed Hellas" (1383). She tells her mother not to mourn for her and not to hate Agamemnon.

It is likely that Iphigenia gives herself over to the total idealization of her father and, simultaneously, to uttermost self-debasement by dying to preserve *his* honor. Perhaps taking her fate "like a man" is also an effort to win his approval. Agamemnon has made use of his daughter both to aggrandize himself and to debase his wife. His daughter is not real to him as a person, and he easily abandons, exposes, and even sacrifices her if he stands to achieve personal gain by such action, even if that gain is merely to buttress his own shaky ego in his relationship with his wife.

Oedipus and Antigone

A second suicidogenic relationship between father and daughter is that of Oedipus and Antigone. Antigone is obsessed with the incestuous sin of her parents: "Alas for the wretched mother's slumber at the side of her own son, — and my sire! From what manner of parents did I take my miserable being!" (Sophocles, *Antigone*, 859-68). She sees this sin as a curse leading to her own death: "And to them I go thus, accursed, unwed, to share their home" (869). Antigone seems obsessed with dying to fulfill her relationship with Oedipus. She even sees death as a kind of marriage. Furthermore, her suicide by hanging mimics that of her mother, Jocasta. Perhaps this is Antigone's way of replacing Jocasta as his wife, or even his mother.

Even more curious is Antigone's obsession with burying her dead brother in defiance of Creon's order. Her defiance has been interpreted by many scholars as the height of individualism. Nevertheless, her more fundamental enmeshment with her family of origin is revealed in a bizarre speech in which she states that she would not have felt compelled to bury a husband or child as she would a brother: "The husband lost, another might have been found, and child from another to replace the first born:

but father and mother hidden with Hades, no brother's life could bloom for me again" (913-18). This enmeshment is bad enough if we take Antigone's concern to be directed toward her slain brother, Polyneices. But we should remember that her father, Oedipus, is also her brother! This desire to merge is clearly expressed in her desire to lie with her "brother" in death: "I shall rest, a loved one with him whom I have loved."[9] Like Iphigenia, Antigone is deeply enmeshed with her father; nonetheless, she shows great indifference toward her lover, Haemon, and severe independence from King Creon. One doubts that Iphigenia has this capacity for independence.

The Electra Complex and Suicide

The Electra complex, based on the myth of Electra that we have summarized above, is a term proposed by Carl Jung (1961, 347-48) for the Freudian concept of the "feminine Oedipus attitude" in young girls. It denotes the ambivalent desire of the daughter to abandon her mother and possess her father. It is neutralized through the daughter's giving up her father as a sexual object and coming to identify with her mother. Since the basis for this identification is not punitive, as in the male Oedipus complex, it may be accomplished through the introjection of an ego ideal rather than that of a superego.[10] In Freud's view, however, the daughter does not rest easy, because she has already been castrated and because of the remaining penis envy she feels toward her father.

According to Freud, the girl is originally attached to the mother.

9. The pattern of a daughter committing suicide to rejoin a dead father has been vividly illustrated in Sylvia Plath's poem "Daddy." Here she describes weeping at her father's grave immediately before swallowing fifty sleeping pills in her mother's cellar:

> At twenty I tried to die
> And get back, back, back to you.
> I thought even the bones would do. (Alvarez 1982, 20; Plath 1986, 134-37)

10. Ego ideals emerge out of the earlier anaclitic identifications of a child, primarily with the mother. In current psychoanalytic thinking, it has become the convention to reserve the term "superego" for the punitive basis for conscience achieved in the boy child through the resolution of the Oedipus complex and the term "ego ideal" for the seemingly more benign basis for conscience that is available to the girl child in the resolution of the Electra complex (cf. H. B. Lewis 1976).

However, she discovers that she lacks a penis, and she feels inferior to the male. She becomes angry toward her mother and holds her responsible for her condition. Therefore, she turns her libidinal attachment onto the father and imagines that she will become pregnant by him. She believes that the pregnancy would replace the missing penis that she envies, and that it would allow her to gain equal status with the father.

This argument is obviously less convincing than that underlying the Oedipus complex. We would suggest that a missing dynamic in this process is shame of menstruation elicited in the daughter by the mother as a means of neutralizing the mother's own fear of abandonment. There is no question that, in many cultures, menstrual shame has led women to feel impure and envious of males (cf. Stephens 1962). This would explain a daughter's willingness to abandon her mother and to look to her father. But penis envy may be a result rather than a cause of this process.[11]

The mother's defense in this regard is to lower her daughter's self-esteem by eliciting even further shame about the latter's menstruation and femininity, to make it risky for the daughter fully to abandon the mother lest she herself wind up totally alone, without either mother or father. Such action on the part of the mother results in the daughter's feeling worse about her than she did previously. Attachment between Greek mother and daughter is thus permeated by a negative symbiotic quality, leaving the daughter unable to cope in a healthy way with the stresses of life.

More generally, the place of the daughter in the Greek family is tenuous at best. She idealizes her father because she needs him. At the same time, he typically ignores or rejects her because he is preoccupied with his own needs. Her mother may neglect her, as Clytemnestra does Electra, or may find it difficult to see her as an independent being. The daughter is thus caught between rejection and smothering, and her shaky self-esteem is further diminished by her mother's attempt to bind her. She remains highly vulnerable to a variety of pathologies, including suicide.

Figure 8.2 diagrams the link between the Electra complex and suicide. The Greek wife-mother is enmeshed (A), envying her husband (WM)

11. In a cross-cultural study, William Stephens (1962) has found a relationship between indices of "castration anxiety" and the severity of menstrual taboos, and one may argue not only that severe menstrual taboos presuppose a high castration anxiety among males but also strong penis envy and resentment of males by females (cf. Slater 1968). The disorders of anorexia nervosa and amenorrhea may represent reactions to strong menstrual shame. Note the wasted states of Medea and of Echo, the ultimate idealizing narcissist.

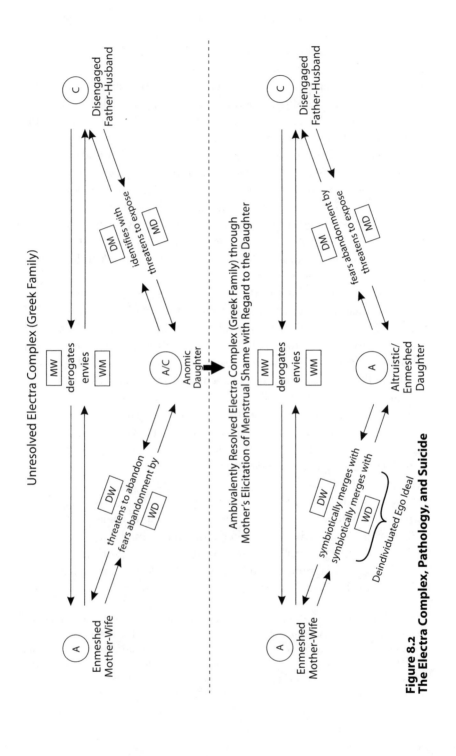

Figure 8.2
The Electra Complex, Pathology, and Suicide

yet terrified of abandonment by him. She also fears abandonment by her daughter (WD) and seeks to arouse menstrual shame in her. In contrast, the Greek husband-father is disengaged (C), deprecating his wife (MW) and yet terrified of absorption by her. He is willing to abandon, expose, or sacrifice his daughter (MD). This, of course, evokes the classic Electra complex for the daughter, who is eager to abandon her mother (DW = C) in her idealization of her father (DM = A). The daughter thus becomes a potential anomic (A/C) suicide (see Figure 8.2, top).

Classic psychoanalytic thinking gives an unsatisfactory account of how this conflict may be neutralized, arguing that the mother has no real deterrent since the daughter has already been castrated. We suggest an alternative explanation: the mother counters the daughter's threat of abandonment by activating her shame of menstruation.[12] This lowers the daughter's sense of self-esteem and merely blocks the daughter's desire to abandon her (both FD and DF = A) without resolving it. However, the wife-husband relationship remains unchanged: the wife still envies her husband (WM = A), and the husband still deprecates his wife (MW = C). As such, the father will try to abandon his daughter (MD = C), but the daughter still idealizes her father (DM = A). In other words, the neutralization of the Electra dilemma between father and daughter leaves her enmeshed (A) with both her father and her mother, vulnerable to threat of abandonment and at risk of altruistic (A) suicide.

The Greek daughter is also thus at risk for suicide, albeit of the altruistic type. Her relationship with her mother remains basically unresolved. The drive to escape her mother is still there, though it is inhibited by low self-esteem. As the ego ideal is internalized, a girl's sense of morality must have an enmeshed and undifferentiated aspect to it, as is apparent in many of Euripides' self-sacrificing female martyrs. Furthermore, this pathology, when left untreated, is likely to recur from generation to generation. The enmeshed (A) daughter will grow up to be an (A) enmeshing woman who is likely to find a disengaged (C) man to marry. Together, this couple will pass on the unresolved Electra conflict and suicidal vulnerability to yet another generation of daughters.

---

12. This may involve invoking a prepubescent girl's anticipation of menarche.

9. The Life-Promoting Structure of
the Biblical Family: Isaac and Ruth

Behold, I will send you Elijah the prophet before the coming of
the great and terrible day of the Lord. And he shall turn the
hearts of the fathers to the children, and the hearts of the children to their fathers; lest I come and smite the land with utter
destruction.

Malachi 3:23-24

A woman of valor who can find? For her price is far above rubies.
The heart of her husband doth safely trust in her. . . . She looketh
well to the ways of her household, and eateth not the bread of
idleness. Her children rise up and call her blessed; her husband
also, and he praiseth her.

Proverbs 31:10-11, 27-28

Therefore shall a man leave his father and mother and shall
cleave unto his wife, and they shall be one flesh.

Genesis 2:24

The biblical and Greek literatures present very different ideas and views of
married life. The Greek theogony portrays a primal and fatal antagonism
between husband and wife. Husband is sky, wife is earth, and their descendants are destructively pulled between a disengaged, freedom-seeking

sky-father and an intrusive, devouring earth-mother. The biblical world has no such view: "In the beginning, God created the heaven and the earth" (Gen. 1:1). The two elements of the universe are harmonious rather than in conflict: they are not divided in a male-female conflict. Adam himself is made of the ground and is given a soul: "Then the Lord God formed man of the dust of the ground, and breathed into his nostrils the breath of life; and man became a living soul" (Gen. 2:7).

The biblical relationship between husband and wife has an essential compatibility. Normal strains and conflicts occur, but there is no sense of a primal antagonism between man and woman that is so endemic to the Greek literature, nor are children suicidally torn between the two. The success of the biblical family structure in meeting challenges is only partly a result of the character of the people who constitute that family. The biblical family is based on the premise that every human — woman or man — is created in the divine image, is therefore worthy of respect and consideration, and likewise has certain well-defined but not rigid obligations toward others. The divine love for a person is unconditional, and it is the person's role to fulfill that trust.[1]

Biblical accounts of families often portray supportive relationships in what could be very trying circumstances. Abraham, Isaac, and Elkanah show the highest respect and affection toward wives who are barren. When Hannah becomes depressed over her infertility and does not eat, Elkanah responds tenderly that he loves her as much as if she had borne him ten sons (Malbim on 1 Sam. 1:8). Not all men in the Bible are that exemplary. The patriarch Jacob is not sufficiently supportive when Rachel complains to him about her barrenness (Gen. 30:1-2), and the Midrash criticizes him for this. The importance of harmony between husband and wife is a ubiquitous theme in the rabbinic understanding of the Bible. Sarah refers to her husband Abraham as "old," and God himself modifies the statement before repeating it to Abraham. Again, the Midrash says that the Hebrews mourned more at the death of Aaron than at Moses' death, because Aaron

---

1. These characteristics seem to have insulated the Jewish family to some degree, even in modern times. In a national survey conducted in America during a six-month period in 1965, the National Opinion Research Center (NORC) studied the family background of child abuse victims: 164 fatalities resulting from child abuse were reported. Although Jews represent approximately 3 percent of the American population, not one of the above fatalities involved a Jewish mother.

had done much to help improve relationships between couples with marital problems (Rashi on Deut. 34:8).

The Bible rejects the suicidal, incestuous sexual, and emotional patterns so destructive in the Greek world. Leviticus provides a list of the blood relatives whom a man may not marry or have sexual contact with: these include his father, his mother, his father's wife, his sister, his half-sister, his granddaughter, his daughter-in-law, or his aunt, whether natural or by marriage (Lev. 18:26). Nowadays this passage is read in the synagogue on the afternoon of Yom Kippur.[2]

The Greek child, according to the pattern discussed above, is put in the position of an unwanted burden, a threat to his parents, and is raised to feel expendable, indeed guilty for existing. No wonder suicide is such a high-risk outcome. By contrast, the Hebrew child is greatly anticipated and desired before his birth and prized afterwards, and this knowledge helps him withstand the normal stresses of life. The resilience given to the child by the parents helps him give the same to his own offspring. Instead of a drive to destroy one's family and oneself, as with the children of the house of Labdacus, there is every incentive to continue the family tradition. Although the deeds of the parents clearly affect the children, there is no sense of predetermination or fate.

This chapter will examine narratives illustrating the ways in which biblical families protect their offspring from self-destruction and encourage them toward development and creativity. Table 9.1 first examines the position of sons, and then of daughters.

Hebrew Fathers and Sons

Parental aggression toward children, which so dominates classical Greek thought and Freudian psychology, has no place in biblical or rabbinic

---

2. The Hebrew Bible allows polygyny, but definitely not incest. Nevertheless, several seemingly incestuous relationships are described, for example, Lot and his two daughters (Gen. 19) and Judah and Tamar (Gen. 38). Lot's daughters, for example, mistakenly believe their father to be the last man on earth. The widowed Tamar feels rejected by her father-in-law with regard to his promise to marry her to his youngest son. In neither case is the man aware of the incestuous nature of the sexual act. Lot is made drunk by his daughters, while Tamar disguises herself as a harlot. Significantly, the rabbis have not seen Tamar's act as incestuous under the religious law of that time.

Table 9.1
Biblical Parent-Child Narratives

	Fathers	*Mothers*
Sons	Abraham — Isaac - - - - - - - - - - Jacob — Sons	Rebecca — Sons - - - - - - - - - - Hannah — Samuel
Daughters	Amram — Miriam - - - - - - - - - - Jephthah — Daughter	Naomi — Ruth

thought. Indeed, biblical narratives take it as natural that a father will be happy if his child surpasses him. God expresses his pleasure when the rabbis base a legal decision on their own scholarship despite heavenly signals to reverse the decision (*Baba Metzia,* 58).

Abraham and Isaac

The covenant of circumcision signals an important victory over the terrible conflict between fathers and sons. In the Bible, God makes a covenant with Abraham and his descendants: God will bless Abraham and give him the land of Canaan as his own; in return, Abraham and his progeny will follow God's law (Gen. 17:9-11). The father is not the owner of his son as with the Roman *patria potestas,* nor does he hold the power of infant exposure. The Bible sees the relationship between father and son in terms of the fulfillment of the covenant. The child honors his father and mother as something that follows from his obedience to God, not from personal obligation to the parent. The urge of father and son to destroy each other is superseded by the obligation of both to fulfill and continue the covenant. One of the most significant themes in the rabbinic literature is the command to the father to teach his children thoroughly (Deut. 6:7; *Kiddushin,* 30a). The father's identity is not threatened by the son; he wants to see his son develop and surpass him.

The son does not learn that he is an unwanted burden, but that his well-being is beneficial both to God and to his father. He does not need to feel guilty for existing, nor does he entertain thoughts of self-destruction, even in his darkest hour. For example, Isaac gets up on the altar on Mount Moriah not to fulfill a wish for suicide but in obedience to God. Neither Abraham nor Isaac wants Isaac's death, but they wish to fulfill the will of God (*Genesis Rabbah*, 56:8).

Psychologically, it is particularly significant that the covenant is partly symbolized by physical circumcision *(berith hamilah)*.[3] The Bible seems to offer an unambivalent resolution for both the father's fear of displacement and the son's fear of castration and murder. The father willingly passes down the covenant, making it unnecessary for his son to displace him.[4] The son becomes aware that the father could have castrated him and destroyed his power of procreation and creativity but chose not to; instead, the father has offered a sanctified and noninjurious circumcision as the very symbol of his love and assent to the son's right to succession.[5] This pattern results in increased security, making attacks by the father on the son or by the son on the father unnecessary.

Abraham goes through a series of tests, culminating in the binding of Isaac, that demonstrate that his devotion to God is of a different order than that of the idolater who actually does sacrifice his children to his deity. The final test is God's command to Abraham to sacrifice his son Isaac on Mount Moriah (Gen. 22). Abraham binds Isaac on the altar, but God will not allow the sacrifice:

> But the Angel of the Lord called to him from heaven and said, "Abraham, Abraham!" So he said, "Here I am." And He said, "Do not lay your hand on the lad, nor do anything to him; for now I know that you fear God, since you have not withheld your son, your only son, from me." (22:11-12)

3. A sense of participation in the covenant is experienced even among those sons for whom the law forbids circumcision for medical reasons.

4. It is noteworthy, too, that although a double portion of the material inheritance generally goes to the firstborn son, there is no comparable notion of primogeniture in carrying on religious leadership. In this, all sons are equally responsible, and the leaders attain their status through ability and merit. Isaac, Jacob, and Joseph are not the firstborn to their fathers, nor are Levi and Judah, upon whom priesthood and kingship later devolve.

5. Covenantal circumcision must be distinguished from circumcision that is simply used as a rite of passage into manhood. Despite these social-benefit arguments, Judaism emphasizes that only God knows the deepest reasons for the laws of Torah.

God leads Abraham through an experience in which Abraham comes to realize something very significant. Unlike the Greek earth-mother, the God of Genesis will never demand ritual murder, heroic self-sacrifice, or human suicide. Full obedience to this God instead demands a rejection of these destructive tendencies. This understanding has to be lived through and understood so that Abraham, Isaac, and all their descendants are released from the terrible forces that bludgeon a thinking Greek like Antigone into self-destruction.[6]

Jacob and His Sons

The story of Jacob and his sons offers another situation of great potential destructiveness. Joseph's special talents and Jacob's recognition of them arouse fear and jealousy among his brothers, to the point that they contemplate killing Joseph, and they do actually sell him into slavery, while they convince Jacob that Joseph has been killed by a wild beast (Gen. 37). But Joseph thrives and develops morally in Egypt, even as a slave. In one particularly challenging moment, the love that he still feels from his father gives him the moral strength to reject the adulterous advances of Potiphar's wife. In this moment of trial, the image of his father comes to his mind (*Sotah*, 37). Years later, as viceroy of Egypt, Joseph orchestrates a reunion with his brothers in which they are able to demonstrate, both to their satisfaction and to his, their sincere regret over their treatment of Joseph and their acceptance of the obligation to support all their brothers and their father (Gen. 42–45).

Jacob, now a very old man, provides the successful denouement to the drama. He comes to Egypt, renews his relationship with Joseph, and makes certain that Joseph's sons, Ephraim and Manasseh, even though born in Egypt, are included within the family and are full recipients of its

---

6. Erich Wellisch has argued that the entire experience produces a fundamental modification of instinct in Abraham:

> A fundamental effect of Abraham's change of outlook was the realization that God demanded life and not death. Abraham realized that the meaning of the commanded sacrifice was not to kill his son but to dedicate his son's lifelong service to God. He completely rejected the former dominance of his death instinct and entirely abandoned his aggressive tendencies against Isaac. His life instinct was tremendously prompted and with it a new love emerged in him for Isaac, which became the crowning experience of his religion. (1954, 89)

teachings and traditions. Finally, Jacob blesses his sons in terms of each one's unique strengths and weaknesses, affirming each as an individual personality and recognizing his unique role and creativity in the covenant (Gen. 49): "All these are the twelve tribes of Israel, and this is what their father spoke to them. And he blessed them; he blessed each one according to his own blessing" (Gen. 49:28).

This individual recognition of both the strengths and weaknesses of each son provides a high degree of approving acceptance for the son to develop and carry on the covenant according to his special emotions and abilities. Such a paternal blessing is the very essence of a non-suicidal society and the strongest possible antidote to the destructive curse of Oedipus on his own sons, who fight and kill each other. The destructive pathology and determinism of the Greek family undermines the basically well-meaning Oedipus; in contrast, Jacob's blessing softens the rivalry between his sons, encouraging each to develop his own talents. We will discuss this contrast at length in chapter 10.

Hebrew Mothers and Sons

The role of the mother in both biblical and later Jewish families also is fundamentally different from that in the Greek family. She, too, is part of the covenant and plays a major role in its continuance. She has no need to defend or avenge herself by pitting her husband and sons against each other (Gen. 28:5; Hirsch 1876 on Gen. 27:42).

The Greek pattern of a mother seducing her son to displace her husband or murdering her son to deprive her husband of an heir is totally foreign to the Hebrew family. Biblical sons do not simply represent extensions of the mother, as do Medea's sons; they are human beings in their own right. Perhaps because the woman's status in the biblical family is highly respected, she feels less need to compete with her husband and sons. Rather than encourage and exploit the primitive impulse toward rivalry between fathers and sons (the Oedipal conflict), she helps to promote a sense of harmony between them. Rather than evoke fears of incorporation and suicide in the son through the threat of either seduction or murder, she helps guide the son to manhood as a potential heir of the covenant. Her role is different from that of her husband, but no less integral. An ideal of womanhood is the *eishet chayil* (the woman of valor in Prov. 31).

Rabbinic literature emphasizes the significance of woman's support for the Torah study of her husband and sons (*Berakhot,* 17a; *Ketubot,* 62b). Numerous stories are told, such as that of the mother of Rabbi Joshua (ca. 50-125 CE), who brought him, while he was still in the cradle, to the house of study of the Torah. The rabbis of the Talmud also showed a great respect to their mothers. When Rabbi Joseph heard the footsteps of his mother approaching his house, he would hasten to meet her, saying, "Let me rise to meet the Divine Presence" (*Kiddushin,* 31b).

Rebecca and Her Sons

Rebecca is a classic example of the Jewish mother. Abraham has sent his servant, Eliezer, to Haran to find a suitable wife for Isaac, and Eliezer plans to test the women of Haran by asking them for a drink of water from the well. Rebecca is the first to respond to his request, and she also volunteers to draw water for his ten camels, which are thirsty from their long journey. By this act of kindness and lively intelligence, she proves herself to be a fit wife for Isaac (Gen. 24:12-20; see also Abravanel 1964, on Gen. 24:12).

During her marriage to Isaac, and particularly in the incident of the passing down of the blessing, Rebecca proves her compassion, ability, and courage as a wife and mother. Isaac, now an elderly man and losing his eyesight, lives a retiring life. He is drawn toward the vigorous Esau, perhaps because the latter has a kind of earthy physical strength, a wildness, that Isaac himself lacks (Hirsch 1976, on Gen. 25:28). Apparently realizing that Jacob is the more fit of his two sons in spiritual matters, he decides to bestow his blessing of material wealth and power on Esau, who will likely need it more than Jacob. Rebecca learns of Isaac's intention and feels that he is mistaken. Jacob will be the follower of Abraham's covenant, and he will also need the support of material well-being. Rather than confront Isaac directly, she plans a deception that will obtain the material blessing for Jacob without bruising Isaac's feelings. When Jacob hesitates, Rebecca assures him that she is the mother and is assuming full responsibility for the plan (Gen. 27:13). The plan succeeds, and Jacob receives the blessing of material well-being: the "dew of the heavens and the fat of the land and much corn and wine" (27:28-29).

Rebecca bears no hatred toward Esau, even through the hard times that follow. She does not desire his destruction, but she sees more realistically than does Isaac the threat to the continuity of the covenant should Esau, not Jacob, receive the blessing. When Rebecca hears of Esau's fury and his threats to murder Jacob, she again acts to save Jacob's life and sets up the basis for the ultimate restoration of harmony to the family. She protects both her sons, each of whom she still loves (in Gen. 27:43 and 28:5 she is still the "mother of Jacob and Esau"), and she again avoids hurting Isaac. Without informing Isaac of Esau's threats and without filling his ears with "I told you so's," she suggests that it would be suitable for Jacob to go to Haran to find a wife, as Eliezer had done for Isaac himself. Rebecca does not try to hold on to Jacob; instead, she arranges for him to be sent away to save his own life. Isaac agrees, without even realizing the full danger in the situation, and he gives Jacob the spiritual blessing that he had planned for him all along (28:3): "And give thee the blessing of Abraham and to thy seed with thee" (28:4). Jacob now has both the spiritual blessing and the material assurance of carrying on the covenant. Family harmony has not been shattered, and when Jacob returns to Canaan years later, he and Esau are reconciled. Rebecca does her best to preserve the self-esteem of her two sons — each in his own way. Neither is driven to fratricide or to suicide.

Rebecca's role as a mediator in the Hebrew family ensures the successful passing down of the covenant and the restoration of family harmony. Throughout her sons' growing-up period, she avoids creating a father-son rivalry. She is not interested in destroying either her son or her husband.

Hannah and Samuel

The relationship of Hannah and her son exemplifies the importance of the interplay of a supportive mother — indeed, of a supportive family. Hannah is deeply saddened over her failure to bear children (1 Sam. 1:5-10), though Elkanah, her husband, is very supportive of her. Hannah goes to the tabernacle to pray, and when the priest, Eli, hears of her problems, he is also supportive (1:17). Hannah, who is basically a positive thinker, accepts Eli's reassurance (1:17). Within a year, Hannah gives birth to a son, and in her gratitude to God she names him Samuel, "because I have asked him of the Lord" (1:20).

When Samuel is old enough, Hannah brings him to serve at the tabernacle. She reminds Eli that God has answered her prayers for a child: she feels that God lent her the child, and now she is lending him back.

Hannah then recites a poem of praise and thanks to God in which she expresses her strong sense of closeness and hope in him "who guards the steps of His holy ones" (2:9). Although still young in years, Samuel is clearly a child of exceptional sensitivity and intelligence, and he takes a serious part in the divine service in the tabernacle. He is not merely a servant but more like a son to Eli, who loves him deeply; Samuel seems to be far brighter and of better character than his own two sons (2:12-20).

Hannah makes Samuel a special robe *(me'il)* and brings new ones to him as he grows. This is a garment typically worn by the leading priests and is a means by which Hannah can express her love and confidence in her son (2:19; see Radak). Hannah continues to love Samuel; however, she does not wish to control him, because she feels that what they both owe to God and to Samuel's own development far exceeds in importance the pleasure she would derive from keeping him at home. It is noteworthy that all through his life Samuel wears a *me'il* and even wears it in the other world (28:14; see Rashi and Radak). Hannah goes on to bear five other children.

In strong contrast is Hagar's treatment of Ishmael in the desert. After the bread and water given to them by Abraham are gone, she casts the child under a shrub and goes some distance off, saying, "Let me not look upon the death of the child" (Gen. 21:16). This pattern should remind the reader of Artemis's withdrawal from the dying Hippolytus (Euripides, *Hippolytus,* 1432-33) rather than the Hebrew mothers. Hirsch (1976) has argued that Hagar's behavior is not characteristic of a Jewish mother, who would not forsake her child and would help him in any way she can. Hagar, in discarding her child behind some bushes, is quite indifferent to where he may fall and is possibly even adding unnecessary pain to his thirst (356-57).

The Akedah Motif, Suicide Prevention, and Life Promotion

The biblical stories provide a model for transforming the pathological position of the child in the Greek family into the life-affirming orientation of the biblical family. The child feels that she is valued in her own independence and creativity. She is not presented with the intolerable choice of deep enmeshment versus estranged isolation. Instead, she can remain part of the tradition while becoming a worthy individual.

In *Isaac and Oedipus* (1954), Erich Wellisch has pointed to the Akedah narrative as the foundation story of this process. A good father-son relationship, which is unavailable in the story of Oedipus, establishes an effective encouragement to life, which prevents suicide in biblical families. Wellisch has postulated that the Akedah experience encourages "instinct modification" in the attitudes of fathers toward sons and vice versa. In psychoanalytic circles, his view has been severely criticized as mixing religion with psychology. Even someone as sympathetic to Wellisch as Theodore Reik has viewed Wellisch's claim for a modification of instincts in the Akedah experience as a psychological impossibility (Reik 1961, 225).[7]

However, Wellisch's claim for instinct modification is supported by a closer examination of Freud's analysis of the Oedipus complex.[8] The son threatens to displace his father, taking over his power as symbolized by his possession of the mother.[9] The father threatens castration in response. The ambivalent neutralization of the Oedipus complex available to Greek society may be seen as a cold war between these two forces: the threat of displacement balanced by a threat of castration. Covenantal circumcision provides for a modification of the entire familial situation. The father knows that the son will inherit the covenant and thus will not try to displace him (the father); the son knows that the father could have castrated him but did not. Instead, circumcision becomes the very symbol of the son's right of inheritance and to his own life (Kaplan 1990a).

The suicide-preventive aspects of the Akedah story are diagrammed in Figure 9.1 (bottom). The covenantal matrix within which the son develops, as expressed in circumcision, changes all of the familial relation-

---

7. Wellisch has suggested that the moral relationship of parents to their children can be considered in three main stages. The first and most primitive stage is characterized by intense aggression and possessiveness of the parents. The aggression is particularly severe in the father and directed mainly at his sons, in the first place at his firstborn son. In early societies, it could often culminate in infanticide. The second stage is caused by a reaction of guilt about aggressive and possessive tendencies, especially about committed infanticide. It results in a compromise solution between the opposing tendencies of the wish to possess the child completely, or even kill the child, and the desire not to do so (i.e., Freud's Oedipus complex). These mental sufferings can be overcome only when the third stage of moral development of the parent-child relationships is reached: it consists in the almost entire abandonment of possession and in a covenant of love and affection between parent and child.

8. Significantly, the possibility of the modification of instincts is accepted in rabbinic thought and particularly emphasized in the Musar teaching of Rabbi Israel Salanter and his school.

9. The mother, though seemingly the center in a sexual triangle, is again not valued in her own right. She represents the "keys to the kingdom" rather than an end in herself.

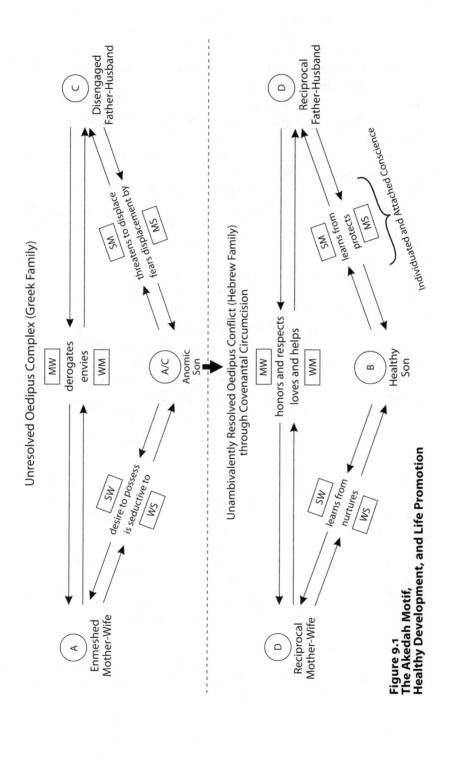

Figure 9.1
The Akedah Motif,
Healthy Development, and Life Promotion

ships. The Hebrew husband (position D) honors and respects his wife (MW); in turn, she loves him and helps him pass on the covenant (WM = D). Her role as a mother is to nurture her son to his covenantal responsibilities, not to dominate his individuality (WS = D); in turn, the son overcomes the Oedipal dilemma with his father. Not fearing displacement by the son, the father instructs him in the covenant (MS = D). The son does not need to desire to possess his mother or displace his father (thus resolving the Oedipal dilemma); instead, he accepts protection and nurturing from his parents and learns from them. It is this assurance of outside protection that allows the son to develop and be an apprentice in a balanced way (SM = B, SW = B), moving toward his own role as a husband and father, and ultimately his own place as an adult male in the tradition (position D).

In summary, the Akedah experience provides an unambivalent resolution to the potentially suicidal Oedipal conflict.[10] The son's existence is not conditional on his staying infantile or becoming disengaged. He receives full support to develop into healthy manhood (BED axis). The biblical family pattern blocks the transmission of narcissism and the Oedipal conflict from one generation to the next. The son does not grow into the male participant (position C) in a suicidogenic parental collusion in the next generation. Rather, he carries the potential of emerging as a developed male participant (BED axis) in a healthy, suicide-preventive (DD) parental relationship.

---

10. Christianity, of course, has its own primal relationship between father and son, that of God the Father and his son, Jesus Christ. The Akedah experience works to eliminate tendencies toward child sacrifice in the human being. God cannot and does not allow the sacrifice of a human being, nor does God allow the sacrifice of the child of the promise. The Golgotha narrative reintroduces the child-sacrifice theme that is so apparent in Oedipus and other Greek myths, but with a twist. It is connected to God's love for the world; indeed, this is the central Christian proclamation: "For God so loved the world, that he gave his only begotten son, that whoever believes in him should not perish, but have eternal life" (John 3:16). The question of why God does not intervene to save his own son, as he did to save Isaac, is the theme of *The Last Temptation of Christ* by Nikos Kazantzakis (1960). This connection between love and sacrifice fits the altruistic suicide theme so typical in the plays of Sophocles and Euripides. The proclamation in John reads like an altruistic suicide note: "I have died to save you." Christianity opposes suicide, yet its central figure can be seen as an altruistic martyr whose aim is to save the world rather than just Thebes. The question can be raised as to whether believing Christians may experience "survivor guilt."

Hebrew Mothers and Daughters

Although the Bible is filled with stories of women of great character and significant accomplishment, there is almost no information in the biblical text specific to mother-daughter relations. We can only assume that highly developed and revered women such as the matriarchs Miriam, Huldah, Abigail, Esther, and Ruth came out of a healthy familial and societal background. Nevertheless, the story of Ruth and her mother-in-law, Naomi, provides a biblical example of an intergenerational relationship between women.

Naomi and Ruth

Naomi and Ruth support each other in very sensitive areas. Naomi offers Ruth a sense of belonging, even after her son, Ruth's husband, has died; she also helps her find a fine husband and position in her new nation. Ruth refuses to abandon Naomi, even when they seem to have lost everything. This relationship is far removed from the enmeshment and abandonment conflicts of the classical Greek families. Ruth shows no desire to abandon Naomi in order to marry; indeed, her loyalty to Naomi is exemplary. In turn, Naomi does her best to enhance Ruth's self-esteem, and she instructs Ruth about how to approach her kinsman Boaz. After Boaz and Ruth do marry, Naomi is included in their happiness: she becomes the nurse to their son Obed, who becomes the father of Jesse, the father of David.

The story begins when Naomi, her husband, and their two sons leave Judah to reside in Moab. After the death of her husband, Naomi's two sons marry women of Moab, Orpah and Ruth. When Naomi's sons also die, she sets out to return to Judah, where, she has heard, food is no longer scarce. Naomi is accompanied by her two daughters-in-law at first; but at some point Naomi blesses her daughters-in-law and tells them to remain in Moab with their own people. Both daughters-in-law weep, insisting that they will return with their mother-in-law to Judah. But Naomi again urges them to go, saying that she is too old to have more sons for them to marry. Unlike Clytemnestra, Naomi does not try to bind her daughters-in-law to her; rather, she unselfishly urges them to go on their way to find new husbands. Because they are not simply objects to serve her, she recognizes their right to their own lives.

Orpah kisses her mother-in-law and departs, but Ruth will have none of it. In a moving speech, Ruth expresses her devotion to Naomi as a person, rather than as just a producer of sons for her. Unlike Electra, Ruth refuses to abandon Naomi:

> And Ruth said, "Entreat me not to leave you, or to turn back from following after you; for wherever you go, I will go; and wherever you lodge, I will lodge; your people shall be my people, and your God, my God. Where you die, will I die, and there will I be buried. The Lord do so to me, and more also, if anything but death parts you and me." (Ruth 1:16-17)[11]

This beautiful reciprocity continues throughout the story: Naomi continuously encourages and helps Ruth to fulfill her own needs, and Ruth is certain to include Naomi in any good fortune she may experience. Ruth meets Boaz, a relative of Naomi's late husband, and he is greatly moved by Ruth's treatment of Naomi: "It has been fully reported to me, all that you have done for your mother-in-law since the death of your husband" (2:11). And Naomi unselfishly continues to look out for Ruth's welfare. Rather than diminish Ruth's self-esteem (as Clytemnestra does to Electra), Naomi instructs Ruth on how to win Boaz. Ruth follows Naomi's advice, and when she ultimately does marry Boaz, she does not fail to include Naomi in her happiness. Naomi becomes the nurse to their son and is even described by the neighbors as the child's mother:

> "And may he be to you a restorer of life and a nourisher of your old age; for your daughter-in-law, who loves you, who is better to you than seven sons, has borne him." Then Naomi took the child and laid him on her bosom, and became a nurse to it. Also the neighbor women gave him a name, saying, "There is a son born to Naomi." And they called his name Obed. He is the father of Jesse, the father of David. (4:15-17)

The Moabite woman Ruth is a fit ancestress of the Davidic dynasty.

---

11. The Midrash amplifies the religious intent behind Naomi's words. When Naomi tells Ruth to remain behind because Jewish women do not frequent theaters and circuses, Ruth replies, "Whither thou goest, I will go." When informed that Jewish women dwell only in houses sanctified by mezuzot, Ruth responds, "Where thou lodgest, I will lodge." The phrase "thy people will be my people" reveals Ruth's intention to give up idolatry, and "thy God shall be my God" indicates her acceptance of the Torah (*Midrash Ruth Rabbah* and Rashi on Ruth 1:16).

Hebrew Fathers and Daughters

The attitude of the father in the Greek family — inducing his daughter to abandon her mother and then sacrificing her — is unthinkable within a Hebrew covenantal family, nor does the daughter idealize her father in the same desperate way. The father sees the daughter as a real person and does not use her against her mother. We consider here two father-daughter stories: first, Amram and Miriam, and second, Jephthah and his daughter.

Amram and Miriam

The Hebrew father sees his daughter as a full person in her own right, as one whose advice and opinions are worthy of respect and attention. This attitude finds full expression in the relationship of Amram and Miriam. Miriam is the daughter of Amram and Jochebed and the elder sister of Moses and Aaron. The Talmud (*Sotah*, 12b) fills out the rather cryptic account in Exodus 1–2 by telling how, when Pharaoh decrees that all Israelite infant boys be killed, Amram and Jochebed separate in despair over the doom that is to fall on any male child they would have. Miriam, still a very little girl, goes to her father and argues: "Pharaoh's decree affects only the sons; your act affects daughters as well."

Amram accepts his daughter's advice and her sense of faith, and he and Jochebed remarry (Miriam actually dances at their wedding). In due course, this reunion produces Moses. Exodus 2 tells the story of Moses' birth and the efforts of his family to hide him. When it is no longer safe to hide him in the house, his mother puts him in a little ark and places that in the reeds along the river's shore. Miriam is the daughter who is sent to watch over him. She does not hesitate to approach the Egyptian princess who finds the ark, suggesting that the boy be nursed by a Hebrew woman, but not letting on that the woman she has in mind is the baby's own natural mother. The critical issue here is that Amram trusts and respects his daughter. This trust should enhance Miriam's self-esteem and resilience and give her the confidence to grow in a healthy and an integrated way.

The incident (Num. 27) of the five daughters of Zelophehad supports this picture of father-daughter relationships. Zelophehad dies, leaving five daughters but no sons. The five daughters are as yet unmarried and therefore presumably rather young. They approach Moses with the claim that, since they have no brothers, they themselves should inherit the father's portion of the land, so that his name should not be removed from his family. The Talmud (*Baba Batra*, 119b) says that the daughters argue their case wisely and make their case well. Moses is impressed by them, and he brings their case straight to God himself. God agrees with the young women's argument and praises them (*Sifre* on Num. 27:7). Rashi records this comment: "Happy is a person to whose words the Holy One gives agreement." Although there is no description of Zelophahad, his daughters are clearly independent and capable. They are also realistic about their father, neither idealizing him nor showing hostility toward him (Num. 27:8).

Jephthah and His Daughter

Consider the single example of father-daughter sacrifice in the Hebrew Bible: Jephthah and his daughter. A child sacrifice story is naturally repugnant; however, a number of striking differences emerge between this sacrifice story and that of Agamemnon and Iphigenia. First, though both Agamemnon and Jephthah are offering a sacrifice in return for military success, Jephthah does not realize that he will be sacrificing his daughter. Rather, he offers to sacrifice "whatever comes out of my house to meet me when I return" (Judg. 11:30-31), apparently expecting it to be an animal. Second, on seeing his daughter emerge from his home, and realizing the full import of his earlier vow, Jephthah shows genuine remorse: "He tore his clothes and said, 'Alas my daughter! You have brought me very low! . . . I have given my word to the Lord, and I cannot go back on it'" (11:35).

Therefore, though Jephthah's vow is ill-considered and foolish, it is not premeditated and callous, as Agamemnon's vow is. Furthermore, he does not use deceit to carry out the vow the way that Agamemnon creates the ruse of a marriage. Finally, Jephthah's response to his daughter is not self-centered in the same sense that Agamemnon's is. This is especially dramatic in light of the greater insecurity in Jephthah's social and political position. Nevertheless, the rabbis have been quite harsh in their evaluation of Jephthah. The Talmud uses him as an example of one who is unfit to rule, and the rabbis also criticize Jephthah's obstinacy in not going to a priest or a sage to have his vow annulled (*Genesis Rabbah*, 60.3; *Midrash Tanhuma Buber Behukotai*, 112-14).[12]

The biblical narrative does not idealize the death of Jephthah's daughter, nor is there any sense of self-sacrificing altruism. In fact, it is not clear that she actually is sacrificed. Some say she is (*Midrash Tanhuma Buber Behukotai*, 112-114), but others maintain that she is not put to death but instead becomes a recluse (see *Tanach Mikraot Gedolot*, glossators on Judg. 11). There is no sense of self-sacrifice or altruistic suicide in the death of Jephthah's daughter. She is willing to go along with her father's vow, but only after she goes away for two months of mourning (Judg. 11:39-40).[13]

The Ruth Motif and Suicide Prevention

The typical biblical mother-daughter relationship is thus very unlike the Greek form. The emphasis shifts from competition between mother and daughter to a united effort toward fulfilling the covenant. The father also teaches children as a fulfillment of the covenant (Bakan 1979). And the child honors his father and mother as an aspect of obedience to God, not simply out of a personal obligation to the parent.

The daughter's role in the Hebrew family is quite different from the son's, but it is no less important. Menstruation does not cause the same shame and diminution in self-esteem as in the Greek society. Rather, it is transformed in Judaism into part of the woman's unique role. It is her task to observe carefully the laws that govern and sanctify the physical aspects of her role as a woman. In practice, the essential law of *nidah* is that a woman ceases sexual contact with her husband at the onset of her menstrual period. Seven days after the termination of her menstrual flow, she may immerse herself in the ritual water, after which full sexual contact between husband and wife may be resumed (Blumenkrantz 1969; Tendler

---

12. It is instructive to compare Jephthah's vow with Abraham's binding of Isaac: Jephthah's vow is a thoughtless, unilateral act; by contrast, Abraham is commanded directly by God to offer up Isaac. This is not a vow but a divine command.

13. We should point out that there is some disagreement about the ultimate fate of Iphigenia as well. While most accounts of the myth claim that Iphigenia was indeed sacrificed at Aulis by Agamemnon, one version maintains that she was miraculously snatched away to safety by Artemis at the last moment and subsequently became the priestess of a human sacrifice cult (see Graves 1955, 2.73-80; Euripides, *Iphigenia at Taurus*).

1982). A woman's sexuality is accepted as part of civilized society, and she need not be ashamed of it.[14] Therefore, a young girl does not need to attempt to abandon her mother and possess her father to achieve security. Likewise, a mother need not evoke her daughter's shame of menstruation. A girl is not an expendable object, but a person with her own unconditional right to exist.[15]

This covenantal structure also overcomes the daughter's fear that her father will abandon her. Leaving her father's house to become a wife and mother on her own is a joyous and sacred fulfillment of her duty as an *eishat chayil* (a woman of valor). The Midrash recounts that when Rabban Gamaliel's daughter was getting married, he blessed her thus: "May you never return to my house, and may the word 'woe' never depart from your mouth." He then explained to her: "May you be so happy with your husband that you have no need to return to your parents' home; and may you have children and be devoted to raising them well" (*Genesis Rabbah*, 26:4).

The relationship between the Ruth narrative and suicide prevention is presented in Figure 9.2. The covenantal matrix within which the daughter develops is symbolized by the ritual purification relative to menstruation (*nidah* and *mikva*). This matrix fundamentally changes all of the family relationships. The Hebrew husband honors and respects his wife (MW = D). She, in turn, helps him pass on the covenant (WM = D). Her role as a mother is to guide her daughter on the path to spiritual, emotional, and material fulfillment with God and her family. Essential to this is that both mother and daughter accept their femininity without shame (WD = D). The daughter gives up any attempt to abandon her mother and ally with her father (thus resolving the Electra dilemma); instead, she comes to accept nurturing, and she learns from her mother without being symbiotically connected to her. It is this assurance of nurturing that allows the

14. About Num. 23:9, the Midrash says that a man cannot number the *mitzvot* that he fulfills with the seed of sexual intercourse. Semen and menstrual blood are both sacred parts of God's creation.

15. The mother may be seen as the person who prepares the daughter to accept her role as a wife and mother in marriage. Rather than eliciting menstrual shame in her daughter, a mother may set the stage for the daughter's subsequent attention to the laws of purity. The daughter must purify herself with respect to sexual relations with her husband, but in a manner that enhances her self-esteem as a woman rather than diminishes it. It is important to note that the ritual of purification occurs among women and does not require male participation.

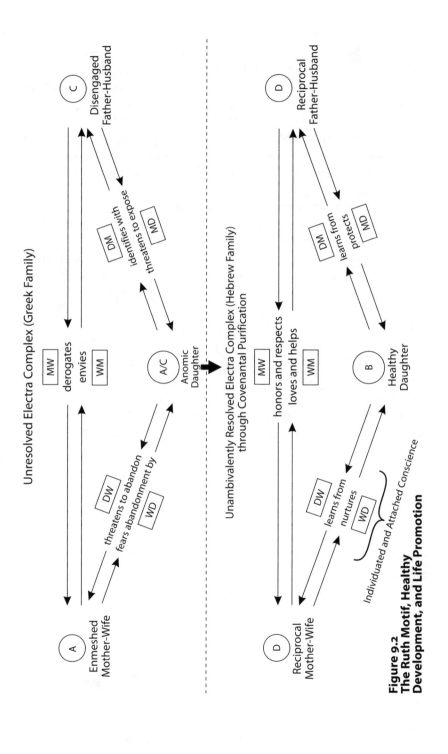

**Figure 9.2
The Ruth Motif, Healthy
Development, and Life Promotion**

daughter to be a daughter (DW = B). The daughter does not fall into the oral-narcissistic dilemma with the father, neither fearing abandonment by him nor desiring to fuse with him. She comes to trust him not to use her for his own interests, and she allows him to protect her.

The mother knows that her daughter is a partner in the tradition and that she need not try to abandon the mother; the daughter knows that the mother need not evoke shame in her. The father's transformation in the family is pivotal. He is transformed from child exposer to protector, resolving the daughter's Electra complex and strengthening her hold on life. Parents can relate in a truly nurturing (D) way to their daughters and to each other, and they provide the genuine protection and support the daughter needs for healthy development (along the BED axis).

The daughter's avoidance of the enmeshment-abandonment pathology endemic to the AC axis has profound implications for blocking the transmission of narcissism and suicidogenics from one generation to the next. The daughter avoids becoming the enmeshing partner in her own pathological (AC) marriage. Rather, her development (along the BED axis) facilitates life-affirming, healthy (DD) parental and marital relationships.

No family pattern is totally foolproof against suicide for either daughters or sons. As we shall see in chapter 13, however, all is not lost in the biblical scheme of things, for God himself provides a safety net for the family. God will provide the stopper to prevent the pattern of suicidal destruction.

10. Oedipus's Curse vs. Jacob's Blessing: Sibling Rivalry and Its Resolution

"A curse prophetic and bitter (of Oedipus on his sons) — *The glory of wealth and pride, with iron, not gold, in your hand ye shall come, at the last to divide*"

Aeschylus, *The Seven Against Thebes*, II. 785-786

"All these are the twelve tribes of Israel, and this is it that their father (Jacob) spoke unto them and blessed them; every one according to his blessing he blessed them."

Genesis 49:28

We can cite several basic differences between the biblical narrative and the literature of ancient Greece in how they present stories of sibling rivalry and family conflict. First, the stories of Genesis abound with sibling conflict, beginning with Cain slaying Abel, continuing with the rivalry of Isaac and Ishmael and the conflict between Jacob and Esau, and culminating with Joseph's brothers' anger and their selling of him into slavery. Many of these stories involve sons vying with each other for their father's blessing or favor.

The earliest myths of ancient Greece are very different: they portray conflict between father and son rather than between and among brothers; indeed, the brothers often band together and/or are joined by the mother (as in Freud's historical reconstruction in *Totem and Taboo*, Freud, 1913) to kill or castrate the menacing father. Several examples come to mind.

Hesiod's *Theogony* begins significantly not with God but with nature polarized into sky-father (Uranus) and earth-mother (Gaea). They marry and produce children, but Uranus is angry over the birth of the offspring, and he shoves them back into Gaea as they are born. Groaning in pain, Gaea incites their son Cronos to castrate Uranus and overthrow his rule. But Cronos then repeats his father's pattern: he imprisons his brothers, the Titans, in Tartarus. He then marries his sister, Rhea, and, fearful of the prophecy of Earth and Sky (his parents) that he will lose the rule to his own son, he devours his offspring as they are born.

The second basic difference between the literatures is even more striking. The Bible offers a plan to resolve family conflict by using the father's blessing. Originally the source of the sibling conflict, this blessing may work to achieve some level of reconciliation between the sons. As the father becomes more involved with his family, his blessing becomes more potent; the blessing, in turn, reduces the degree of sibling rivalry.

Greek literature offers no such balm. The father represents an obstacle rather than a blessing, and a rival rather than a teacher. While the father remains an active threat, the sons remain united against him for survival. As the power of the father diminishes, the sons become free to turn their enmity on each other. As his power completely recedes, the father leaves the sons with a curse regarding their relationship.

In this chapter we will focus on two critical events in the respective literatures that highlight these transformations: Jacob's blessing and the curse of Oedipus.

The Biblical Pattern

Let us examine these two patterns more closely. In the Genesis story of the biblical patriarchs, the succession of generations is accompanied by blessings of the father to the sons, and by some level of reconciliation, or at least cooperation between the sons. The practice of the fathers blessing their children is introduced in the Bible with the patriarchs. The blessing registers in a formal way the father's recognition of the son and his confidence and hope that the son will find fulfillment in his natural gifts. It is not a magical formula designed to bring on good fortune. Though the father administers the blessing in a formal way, it is clear that the mother also plays an important part in deciding what blessing will be given to each son.

The Scriptures do not mention fathers blessing sons before Abraham. However, the blessing became increasingly important with each generation of the patriarchs, until Jacob was able, with his blessing, both to affirm the unity of his twelve sons as the basis of the twelve tribes of Israel and to recognize and encourage the unique individual qualities of each.

We focus on four generations of biblical family: (a) Adam, (b) Abraham, (c) Isaac, and (d) Jacob. We will attempt to demonstrate an increase in the father's involvement across these four generations, a greater degree of blessing, and ultimately the resolution of sibling rivalry (see Table 10.1).

Adam and His Sons

God alone gave blessings to all mankind at creation: "Then God blessed them, and God said to them, 'Be fruitful and multiply; fill the earth and subdue it; have dominion over the fish of the sea, over the birds of the air, and over every living thing that moves on the earth'" (Gen. 1:28). God also gave blessings directly to Adam and Eve (1:28) and to Noah and his family (9:1). But there is no indication that God blessed Cain and Abel directly, or that Adam gave either son a blessing.

Consider the Genesis accounts. Cain, the elder, is a tiller of the ground, while Abel, the younger, is a keeper of sheep. Each brings an offering to the Lord, who has respect for Abel's offering, but not for Cain's. According to the traditional interpretation, God rejects Cain's offering because of the difference in spirit in which Cain offers it. In any case, Cain's countenance understandably falls. God is aware of this and tries to intervene. First, he acknowledges Cain's disappointment: "Why are you angry? And why has your countenance fallen?" (Gen. 4:6) Then he offers Cain the potential for acceptance if he changes: "If you do well, will you not be accepted?" Finally, God warns Cain of the dangers of a continuing bad spirit: "And if you do not do well, sin lies at the door. And its desire is for you, but you should rule over it" (4:7).

God's intervention fails, and Cain goes out and kills Abel. Notably absent in this account is any mention of direct communication between Adam (or Eve) and the two sons. Could Adam and Eve have been that unaware of the rivalry developing between Cain and Abel, and of Cain's jealousy toward Abel? Adam's direct blessing of his sons, showing each his place in the larger divine purpose, may have helped prevent the murder.

Table 10.1
Paternal Blessing and the Relationship between Brothers in Biblical Narratives

Father	Sons	God's Blessing of Sons	Father's Blessing of Sons	Outcome of Relationship between Brothers
Adam	Cain and Abel	No statement of God blessing Cain or Abel	Adam does not bless Cain or Abel	Cain murders Abel
Abraham	Isaac and Ishmael	God blesses Ishmael but reserves covenant for Isaac	Abraham circumcises Ishmael and gives him gifts, but reserves his blessing for Isaac	Ishmael reconciles with Isaac but without mutuality of purpose
Isaac	Jacob and Esau	God tells Rebecca that two nations will come from her womb but reserves blessing for Jacob	Isaac blesses both Jacob and Esau as separate nations	Esau reconciles with Jacob as separate nation with potentialities for mutuality or discord
Jacob	Joseph and his brothers	No statement of God blessing any of Jacob's sons	Jacob blesses each son according to his own potential, but with a common purpose	Joseph and his brothers finally reconcile and cooperate in the building of a nation

But that blessing was absent, and God's intervention alone, without the underlying blessing, did not seem sufficient to prevent the killing. In other words, Cain may not have felt sufficiently loved to withstand his sense of rejection.

Abraham and his Sons

God told Abraham that he himself would be a living blessing and that through him all the peoples of the world would be blessed. The ability to bless people was given over to Abraham and passed on to his descendants (cf. Gen. Rabbah 39:11; Tanhuma Buber Lekh Lekha 5; Numbers Rabbah 11:2; BT Sota 14). It seems clear that Abraham has developed a strong affection for Ishmael, his son by the Egyptian woman Hagar. Indeed, he entreats God on Ishmael's behalf when he is told that Sarah would bear him a child. "And Abraham said to God, 'Oh that Ishmael might live before You!'" (Gen. 17:18). Significantly, God responds to Abraham's entreaty by informing him that he has blessed Ishmael but will establish his covenant only with Isaac. "And as for Ishmael, I have heard you. Behold, I have blessed him, and will make him fruitful, and will multiply him exceedingly . . . and I will make him a great nation. But my covenant I will establish with Isaac, whom Sarah shall bear to you at this set time next year" (Gen. 17:20-21).

Abraham circumcised both Ishmael and Isaac. According to some interpretations (Rabbi Nehemiah), Abraham gave his blessing only to Isaac, though others (Rabbi Hama) interpret Abraham as giving only gifts to Isaac (Gen. Rabbah 61:6; Rashi on Gen. 25:9).[1] What is clear is that Abraham sends Ishmael out into the desert because he scoffed at a feast celebrating the weaning of Isaac. Subsequently, Abraham trains Isaac as his successor and the receiver of God's special covenant. He gives his other sons gifts and sends them away eastward. Meanwhile, Abraham has apparently become close to Ishmael after a period of estrangement, and Ishmael and Isaac join together to bury Abraham.

Nevertheless, there is no indication of any real meeting of minds between the two sons. Isaac and Ishmael do seem to be able to cooperate

---

1. The rabbis here disagreed as to whether Abraham blesses Isaac or defers for fear of having to bless the other children as well. In this second view, Abraham says that God, the source of blessing, would bless whom he chose.

when necessary, and one does not kill the other. However, they seem to pursue largely separate paths without any real common purpose, though Isaac's son Esau does later marry the daughter of Ishmael (Gen. 28:9).

Isaac and his Sons

Esau, the son of Isaac and Rebecca, has angrily threatened to kill Jacob, his twin brother. He accuses Jacob of stealing his birthright and his father's blessing. However, years later the brothers are reconciled and they coexist at least in peace if not in harmony of purpose. These peaceful outcomes of potentially explosive sibling clashes could result only because the parents, Isaac and Rebecca, did not saddle their sons with insurmountable emotional burdens; instead, they tried to be supportive of their sons. God first told Rebecca, when she was still pregnant with Jacob and Esau, that there were two great nations in her womb and that the older would serve the younger (Gen. 25:23-24). This is more a prediction than a blessing per se. God subsequently does bless Jacob but does not seem specifically to bless Esau.

Isaac, however, did bless both Jacob and Esau, repeating God's prediction that the older (Esau) shall serve the younger (Jacob). Significantly, however, he gave each son a blessing that seemed suitable for each one. First Isaac blessed Jacob, who had disguised himself as Esau, with the dew of the heaven and the leadership of other nations. Esau, distraught over Jacob's trickery, also received a blessing of the dew of the heaven; but he was destined to live by the sword and to serve his brother (Gen. 27:39-40).

Esau naturally hated Jacob because he believed that the latter had stolen his blessing from him, and so he threatened to kill him (Gen. 27:41). But their mother's intervention restored peace between the brothers, and ultimately Esau indicated satisfaction with his portion: "I have plenty, my brother" (33:4). The fact that Esau had also been blessed by his father gave him the resilience to gain great success. Significantly, both of the twins founded successful families and lines of kings.

Jacob and his Sons

In the succeeding generations each father blessed his own children, joining them closer to the covenant with God and helping each son define and affirm his own sense of identity. The father permitted and encouraged them to enjoy the good things of life, both spiritual and material. Jacob, however, had the joy of seeing his sons reconciled despite their many problems with both him and each other. Even the selling of Joseph into slavery ended happily when Joseph, as viceroy of Egypt, saved his family from famine in such a wise way that the old wounds were appreciably healed.

There is no mention of a direct blessing that God gave to Jacob's sons. But Jacob, in his last moments, conscientiously and lovingly blessed his sons, each according to his own personality and his own needs. Going a step further, he also blessed his grandsons Ephraim and Manasseh (Joseph's sons) and added that they would be the highest examples of blessing: "By you Israel will bless, saying, 'May God make you as Ephraim and as Manasseh'" (Gen. 48:20). It is important to note that Jacob uses the blessing to prepare each son for the unique problems and challenges of his own personal situation. This recognition of the importance of each son does much to deflate the potential dangers of sibling rivalries and of parent-child conflicts. For example, when Jacob blesses his sons, he criticizes Simeon and Levi for their violent ways. "Simeon and Levi are brothers; instruments of cruelty are in their dwelling place" (49:5). Brotherhood must have a positive purpose and consist of more than simply being violent together. Still, Jacob does not disown Simeon and Levi; instead, he scatters them in Israel rather than giving them their own territory.

An Overview of the Biblical Family

The biblical matriarchs were devoted both to their husbands and to the raising of their children as continuations of the covenant with God. They intervened forcefully and successfully in family affairs and were profoundly important in maintaining both the high quality of the covenantal relationship and the unity within the family. The Bible and the rabbinic writings regard women as equal and sometimes superior to their husbands in spirituality and in prophecy.

Through the various vicissitudes and disagreements of the lives of the founding families, the husbands and wives were able to support and enjoy each other while carrying out the duties that God had placed on them. The children in these families grew up in an atmosphere where fulfillment was not found in narcissistic acquisition of goods or by destroying their relatives. Instead, there was a steady development toward building a nation with a unique theocentric unity. This development was affirmed anew in each generation by the fathers' blessing of the children.

Of course, there were also some sad failures in biblical families. Abimelech, the son of Gideon and his concubine, murdered all but one of his seventy brothers in an attempt to become ruler. Perhaps his outsider status left him feeling unblessed by his father (Judg. 9:5). David's family saw its share of evil as well: his son Amnon raped his half-sister Tamar; Amnon was then murdered by Absalom, his half-brother. And Absalom himself later led a revolt against David. Another son of David, Adonijah, tried to seize the throne from Solomon, the designated successor. The text explains that David had not sufficiently disciplined him (1 Kings 1:6). But after the prophet Nathan and Solomon's mother, Bathsheba, successfully lobbied King David to have Solomon installed as king, the latter had Adonijah put to death. Yet, despite these troubles, David still managed to build a line of royal succession that ruled Judah for over four centuries — until the Babylonian conquests. Some of the Davidic kings were outstanding personalities, among them Solomon, Hezekiah, and Josiah.

The Greek Pattern

The Greek myths, in contrast, never develop the idea that a father should bless his children. The result is that conflict in the families grew more angry and nasty in each succeeding generation, until the families self-destructed, as the family of Oedipus did. Not only do successive generations of parents not bless their offspring, they actively reject them. Indeed, Oedipus cursed his sons to kill each other. And it was common enough both in myth and in historical reality for Greek parents to kill newborn children by exposing them.

Many children were born out of wedlock or by incest, so it is not surprising that these children later found it difficult to relate to other people. Narcissus, for example, was born of a rape. His father abandoned him, and his mother showed little affection for him. When the baby was born, his mother went to the seer Tireisias and asked him whether Narcissus would live a long life. A loving parent might express a joyous wish for a newborn child to be a dedicated physician, a great athlete, or a heroic soldier. But Narcissus's mother asked only how long he would live, as though she hoped it would not be a long time. Narcissus grew to be a very handsome young man, but he was a person who could not relate to other people and could not deal with himself at all. He died terribly, either by stabbing himself (Conon, *Narrations,* 24) or by simply pining away in his misery (Ovid, *Metamorphoses* 3, 497-502), according to different versions of the story.

We will now examine four Greek families: (1) Uranus and Cronos, (2) Cronos and Zeus, (3) Zeus and Heracles, and (4) Oedipus and his sons. We will seek to demonstrate a decrease in the threat of violence from the father over the generations, and in the case of Oedipus, the emergence of a paternal curse. The decline of the father allows the emergence of the previously latent sibling rivalry, which culminated in the mutual killing of Oedipus's two sons, Polyneices and Eteocles, at the gate of Thebes (see Table 10.2).

Uranus and His Sons

Hesiod's *Theogony* describes the marriage of Sky (Uranus) and Earth (Gaea). Uranus is portrayed as a menacing figure, hating his sons from the first. As soon as each is born, Uranus shoves him back into Gaea for fear of being usurped. He is described as "enjoying his wickedness." Groaning in pain, Gaea bands her sons together and urges them to take vengeance against their father; she gives Cronos a saw-toothed scimitar. Cronos cuts off his father's genitals while he is lying down, stretched out fully against Earth, longing for love. Uranus reproaches his sons and calls them Titans, for he says, "They strained in insolence and did a deed for which they would be punished afterwards" (Hesiod, *Theogony,* 11.155-210).

This is clearly the model used by Freud in *Totem and Taboo* (1913), where he describes primitive families. According to Freud's historical reconstruction, in primeval times people lived in small hordes, each under the domination of a strong male. All females were his property; if the sons born to these females excited the father's jealousy, he drove them out. Freud argued that this kind of social organization was altered by a banding together of the driven-out sons, who then collectively overcame and murdered their father and ate of his body in an attempt to identify with him through displacing him and incorporating a part of him in themselves.

The sons do have a common purpose, but it is based on fear of the father rather than in any anticipation of a blessing. Indeed, Uranus warned

Table 10.2
Paternal Threat/Curse and the Relationship between Brothers in Greek Narratives

Father	Sons	Father's Threat/Curse toward Sons	Outcome of Relationship between Brothers
Uranus	Cronos and the other Titans	Uranus tries to keep sons from being born. After being castrated by sons, Uranus predicts they will be punished.	Cronos and other Titans band together to castrate Uranus. After the threat of Uranus recedes, Cronos imprisons his brother Titans.
Cronos	Zeus and Olympian Gods	Cronos devours sons as they are born.	Zeus and the Olympians join together to hurl Cronos down to Tartarus.
Zeus/ Amphitiyon	Heracles and Iphicles	Zeus attempts to promise Heracles the rule of Perseus but is rendered ineffectual by his wife, Hera.	Rival Eurystheus forces Heracles to perform dangerous labors.
Oedipus	Polyneices and Eteocles	Blinded Oedipus is exiled from Thebes. He curses his two sons to die at each other's hands.	Polyneices and Eteocles kill each other in civil war.

his sons that they would be punished for their misdeeds. The banding together of the sons is defensive against a hated father who threatens to destroy them. They accomplish identification through incorporation, and the father's curse is lurking in the background, threatening to punish them. Indeed, after the threat of Uranus recedes, the previously repressed sibling rivalry has a chance to emerge: Cronos himself, according to some interpretations, imprisons his brothers, the Titans (Hesiod, 11.504-5).

Cronos and His Sons

This same pattern of a paternal threat to the sons emerges in the next generation that Hesiod describes in *Theogony* as well. Cronos begets many children by force, and he proceeds to swallow them because he has learned from Earth and Sky that his destiny is to be overcome by one of his sons. Rhea, Cronos's sister and wife, appeals to her parents, Gaea and Uranus, who send her to bear her youngest son, Zeus, in Crete. Rhea tricks Cronos into swallowing a huge stone in swaddling clothes by making him think it's Zeus. When Zeus grows up, he leads his siblings, the Olympian gods, to overthrow father Cronos and his allies, the Titans. They hurl Cronos and their uncles down to Tartarus (Hesiod, 11.629-725). Yet, Zeus and his siblings do not need to cooperate after that in any meaningful way.

Once again, we have a case where the sons (Zeus and the other Olympian gods) band together not out of any positive sense of purpose but as a defensive necessity against their threatening father, Cronos. When they have removed him as a threat, their unity dissolves.

Zeus and Heracles

Our third example of the relationship between paternal threat and sibling rivalry can be seen in Ovid's narrative of Heracles and Iphicles. Although the two boys are described as twins born of the same mother, they have different fathers. Heracles is the son of Zeus, while Iphicles, his twin, is the son of Alcmene's husband, Amphitryon. This has occurred as a result of Zeus's impersonation of Amphitryon during the latter's absence.

Despite this trickery, neither father seems to be a threat in the sense of that Uranus and Cronos were. However, they seem largely absent or powerless. Zeus boasts that he has fathered a son whom he provocatively names Heracles (which means "the glory of Hera"), who will rule the noble house of Perseus. However, Zeus is tricked by an enraged Hera, who delays Heracles' birth long enough so that Zeus's promise goes instead to a relative, Eurystheus, who is born just before Heracles (Hesiod, *Shield of Heracles*, 11.35, 56 and 80). Again, note the similarity here to the biblical theme of birth order that is discussed in the Jacob and Esau story — but with a very different purpose. Hera acts out of personal pique; Rebecca — and even Sarah — act out of a sense of suitability of inheritance.

Oedipus and his Sons

The final Greek family we examine is that of Oedipus himself — that is, his relationship to his sons rather than to his father. Two sons, Eteocles and Polyneices (as well as two daughters, Antigone and Ismene), were born of the incestuous union of Oedipus and Jocasta. After the suicide of Jocasta and the self-blinding of Oedipus, Polyneices and Eteocles, who were to share the power in Thebes, mistreat their now powerless father. They allow him to be exiled from Thebes, and he wanders about, cared for by his daughters. But before his death, Oedipus announces a curse on his sons: they shall die each at the hand of the other. According to the legend, Eteocles, now declared king of Thebes, exiles his brother. Polyneices, in turn, leads a vast army from Argos against Thebes in order to seize the throne for himself. In the ensuing battle, the brothers slay each other in individual combat, fulfilling their father's curse.

This episode is so striking that it has been covered from slightly different angles by a number of Greek plays. In Sophocles' *Oedipus at Colonus*, Oedipus disowns his two sons and curses them to kill each other. He says to Polyneices:

> And thou, begone, abhorred of me and unfathered! — begone, thou vilest of the vile, and with thee take my curse which I call down on thee never to vanquish the land of thy race . . . but by a kindred hand to die, and slay him by whom thou hast been driven out. I call the Destroying God who both set that dreadful hatred in your twain. Go with these words in thine ears — that Oedipus has divided such honours to his sons. (11.1386-94)

Oedipus's conduct is diametrically opposite to the blessing of Jacob discussed above, even Jacob's mixed blessing on Simeon and Levi! Jacob criticizes Simeon and Levi for their violent ways, but he does not disown them. Oedipus disowns Polyneices and Eteocles and curses them to be violent against each other.

Aeschylus, in *The Seven Against Thebes*, describes the curse as follows:

> And both alike, even now and here have closed their suit, with steel for arbiter. And lo, the fury-fiend of Oedipus, their sire, hath brought his curse to consummation dire. Each in the left side smitten, see them laid — the children of one womb, slain by a mutual doom! (11.879-924)

Again, note the striking difference between this curse and the prophecy given by God to the pregnant Rebecca regarding Jacob and Esau (Gen. 25:23-24). Polyneices and Eteocles are cursed to a mutuality of doom, within one womb; Jacob and Esau are described as two separate nations, albeit of the same womb. In both Sophocles and Aeschylus, Jocasta is described as already dead. Euripides' *The Phoenissae* presents a revised version: here Oedipus and Jocasta are still alive, and Jocasta engages in a futile attempt to bring about reconciliation between the two brothers. She describes Oedipus's curse as the product of his mental illness:

> He [Oedipus] is still living in the palace, but his misfortunes have so unhinged him that he imprecates the most unholy curse on his sons, praying that they may have to draw the sword before they share the house between them. (11.1-91)

Unlike Rebecca, Jocasta fails to bring about a peaceful reconciliation between her sons, indicating that, even when the Greek mother tries to resolve sibling rivalry, she is unsuccessful.

An Overview of the Greek Family

The narrative of Oedipus illustrates an important principle in the Greek family. As the father recedes as a threat, previously repressed sibling rivalry and hatred become free to emerge. This is because the earlier banding together of the sons was not done out of any filial love or mutuality of purpose, but out of a devil's pact against the murderous father.

Consider, for example, the portrayal of Castor and Pollux, half brothers who by all accounts seem to get along quite well with each other. Perhaps there is no paternal threat. Nevertheless, their friendship seems to be without purpose. They join in adventures that typically involve violence of some kind or other, exploits such as rape or theft, the kind of bonding through violence that is exactly what Jacob criticizes in Simeon and Levi. Castor and Pollux do nothing to build families where they can raise future generations. The children they beget are generally born of rapes and casual relationships (Apollodorus, 3.2.2).

Summary

In summary, then, we argue that the greater incidence of sibling rivalry in narratives in Genesis than in Greek mythology is misleading. It is a function of the underlying purposiveness of the biblical family: that is, the sons compete to inherit the covenant of the father. The father's blessing can resolve this rivalry. We see the culmination in Jacob's blessings on all his sons. By contrast, the Greek family is purposeless. The father is not a source of inheritance but an impediment. Sibling rivalry is initially masked by the threat of the father to the sons, who must band together to protect themselves. However, this bonding is shallow and will disappear as the paternal threat recedes. We see the culmination of this pattern in Oedipus's cursing his two sons to kill each other.

A purposive family therapy would benefit from taking seriously the biblical idea of parental blessing as a means of overcoming potentially disastrous sibling conflict. Each child may require a unique blessing suited for his particular talent, a blessing that will leave him feeling loved unconditionally. This is the biblical message to family dynamics.

IV. Contemporary Confusions about Life and Death

11. Kevorkian, Hippocrates, and Maimonides: Watching Over Patients' Life and Death

> The art consists in three things — the disease, the patient, and the physician. The physician is a servant of the "art" and the patient must combat the disease along with the physician.
>
> Hippocrates, Treatise on Epidemics,
> Section II of the Second Constitution

> I will give no deadly medicine to anyone if asked, nor suggest any such counsel. . . .
>
> The Hippocratic Oath

> Almighty God, Thou hast created the human body with infinite wisdom. . . . Thou sendest to man diseases as beneficent messengers to foretell approaching danger and to urge him to avert it. Almighty God, Thou has chosen me in Thy mercy to watch over the life and death of Thy creatures.
>
> Maimonides, "Prayer for Physicians"

The "right-to-die" debate that has been going on in the United States for several decades now was highlighted by the "physician-assisted suicides" undertaken by Dr. Jack Kevorkian (Kaplan 2000). In the 1990s, Dr. Kevorkian, a previously little-known pathologist in Michigan, conducted a campaign to assist ninety-three documented people to commit suicide.

These people were presumed to be severely physically ill — indeed, terminally ill — and Kevorkian was hailed in many quarters as a great defender of a patient's right to die with dignity. However, we conducted a psychological "autopsy" of these physician-assisted suicides in conjunction with the *Detroit Free Press* and Wayne State University, and we discovered a number of highly disturbing trends:

1. **Gender.** Sixty-three of the ninety-three physician-assisted deaths (68 percent) were women, and thirty (32 percent) were men. This trend is contrary to the usual four-to-one gender ratio among *completed* suicides in America: that is, four out of every five completed suicides are by men. However, Kevorkian's gender ratio is similar to that of *attempted* suicides: that is, 75 percent of suicide attempts are by women. These attempts often seem to be a cry for help rather than an irrevocable desire to exit life. It is significant that Kevorkian seemed totally unaware of these psychodynamic issues.

2. **Terminality.** Only twenty-seven of the ninety-three (29 percent) decedents were judged to be terminal (under six months to live), while sixty-six (72 percent) were not terminal. More male decedents (eleven of thirty, or 37 percent) were terminal than were female decedents (sixteen of sixty-three, or 25 percent).

3. **Anatomical basis for pain.** Only thirty-nine of the ninety-three decedents (42 percent) were judged by the medical examiners at autopsy to have an anatomical basis for pain, while fifty-four (58 percent) were not so judged.

4. **Anatomical sign of disease.** No apparent anatomical sign of disease emerged in six of the ninety-three (6.7 percent) autopsies for which information was available. Five of these were women.

5. **Disability.** Two-thirds of the decedents (sixty-two of ninety-three) were judged by the medical examiners to be disabled at the time of their death.

6. **Depression.** More than one-third (37 percent) of the decedents for whom depression data was available (the first forty-seven cases) were described as depressed. This percentage was higher for women (40 percent) than for men (30 percent).

7. **Fear of dependence.** Ninety percent of the first forty-seven cases were reported as having declared that they had a high fear of dependence on others in their disabled condition.

In this chapter we explore Dr. Jack Kevorkian's philosophical base and his effort to find support in Greek philosophy, culture, and medicine. We offer, in contrast to his worldview, a biblical view of helping a dying patient as it is expressed in the "Physician's Prayer," which is attributed to Moses Maimonides.

Hippocrates vs. Maimonides

Dr. Kevorkian specifically rejects the biblical views of life, death, and healing; instead, he remains trapped inside the views of the ancient Greeks, of which one expression is the Hippocratic Oath. Kevorkian declares his basic case as follows:

> As medical services, euthanasia and assisted suicide were always ethical, widely practiced by physicians and endorsed by almost all segments of society in Hippocratic Greece *[sic]*. The only opposition came from the tiny pagan religious sect called Pythagoreanism (which is said to have concocted the oath erroneously ascribed to Hippocrates). Despite their opposition, the Pythagoreans acknowledged that their contrary tenets could not be imposed on all of Greek society without seriously impairing its functional integrity. Later on there was none of that blunt honesty and respect for mores when the Western Judeo-Christian principles, which coincided almost exactly with those of extremely puritanical Pythagoreanism, dictated harshly punitive laws against euthanasia for all of society. Such laws cannot change but can only abuse and subvert ethics by paralyzing humans through brutal intimidation and fear. Eventually, in spite of all the fearful acquiescence and repressive atrocities born of such transgression, the mores will prevail and ethics will be disabused. (Kevorkian 1992, 9)

In this passage Dr. Kevorkian offers several arguments: (1) Euthanasia and assisted suicide were widely practiced in ancient Greece. (Classical sources clearly support this view.) (2) The Hippocratic Oath, which opposed doctor-assisted suicide, has been construed to be the generally accepted Greek position, when, in fact, it reflected the view of the small Pythagorean school. (Ludwig Edelstein [1943] has argued this point convincingly.) (3) Kevorkian equates Judaeo-Christian principles with abuse, paralysis, and brutal intimidation, on the one hand, and with what he calls Pythagorean Puritanism, on the other. (Here Kevorkian is seriously in error.)

Argument 1: Euthanasia and Suicide Were
Widely Practiced in Ancient Greece

With respect to the first point, there is no question that suicide was widespread in ancient Greece, and that assistance was often offered. The Greeks and Romans saw suicide as freedom (Seneca, *De Ira*, 3.15.34), because they saw life as hopeless, fatalistic, and unfree, and many killed themselves on philosophical grounds. Indeed, the early Greeks and Romans followed a number of practices that modern society would find abhorrent: (1) child exposure, which was so widespread that it caused a population decline by the third century BCE; (2) the killing or beating of people as part of religious ceremonies; (3) the forced enslavement or massacre of prisoners of war, including women and children; (4) the restrictions on women, who were forced to live rather sequestered lives, with very limited opportunities for self-expression and personal advancement. The Greeks contributed much to civilized humankind with their accomplishments in art, theater, government, science, and philosophy; but many of their social and religious practices would hardly be acceptable to us today.

Argument 2: Hippocrates Reflected a
Minority Position in Ancient Greece

Answering Kevorkian's second argument requires some study of the Hippocratic Oath. Here is, in part, what it says:

> I will follow that system of regimen which, according to my ability and judgment, I consider for the benefit of my patients, and abstain from whatever is deleterious or mischievous. I will give no deadly medicine to anyone if asked, nor suggest any such counsel; and in like manner I will not give to a woman a pessary to produce abortion. With purity and with holiness I will pass my life and practice my Art. I will not cut persons laboring under the stone, but will leave this to be done by men

who are practitioners of this work. Into whatever house I enter, I will go into them for the benefit of the sick, and will abstain from any voluntary act of mischief and corruption; and, further from the seduction of females and males, of freemen and slaves. Whatever, in connection with my professional practice or not, in connection with it, I see or hear, in the life of men, which ought not to be spoken of abroad, I will not divulge, as reckoning that all such should be kept secret. While I continue to keep this oath unviolated, may it be granted to me to enjoy life and the practice of the art, respected by all men, in all times! But should I trespass and violate this Oath, may the reverse be my lot!

For Kevorkian (1991, chap. 13), the real source of the doctor's enmity toward death as the arch-enemy of medicine lies less in the Hippocratic Oath per se than in Section II of the Second Constitution of Hippocrates' treatise on epidemics, in which he exhorts physicians "to do good or to do no harm." This document contains the following passage:

> The physician must be able to tell the antecedents, know the present, and foretell the future — must mediate these things, and have two special objects in view with regard to diseases, namely, to do good or to do no harm. The art consists in three things — the disease, the patient, and the physician. The physician is the servant of the "art," and the patient must combat the disease along with the physician.

Kevorkian tries to distinguish Hippocrates' call for "the doctor and the patient to work together to combat the disease" from the position that "the doctor must heroically lead the patient off to do battle with death." Kevorkian attempts to buttress his argument through separating the word "disease" into its component parts, "dis" and "ease." The main — indeed, the only — enemy for Hippocrates, he says, is disease, that is, the disturber of a person's "ease." "In having taken the oath of combating death," Kevorkian argues, "the medical profession wantonly infringes upon both aspects of its special and genuinely Hippocratic obligation. In quixotically trying to conquer death, doctors all too frequently do no good for their patients' ease; but at the same time they do harm instead by prolonging and even magnifying patients' dis-ease."

Kevorkian's attempt at linguistic analysis is erroneous and misleading. "Disease" is from the Middle English word *disese* (meaning "misery," by way of Old French) and not derived from the Greek word used by Hippocrates. Breaking the Middle English word into component parts obviously has no implications for Hippocrates' use of the word. The passage from Hippocrates' Treatise on Epidemics reveals his position on several important points: (1) the physician is the servant of the "art" or "nature"; (2) the "art" consists of three parts — the disease, the patient, and the physician; (3) the disease is the enemy, something to be combated by the patient along with the physician; (4) the physician is exhorted to do good or to do no harm; and (5) the physician swears to "give no deadly medicine to any one if asked, nor suggest any such counsel" (this from the Hippocratic Oath per se).

What is notably absent in these statements by Hippocrates is anything about the doctor's responsibility to care for a dying patient. The doctor must not administer deadly medicine, but what should she do to ward off death, or at least to ease the patient's discomfort? Or should she simply leave the patient to his fate, abandon him as the goddess Artemis abandoned her worshiper, the hero Hippolytus when he was mortally wounded (Euripides, *Hippolytus*)?

Dr. Kevorkian is correct in saying that the Hippocratic Oath is opposed to much that occurred in Greek practice. However, it is very significant that he fails to see that both the Oath and he himself are operating within the structure of a Greek worldview that was obsessed with fatalism, suicide, and child exposure, a worldview that equated death with freedom.

Argument 3: Pythagorean and Biblical
Prohibitions against Suicide Are Equivalent

In his third argument, Kevorkian goes on to incorrectly equate the mathematical Pythagorean position underlying the Hippocratic Oath with Christian anti-suicide dogma and "Western Judeo-Christian principles." In fact, however, suicide was wrong for the Pythagoreans because it upset an abstract mathematical discipline set by the gods. There is a set number of souls, according to the Pythagoreans, that is available in the world at any given time. Killing oneself creates a gap by upsetting this mathematical equilibrium, and thus must be rejected (see p. 18 above).

Furthermore, human beings reject suicide because they fear punishment:

. . . that the souls of all men were found in the body, and in the life which is on Earth, for the sake of punishment. . . . On which account all men, being afraid of those threatenings of the Gods, fear to depart from life by their own act, but only gladly welcome death when it comes in old age. (Athenaeus, *The Deipnosophists,* 2.216)

The punitive, cold, and abstract emphasis of the Pythagorean position was not sufficient to prevent Pythagoras from letting himself be killed (Diogenes Laertius, 8.45), and it cannot be equated with the passionate biblical prohibition against suicide. The Bible describes the Creator being lovingly involved with the world. He created the world solely as an act of kindness and, in the highest expression of love and benevolence toward humans, created them in the divine image. To destroy or damage any human being defaces the divine image, insults and diminishes the whole of God's creation, and reduces the divine plan of love in which the world was brought into being (Soloveitchik 1973). This is not a cold prohibition based on an abstract mathematical principle; rather, it is a passionate commitment to the divine quality within each human being.

The Hebrew position is expressed in the "Physician's Prayer," attributed to Moses Maimonides, the great Jewish thinker and physician of the twelfth century CE:

Almighty God, Thou hast created the human body with infinite wisdom. Ten thousand times ten thousand organs hast Thou combined in it that act unceasingly and harmoniously to preserve the whole in all its beauty — the body which is the envelope of the immortal soul. They are ever acting in perfect order, agreement, and accord. Yet, when the frailty of matter or the unbridling of passions deranges this order or interrupts this accord, then forces clash and the body crumbles into the primal dust from which it came. Thou sendest to man diseases as beneficent messengers to foretell approaching danger and to urge him to avert it.

Thou hast blest Thine earth, Thy rivers and Thy mountains with healing substances; they enable Thy creatures to alleviate their sufferings and to heal their illnesses. Thou hast endowed man with the wisdom to relieve the suffering of his brother, to recognize his disorders, to extract the healing substances, to discover their powers and to prepare and to apply them to suit every ill. In Thine Eternal Providence

Thou hast chosen me to watch over the life and health of Thy creatures. I am now about to apply myself to the duties of my profession.
Support me, Almighty God, in these great labors, that they may benefit
mankind, for without Thy help not even the least thing will succeed.

Inspire me with love for my art and for Thy creatures. Do not allow
thirst for profit, ambition for renown and admiration, to interfere with
my profession, for these are the enemies of truth and love for mankind
and they can lead astray in the great task of attending to the welfare of
Thy creatures. Preserve the strength of my body and of my soul that
they may ever be ready to cheerfully help and support rich and poor,
good and bad, enemy as well as friend. In the sufferer let me see only the
human being. Illumine my mind that it recognize what presents itself
and that it may comprehend what is absent or hidden. Let it not fail to
see what is visible, but do not permit it to arrogate to itself the power to
see what cannot be seen, for delicate and indefinite are the bounds of
the great art of caring for the lives and health of Thy creatures. Let me
never be absent-minded. May no strange thoughts divert my attention
at the bedside of the sick, or disturb my mind in its silent labors, for
great and sacred are the thoughtful deliberations required to preserve
the lives and health of Thy creatures. . . . (Golden, 1900, 414-15)

This approach is fundamentally different from that of Hippocrates
in the following ways: (1) the physician has been chosen by God to watch
over the life and health of God's creatures; (2) the doctor prays for inspiration from God, for love for his art and for God's creatures, the three parties
being God, the physician, and God's creatures; (3) the disease is a beneficent messenger sent by God to warn the patient of danger to the body, and
to urge him to avert it; (4) the physician has been chosen by God, in his
mercy, to watch over the life and health of his creatures; and (5) the physician specifically prays (later in this prayer) that God remove from his patients "all charlatans and the whole host of officious relatives and know-all
nurses, cruel people who arrogantly frustrate the wisest purposes of our
art and often lead Thy creatures to their death."

Thus, Maimonides is a contrast to Hippocrates on at least five questions: (1) Whom does the physician serve? (2) Who are the relevant parties? (3) How does the physician view disease? (4) What is the role of the
physician regarding good and harm, life and death? (5) What is the role of
the physician with respect to inducing death? For Hippocrates, the physi-

cian serves nature, and, along with the patient, combats disease. In contrast, Maimonides sees the physician as serving God, and he sees the disease as God's beneficent messenger to foretell approaching danger and help the person avert it.

Hippocrates, perhaps reacting to the suicidal nature of Greek culture, specifically forbids the doctor to give the patient any lethal medicine or make any suggestions to that effect. But this is a cold injunction, not accompanied by a positive instruction to tend to a patient in his last hours. Maimonides gives no specific instruction to the physician not to give lethal medicine. Indeed, he does not need to, because the biblical civilization does not equate freedom with suicide, as the Greco-Roman Stoics do, but with fulfilling God's commandments in life (*Avot,* 6.2). Maimonides' physician does pray that his patient be shielded from those charlatans, know-it-alls, officious relatives, and cruel people who would lead him to his death. In addition, however, the physician is specifically instructed to watch over the life and death of God's creatures to give them all the help and comfort possible in their last hours.

Where Does Kevorkian Go Astray?

Let us grant that Dr. Kevorkian correctly senses the lack of human compassion in the Hippocratic view and that he sincerely wishes to alleviate the pain of his patients in the most thorough and foolproof manner. On the surface, Kevorkian does not turn his back on the dying patient, as do Artemis and Hippocrates. But he seeks to answer a Greek problem with the classic Greek solution — suicide — which ironically also implies turning away from one's patient, washing one's hands of the patient in distress.

In his practice, Kevorkian follows the way of Sophocles' Antigone. The latter's obsession with burying her dead brother leads to her being buried alive herself. "Not burying the dead" symbolizes the indifference of a medicine that unfeelingly turns away from the suffering patient in need. "Burying the living" represents the approach Kevorkian, who, perhaps because he fears that the patient will reach a point where she can no longer deal with her own pain, kills her prematurely. Dr. Kevorkian is thus a tragic figure in that he is trapped in his own misguided inability to escape the polarized and fatalistic vision of the Greeks.

It does not occur to Kevorkian to use the higher compassion inherent in the biblical approach to medicine as it is reflected in the prayer of Maimonides. Indeed, Kevorkian sees "medicine as a purely secular profession, like engineering and many others." Elsewhere he says, "Any religion ought to be irrelevant to the strictly secular doctor-patient relationship." Medicine is part of the empirical world, while religion belongs to the "uninvestigatable" world, and the two cannot mix.

Dr. Kevorkian strongly opposes religion, and he assumes that it has no place in the doctor-patient relationship. However, a physician's medical skill alone does not in any sense qualify him to make moral decisions about a patient's life and death any more than it qualifies him to serve as a federal judge or a referee at a hockey game. It takes many years of devoted study to learn enough about one's religion to serve as a religious teacher, minister, or rabbi. Obviously, scholars of religion are not qualified to perform surgeries, but they are generally far better prepared than are physicians to make moral and ethical judgments even on medical issues. Remarkably, Dr. Kevorkian makes no effort to tell us about what a patient faces after a suicide. Can we presume that suicide means the utter annihilation and termination of the individual? Or shall we follow the doctrines of Kevorkian's much-admired Greeks, who believed strongly in the continuing existence of the soul. Plato and many others even wrote at length about the transmigration of the soul. Homer depicted the dead warriors of the Trojan War amid the terrible miseries of Hades. What can Dr. Kevorkian promise his patients about their own postmortem continuance?

This blind spot in Kevorkian is extremely unfortunate, for it is the biblical world that contains the hope necessary to counter the Greek sense of despair. Physical, spiritual, and social support of the suffering patient is in harmony with the highest biblical ideal of freedom, emphasizing the preciousness of every moment of life. Who knows how much good can result from a small act or word of kindness by an apparently insignificant person in a seemingly lost moment — even if that person is in great pain. In Maimonides' view, the doctor's caring for his patient is a religious commandment. The patient is offered freedom within that relationship. Kevorkian is too immersed in the tragic Greek vision to see this: in that vision, freedom can only come via suicide. Indeed, suicide becomes the highest expression of freedom, and death becomes a right rather than an inevitable fact. Suicide becomes a worthy goal and objective in and of itself.

It is instructive to compare the death of Jack Leatherman, one of Dr. Kevorkian's later suicides, with that of Joseph Cardinal Bernardin. The two men were of a similar age — Leatherman, 72, and Bernardin, 68 — and had similar diagnoses: terminal pancreatic cancer. And both refused prolonged treatment. But that is where the similarity in their lives' final days ends. A videotape shot by Dr. Kevorkian shortly before Leatherman's physician-assisted suicide reveals his self-expressed insistence that he "control [his] own destiny." With Kevorkian's help, Leatherman commits suicide while he is still functioning fairly well, because he insists that he is less terrified of death than of the end of life. By contrast, Cardinal Bernardin finds peace "by putting himself in God's hands." Giving up this pseudo-control over life and death allows Bernardin to live as fully as his strength permits to the very end, completing many final tasks he had set for himself. These two postures vividly reflect, respectively, the Greek and biblical views of freedom.

We emphasize the terminal situation of a patient because we are afraid to face the fact that, as mortals, we are all terminal. We obsess about control because we sense that we really have very little control over the most important things in our lives. Is not Kevorkian as phobic about death as the medical establishment that he opposes? Shall the physician's role be to bring death or to apply as best she can the many methods, physical and psychological, of relieving pain? As Maimonides acknowledges, the physician can help bring a person into the world; and she need not abandon the patient when he leaves the world, but can help him with a similar application of technical skill and compassion.

To assist a suffering patient in killing himself is, in a sense, to help collude with the world's abandonment of him. In Maimonides' view, God does not abandon the patient even in great suffering or at the moment of death. The physician acts as representative of God, who cares deeply about human life and who does not rejoice in the death even of the wicked. Maybe that wicked patient will repent and "seize his world" even in his last moment (Babylonian Talmud, *Avodah Zarah*, 11a).

The fact that Hippocrates was wrong does not make Kevorkian right. In the last analysis, they represent two sides of the same coin. The Hippocratic posture is too disengaged from the dying patient, while Kevorkian becomes overly enmeshed in the dying process. Maimonides stands as a bright and hopeful alternative to the two: he provides a model for the physician, who watches over the life and death of his patient as God's creature.

12. Zeno vs. Job: The Biblical Case against "Rational Suicide"

But if he gives the signal to retreat as he did to Socrates, I must obey him who gives the signal, as I would a general.

(Epictetus, *Discourses*, 1.29)

Though He slay me, yet will I trust Him.

(Job 13:15)

The previous chapter has contrasted the Hippocratic Oath and the "Prayer to Physicians" (attributed to Maimonides) concerning the physician's responsibility to both the life and death of a patient. We investigated this contrast to examine the thinking and practice of Jack Kevorkian regarding his campaign of ninety-three recorded physician-assisted suicides in the 1990s (from Janet Adkins on June 4, 1990, through Thomas Youk on September 17, 1998). In this chapter we will attempt to deepen this analysis by comparing the stories of two famous figures of antiquity: the Stoic Zeno and the biblical character Job. Second, we will draw out the implications of this contrast for the question of "rational suicide." Third, we will discuss the clash of the "right-to-die" and "right-to-life" movements in the events surrounding the death of Terri Schiavo in April 2005, a drama that polarized America and galvanized opposing political and religious agendas. We will conclude by returning to our contrast between Zeno and Job — and thus, of course, to Athens and Jerusalem.

Zeno vs. Job

According to the ancient Greek chronicler Diogenes Laertius, Zeno, who was the founder of the Stoic school of philosophy, wrenched his toe on the way home from lecturing at the Stoa (porch) and afterwards voluntarily held his breath until he died (Diogenes Laertius, 7.28). Leaving aside the question of whether it is possible to commit suicide by this means, this event certainly seems curious from a commonsense perspective. Why should Zeno kill himself after such a seemingly minor annoyance as breaking his toe? The leap from wrenching one's toe to killing oneself seems monumental.

To understand Zeno's actions, we believe that it is necessary to examine more closely the Stoic school of thought regarding suicide. The Stoics believed that suicide should not be undertaken frivolously, "but if he [God] gives the signal to retreat as he did to Socrates, I must obey him who gives the signal, as I would a general" (Epictetus, *Discourses*, 1.29). Droge and Tabor (1992, 29-39) find a precedent for "rational suicide" in this quote, and it has consequently provided a justification for physician-assisted suicide (PAS). Voluntary suicide is condoned when it is necessary (Greek: *anangke*) and rational, but condemned when it is irrational. A rational suicide is apparently preceded by a divine signal that the time to die is at hand. In other words, Zeno killed himself not because he broke his toe, nor because he was in pain, nor even because he was depressed, but because he, as a Stoic, had bought into the notion that the event of stubbing his toe represented the divine signal to depart (Droge and Tabor 1992, 31).

The biblical figure of Job is a profound contrast: he does not commit suicide even though he has been assailed by far more serious misfortunes. First, Job loses all of his great wealth; next, all his children meet their deaths. Still, Job reaffirms his faith in God: "Naked I came from my mother's womb, and naked shall I return there. The Lord gave, and the Lord has taken away; blessed be the name of the Lord" (Job 1:21). Finally, Job is inflicted with severe skin inflammations all over his body, and he takes a potsherd to scrape at his boils as he sits in the ashes. By this time his wife urges him to "curse God and die" (2:9). But Job rejects his wife's view: "Shall we indeed accept good from God, and shall we not accept adversity?" (2:10). Though he is deeply grieved, he reaffirms his relationship with his Creator. "Though He slay me, yet will I trust Him" (13:15).

However, the question remains: Why does Zeno interpret the wrenching of his toe as a divine signal to depart life, while Job does not react similarly in the face of far greater pains and misfortunes? It may well be that the tendency to find cosmic significance in a minor misfortune (we will call this tendency "zenoism"), as destructive as it proves to be for Zeno, may represent a coping strategy that provides him with a meaningful structure that is otherwise missing in his life. In a certain way, it provides a sense of the heroic: Zeno has been considered important enough to be called by the gods to depart. Although it is pale substitute for a life-affirming religious faith, zenoism may still represent an antidote to states of hopelessness and helplessness, but without any redeeming sense of meaning.

To be sure, zenoism is something of a delusional coping mechanism, imparting meaning to an event where it does not really exist. Furthermore, in Zeno's case it centers that meaning on death and suicide rather than on life. At the same time, however, "zenoizing" may actually give Zeno a sense of the heroic, and it may make him feel important, as well as less depressed and hopeless. Zeno is aging and feels alone, and he inserts meaning into his life by giving cosmic significance to his relatively minor misfortune. In effect, his interpretation of this rather innocuous mishap as a divine signal to depart life provides him with permission to commit suicide (Plato, *Phaedo*, 62b-c; Cicero, *De Finibus*, 3.60-61). In this sense, his suicide is *rationalized* rather than *rational,* which masks the underlying psychodynamic issues of gerophobia and loss of control.

By contrast, Job does not need this interpretive structure because he is in a relationship with a Creator who gives his life intrinsic meaning. Job's meaning is to live — and to overcome his misfortunes. In the biblical framework, God gives and takes away life; but this is not the same as searching for a divine signal that it is time to depart. Therefore, Job is not goaded to see his far greater misfortunes as a sign to exit this world, but rather as a test of his faith.

The Question of Rational Suicide

The idea of "rational suicide" has been championed by Derek Humphrey, founder of the Hemlock Society (1987, 1991), who has argued that an individual has a "right to die." This idea has been discussed — if not necessarily advocated — by a number of current mental health professionals (e.g., Battin and Mayo 1980; Beckerman 1995; Maris 1982, 1983; Siegel 1982, 1986).

Prominent among them is the counseling psychologist James Werth, who has written a book entitled *Rational Suicide? Implications for Mental Health Professionals* (1996), in which he draws on a definition of rational suicide offered by K. Siegel ten years earlier.

> The defining characteristics of a rational suicide are: (1) the individual possesses a realistic assessment of his (or her) situation, (2) the mental processes leading to his (or her) decision to commit suicide are unimpaired by psychological illness or severe emotional distress, and 3) the motivational basis of his (her) decision would be understandable to the majority of uninvolved observers from his (or her) community or social group. (Siegel 1986, 407)

Werth himself recommends three criteria for determining whether a patient's decision to die is "rational," and thus "sound": first, the person considering suicide must have a hopeless condition; second, the person must make the decision as a free choice; third, the person must be engaged in a sound decision-making process (1996, 61). All these criteria are extremely problematic. Let us consider them one by one.

Hopeless Conditions

Consider first Werth's definition of "hopeless conditions," which "include *but are not necessarily limited to,* terminal illnesses, severe physical or psychological pain, physically or mentally debilitating conditions, or quality of life no longer acceptable to the individual" (62). Wesley Smith, the attorney for the International Anti-Euthanasia Task Force, points to the Achilles' heel of this definition:

> All suicidal people have severe psychological pain or mentally debilitating conditions. Every suicidal person by definition believes that his quality of life is unacceptable. In the name of nonjudgmentalism, rational suicide transforms self-destruction into just another choice. It is also a warrant for the abandonment of suicidal sufferers by psychologists, psychiatrists, and social workers, the very people who are often the last line of defense between a despairing person and a leap into eternity. (Smith 2000, 26)

Let's consider a case in point, one of the Kevorkian cases: No. 70, Martha Wichorek. Mrs. Wichorek sent a series of letters to a number of public officials and professionals, including one of the coauthors of this book (Kaplan), in which she advocated for a state euthanasia clinic. Below is an excerpt from a letter by the highly functioning woman named Martha Wichorek (Dec. 2, 1996):

> When "life" (being able to do things for yourself and others) is taken away, unless a heart attack or accident strikes first, every human being usually descends into the "miserable existence" stage (cannot do any-thing for yourself or others — totally helpless). This stage of that life-death cycle can last weeks, months or years and is the most dreaded of human experiences. . . . (Kaplan and Leonhardi 2000, 268)

Mrs. Wichorek went on for three full pages speaking about the suf-fering of those in the "miserable existence stage," which she also called the "other death row." Among the indignities of the "miserable existence stage" she included (1) nursing home or hospital tests and procedures; (2) living with children; (3) hospice; (4) in-home and visiting nurse ar-rangements; (5) living wills; and (6) committing suicide without the help of a doctor. She called for a state-approved euthanasia clinic, and she signed the letter, "A still clear thinking 81-year-old human being."

Since we were concerned about Mrs. Wichorek, we called her as soon as we received this letter. Our conversation with her revealed that Martha had lost her husband to cancer three years before, and that she had three grown daughters. She lived alone and, aside from some normal ailments associated with aging, was in reasonably good health. She was not terminal nor in acute physical pain. In fact, she seemed to be active in her commu-nity and had a very sharp mind.

In April 1997, many of us again received letters from Martha, this time from a hospital where she had undergone a hysterectomy after epi-sodes of vaginal bleeding. She was doing fine and acknowledged that "she was getting stronger," but she described the "torture" she was enduring, specifying the following: (1) "IVs with anesthetics, nutrients, etc."; (2) "tight rubber stockings that stretched from my toes to the crotch, and expanding and contracting legging attached to a motor for better blood circulation"; (3) "tubes in my nose, for oxygen"; (4) "breathing tubes to ex-ercise my lungs"; (5) "blood pressure and temperature checks every hour, an EKG, blood drawn for lab tests, etc."; and (6) "I was expected to walk, one day after surgery, alone from the bathroom, holding onto the IV pole."

All of us who have undergone surgery recognize these "tortures" as unpleasant but temporary and recognize that they are quite necessary to facilitate a quick and complete recovery. Martha's comments indicate that she also recognized the reason these measures were undertaken; yet she seemed to regard each of these measures as an assault to her dignity that made "life not worth living." Martha spent only three days in the hospital and recovered quite quickly from her surgery. Yet it was scarcely eight months later, on December 3, 1997, that Martha became the seventieth documented physician-assisted suicide conducted by Jack Kevorkian and his associates. The physical autopsy revealed no anatomical evidence of any disease, indicating that her sense of hopelessness had little to do with her physical condition.

Freedom of Choice

Consider now Werth's second criterion of freedom of choice. Our own experience in studying the Kevorkian cases (see chapter 11 above) shows how sensitive a physically ill person is to what she perceives to be the attitude of people around her as to whether she is a burden, and how this seems disproportionately to influence more vulnerable portions of the population to commit suicide, including women, elderly people, and people with disabilities (Kaplan, Lachenmeir, et al. 2000; Kaplan, O'Dell, et al. 2000; Kaplan, Harrow, and Schneiderman 2002). The fear of being a burden also arises as a leading reason given by people who prematurely ended their lives in studies in Oregon (Foley and Hendin 2002), in the Netherlands (Hendin 2002), and in the northern territories of Australia (Kissane 2002; Street and Kissane 2000). So what exactly does a free choice mean in such situations of illness and disability (Coleman 2002)? This is especially true in the Western world, which is very counterphobic about dependence, because it carries forward this fear of attachment from the Greek and Roman world, as we have argued throughout this book.

Sound Decision-Making

Werth's final criterion of sound decision-making is also problematic. An analysis of Martha Wichorek's reasoning described above suggests that an argument can be rational in a narrow sense of the word, yet deeply disturbed. The themes that stand out in Martha's statements are: (1) black-and-white negative thinking; (2) a counterphobic stance toward dependency (she has rejected all help or assistance); (3) insistence on a nonbiological definition of life (she defines life as being able to take care of herself); (4) use of euphemisms (she has created a new life stage, "miserable existence," rather than simply describing herself as feeling miserable); (5) unsolicited speaking for others (she advocates for a state-sanctioned euthanasia clinic for "us terminally ill, elderly, Alzheimer's," though she herself falls into none of those categories); (6) an overly rational, legalistic analysis of the problem of euthanasia and doctor-assisted suicide; (7) exaggeration of annoying but relatively minor and temporary discomforts; (8) an irrational tunnel vision behind her seemingly logical arguments; (9) an apparent blurring of her personal situation with the campaign to legalize euthanasia and her eagerness to make herself a martyr for the cause; (10) her plan to kill herself and to give her grandson a car with the medication money she would save; (11) reluctance to accept family support (she finds death preferable to living with her children); (12) her choice to die (and be in control) rather than accept her current relatively healthy — though somewhat diminished and dependent — condition.

The suicide note Martha sent out to people insisted that she was rational and competent: "I am not stressed, oppressed, or depressed. I don't have Alzheimer's and am not terminally ill, but I am 82 years old and I want to die." Why does Martha Wichorek want to kill herself? It is difficult to see her as much different from Zeno the Stoic, sadly hoping to find in her suicide a meaning to her life.

Kevorkian himself may have reinforced or even provoked this sense that death is somehow heroic in some of his patients. Kevorkian's first assisted suicide, Janet Adkins, was a highly intelligent and accomplished 54-year-old woman who was likely in the very early stages of Alzheimer's disease, though she had been told by her physician that she had a number of quality years ahead. She had been a musician, but she no longer seemed able to sight-read music. She was still quite alert and physically active, and was quite a good tennis player: she had defeated her son in tennis three days earlier, though she was having problems keeping score. One of the problems was that Janet's husband was very negative about her achievements; he focused on the losses she had experienced and labeled Janet "terminal in a mental sense" — in her presence. Kevorkian agreed with this assessment: he focused on her decrements and the diminution of her quality of life that made "her life not worth living." Rather than explore the emotional and relational reasons for Janet's desire to die, Kevorkian framed the discussion in terms of "autonomy and self-determination," and he praised Janet as a heroine for dying, because this was the first time this had happened since classical Greece. He insisted that the world would thank her for her heroic gesture. Therefore, at the same time that her life was being stripped of meaning, her death was being invested with meaning.

Terri Schiavo: The Right to Die and the Right to Life

The collision between the "right-to-die" and the "right-to-life" movements occurred during the events surrounding the death of Terri Schiavo in April 2005. The controversy came into the public consciousness as a parallel issue to the legalized abortion issue that had resulted from the 1973 *Roe v. Wade* decision of the United States Supreme Court. Abortion-rights supporters marched under the ambiguous banner of "freedom of choice" and framed their argument as a civil liberty; those opposing abortion promoted the "right to life" on the grounds that abortion represented nothing short of murder, and that they represented the protection of the defenseless and innocent fetus. In reality, the issue of abortion inherently involved the balancing of two rights, that of the mother and that of the unborn fetus, and much of this turned on the question of when life begins and when a fetus achieves legal personhood. Advocates of abortion rights did not advocate the right of a mother to commit infanticide, nor did opponents of abortion rights typically deny a mother the right to make other private decisions about her health.

The controversy came under a new light and into different focus with the issue of physician-assisted suicide and *euthanasia* (derived from the Greek, meaning "good death") and was spurred on by the continuing de facto physician-assisted suicides (PAS's) performed by Jack Kevorkian and his associates in Michigan. In 1997, the United States Supreme Court overturned two lower court rulings in denying that there is a constitutional right for physician-assisted suicide (*Washington v. Glucksberg,* 1997). However, the Supreme Court refused to hear the appeal of Oregon's "Death with Dignity" act, which was passed in 1994 and reaffirmed by Oregon's voters in 1998. This is the upshot of the Supreme Court's position: it denies that PAS is a constitutional right; however, it does not preclude individual states from enacting laws to either allow or forbid PAS.

The unsettled nature of this controversy was tested severely in the case of Terri Schiavo. Paul McHugh describes her case concisely in an excellent article in the June 2005 issue of *Commentary*:

> In 1990, when Terri Schiavo was in her mid-twenties, she suffered a severe cerebral anoxic injury (low amount of oxygen in the body's tissues — and coma). From this coma, she emerged gradually, settling for the next fifteen years into an impaired state of consciousness. She could swallow, breathe, sleep, and awaken without assistance and could react to sudden sounds with a glance, or to pain by grimacing or groaning. But she was apathetic to inner needs and external events. She was mute, mostly immobile, incontinent, psychologically blank. (*Commentary* 119 [6]:27-28)

During the several years before her death, Terri Schiavo was being treated in a hospice for terminally ill people. The hospice provided nursing care for Schiavo's basic bodily needs (being bathed and turned on schedule), and she received nutrients through a feeding tube that had been inserted through her abdomen into her stomach. She developed frequent bedsores, and a good deal of tooth rotting, and muscle contractions that twisted her limbs into a fixed contorted position. Schiavo was sustained by the regular attention of a devoted staff and family (her husband, parents, and siblings) and was financially supported by money her husband, Michael, had won for her treatment through a successful malpractice suit.

Schiavo would have remained in this condition until, within a period of years, an infection, a blood clot, or some cardio-respiratory difficulty would have ended her life. "What changed," McHugh says, "was not her physical condition but her husband's mind." Michael Schiavo was Terri's legal guardian and had first battled for her care and support. However, he gradually lost hope in her further recovery. This change of attitude could be seen in his resistance to permitting antibiotic treatment for a recurring bladder infection. He ultimately demanded the withdrawal of all sustaining treatments, including the gastric tube that provided nutritious fluids to Terri or any feeding of her by spoon or cup. However, Terri's parents strongly disagreed with Michael's view that Terri was beyond hope of recovery, and they launched a long legal fight with him for her guardianship. Their intention was to continue her hospice care and her feeding, whether by the feeding tube or by mouth.

McHugh provides a chilling summary as to the disposition of this case:

> Through a series of court battles, legislative enactments, and executive mandates, the husband's right of guardianship was upheld, the gastric tube was removed, and all — hospice staff, parents, siblings, onlookers — were forbidden by court order to give her food or drink orally. Even a chip of ice to relieve the pain of a parched mouth and throat was judicially prohibited, and local sheriffs were alerted to prevent it. Within thirteen distress-filled days, she died of dehydration. (28)

McHugh cogently examines the question of how this terrible state of affairs came to be. He points out that the overarching principle of hospice medical staff is that, while they may help a patient *surrender* to death, by forgoing active medical procedures when these seem to be futile, they must never *betray* a patient to death, or act directly to kill the patient. In a hospice, the staff does not provide a ventilator or cardiac monitoring at a patient's bedside, because there is no plan to transfer a patient back to acute treatment. However, the hospice will treat the symptoms of certain potentially deadly conditions, such as bowel obstructions and blood clots, but will not treat the symptoms themselves. Under no circumstances does hospice care deprive the patient of being kept clean and receiving food and water. In Terri Schiavo's case, just as the team did not withdraw her bladder catheter, which helped to keep her clean, so it did not withdraw the gastric tube. These judgments may be somewhat ambiguous, or even arbitrary, but they are usually clear.

McHugh argues that in this phase the treatment of Terri Schiavo went terribly wrong. Terri's husband, Michael, began to feel hopeless about her and perhaps about his own future as well. No functional studies (such as an MRI) were done to determine whether her cerebral cortex, the brain region most responsible for coherent behavior, showed any evidence of recovering. Furthermore, there was a good deal of inconsistency in the testimony of bedside observers. Some observers reported evidence of some small and slow steps toward consciousness, while others thought that she displayed only reflex reactions. Michael was told that Terri's diagnosis was a "persistent vegetative state," an unfortunately loaded term that encouraged those who no longer saw her as an animate being and infuriated those who believed that it labeled her a vegetable. McHugh suggests that a more dispassionate neuropathological term would have described Terri as being in a "decorticate" condition.

At this point, Michael was no longer willing to allow her to be fed, and under Florida law he had the right to demand that her nutrition be stopped. And it is here that McHugh makes his most telling point.

> As soon as Terri Schiavo's case moved into the law courts of Florida, the concept of "life under altered circumstances" went by the boards — and so, necessarily, did any consideration of how to serve such life. Both had been trumped by the concept of "life unworthy of life," and how to end it. (31)

McHugh uses the term "life unworthy of life" advisedly, because he is certainly aware that the phrase originates in a book written by Hoche and Binding, a lawyer and a psychiatrist, entitled *Die Friegabe der Vernichtung Lebensunwertes Leben* (published in Germany in 1920), which translates into English as "Lifting Constraint from the Annihilation of Life Unworthy of Life." The concept of "life unworthy of life," of course, was instrumental in the Nazi T-4 euthanasia program, and it became the subject of one of the leading propaganda films of the Nazi Party in 1939, *Dasein ohne Leben* ("Existence without Life").

McHugh argues that "Terri Schiavo's husband, and his clinical and legal advisers, believing that hers was now a life unworthy of life, sought, and achieved its annihilation." McHugh asks the question of how this could happen in America in 2005; after all, this is not Nazi Germany. McHugh tellingly argues that we have created our own "culture of death, whose face is legal and moral and benignly individualistic rather than authoritarian and pseudo-scientific." McHugh concludes his incisive analysis with a chilling summary, and it unfortunately mirrors our own clinical and professional experience.

> Contemporary bioethics has become a natural ally of the culture of death. . . . In Terri Schiavo's case, it is what won out over the hospice's

culture of life, overwhelming by legal means, and by the force of advanced social opinion, the moral and medical command to choose life, to comfort the afflicted, and to teach others how to do the same. . . . More of us will die prematurely; some of us will even be persuaded that we want to. (32)

The Biblical Case against Rational Suicide

Let us examine McHugh's analysis within the context of the discussion of Zeno, Job, and rational suicide developed in the first part of this chapter, where we cited Droge and Tabor's argument that Zeno's actions represented a precedent for rational suicide. They may well be correct; however, they may not be focusing on what is rational in Zeno's act. Zeno's rationality lies not in his interpretation that stubbing his toe represents a sign from the gods that he should depart, but in his need for the events in his life to have meaning. Zeno is aging and feels alone, and he deludes himself into thinking that the act of stubbing his toe has cosmic meaning. At least his otherwise indifferent gods notice him, even if their attention is lethal, and Zeno becomes a hero, even if he dies in the process. Its inherent rationality is not that stubbing his toe is a sign to depart, but that it is better to have a world in which one's actions are given meaning, even destructive meaning, than one in which they are not given meaning at all. In the absence of a religious system that gives life meaning, Zeno is cast adrift, and he ends up overinterpreting events in an attempt to feel less adrift and isolated.

Job, however, has no need for these intellectual and emotional tricks: he is anchored in a sense of a personal Creator who is with him from the moment of his birth and will be with him until his death and beyond. Thus he can withstand far greater misfortunes than can Zeno without the need to attribute cosmic meaning to them. Job is able to maintain his sense of innocence before his Creator even while expressing his faith in him. He has no need to be a hero or to provide cosmic interpretation for his misfortune. This does not make Job any less rational; it simply anchors his interpretive structure in his desire to live.

Job knows that his God has created him uniquely in an act of loving kindness. Job knows that his God gives and takes away life, but that he does not give signals that it is time for Job to depart because of an imperfection or disability. The value of each human life is infinite in biblical Judaic and

217

Christian thought (see Jacobovits 1959; Maimonides 1962; Rosner 1998; and Sherwin 1998, for a somewhat different view). Job did not focus on his "quality of his life"; life is life, and it is whole — of a piece. Nor does it allow mathematical operations that compare one life with another. One cannot divide, multiply, add, or subtract infinity. Life is life, indivisible and whole, and each life is of unique and unqualified value and cannot be compared to any other life.

Job does not focus on any particular attributes that make life worth living or not; indeed, that is not a question that has even occurred to Job. Our experience with Nazi euthanasia must make us very wary about any philosophy that suggests that some lives are not worth living. We must even view familiar and seemingly benign bromides such as Descartes's *Cogito ergo sum* ("I think, therefore I am") and Plato's "the unexamined life is not worth living" cautiously and with eyes wide open. Though these are usually interpreted as statements in praise of self-examination and knowledge, they can easily be turned into an attack on the right of the cognitively impaired to live.

This latter direction has emerged in the utilitarian bioethics of Peter Singer (1975, 1979, 1995). While Singer's original work championed animal rights, his argument degenerates into a morally dangerous obliteration of the traditional and biblical distinction between humans and nonhumans. In the biblical world, human beings are distinguished from animals: humans have dominion over the animals and are commanded to watch out for them. For Singer, such distinctions between human beings and animals represent "specieism"; in its place, he offers a functional distinction between persons and nonpersons. Persons, whether human or animal, are beings who feel, reason, have self-awareness, and look forward to a future. In other words, Singer's "persons" are *sentient*; by contrast, nonpersons are beings that do not have these capabilities, that is, who are *nonsentient*. For Singer, the category of nonpersons includes cognitively impaired humans, for example, human beings with Alzheimer's disease.[1] The killing of such humans would not be described as murder because these nonsentient creatures would not be distinguished from nonsentient animals. It is a series of but small steps from Zeno the Stoic to Singer's nonsentient human

---

1. Singer, in fact, has been described as an exceptionally loyal and devoted son to his own mother, who suffered from Alzheimer's disease. However, it is difficult to see how his commendable behavior flows out of his practical bioethics.

being to Terri Schiavo. None of them have sufficient "quality of life" to justify continuing it. For Zeno the Stoic, his death sentence was self-imposed; for Terri Schiavo, it was imposed from outside her.

By contrast, Job knows that his misfortunes do not make his life less worthwhile in the Creator's eyes. If anything, Job's tests deepen his faith. It is true that Job suffers grievously; furthermore, he does not receive an explanation — nor does he understand — why this suffering has come upon him. However, he knows that he has done nothing evil to warrant these miseries. And yet he rejects his wife's suggestion to "curse God and die."

Her suggestion neither makes much sense nor is it at all positive. Was cursing God supposed to cause death? Probably not. Job's wife was merely expressing her deep hurt and anger, her feeling that life is useless and that it would be best to end it. Job's wife's response is similar to the attitudes that relatives too often show to a family member who seems very ill. Either the relatives feel the patient cannot bear continued suffering or, because they themselves do not wish to have to deal with his sufferings, the relatives may actually encourage euthanasia (so-called) or even direct suicide, whether unaided or doctor-assisted. The patient comes to feel that he is no more than a burden to his "loved ones," and he may accept euthanasia or suicide as a means of relieving and releasing them from what he perceives as the burden he places on them.

Job knows that God strongly opposes suicide and greatly prefers life to death. Job rejects his wife's view and begins his long and determined course of questioning. This finally does bring him to a new closeness to God and to a higher level, both intellectual and emotional, of the purpose of human life. Job refuses to give in either to his wife's unthinking rejection of God's gift of life or to his friends' suggestions that he must have sinned and is thus being punished by God. Indeed, Job lives through his many sufferings *despite* the pressure from his wife and his friends.

Job learns many new things about God's world and about himself, and he finds new meaning and joy in his life. He is not obsessed with death, nor does he need to control it, nor does he need to worry that it is timely. Thus he does not need to interpret each event as a signal to exit, in a fruitless attempt to find meaning in the heroic. Job simply needs to live the life that has been given to him in dignity. And this is the best antidote to the obsession with "death with dignity" and "rational suicide" that is so prevalent in Zeno the Stoic, Nazi euthanasia, and contemporary trends in bioethics. These contemporary forces are working to turn the default in medicine from a patient's life to death. A biblical psychology of hope is a good place to start in combating these trends in our current medical culture.

V. Conclusion

13. From Tragedy to Therapy:
The Case for Biblical Psychotherapy

But now, I am forsaken of the gods, son of a defiled mother, successor to his bed who gave me my own wretched being.

Sophocles, *Oedipus the King,* 1359-61

Pray thou no more; for mortals have no escape from destined woe.

Sophocles, *Antigone,* 1336

Cast me not off, neither forsake me, O God of my salvation. For though my father and mother have forsaken me, the Lord will take me up.

Psalm 27:9-10

Even if a sword's edge lies on the neck of a man he should not hold himself back from prayer.

Berachot, 10a

In *The Future of an Illusion* (1927), Sigmund Freud declares his view of "religious doctrines as illusions" (43) and religion as "the universal obsessional neurosis of humanity . . . arising out of the Oedipus complex" (55). Nevertheless, the relationship between religion and mental health has continued to fascinate a number of thinkers and writers (e.g., Niebuhr 1949; Fromm 1950; Bakan 1958; Tillich 1959; Zilboorg 1967; Shoham 1979; Ostow 1982; Rotenberg 1992; Kaplan and Schwartz 1991), and it has been the subject of several books in the last two decades (Gay 1987; Yerushalmi 1991; Schwartz and Kaplan 2004). One of the reasons for the continuing interest in the interface between religion and mental health may be the awareness of the therapeutic function that clergy in traditional societies performed. The situation is very different in contemporary America: the role of clergy is quite truncated with regard to psychological counseling; furthermore, belief in a transcendent God is quite low (40 percent) among trained psychotherapists, though it is very high (90 percent) among the general public (Shafranske and Maloney 1990).

Another reason may be the natural distaste many people have for the Greek foundation stories that underlie the psychoanalytic tradition (e.g., Oedipus, Electra, Narcissus). Phillip Slater (1968) and Bennett Simon (1978) have concluded that these Greek foundation stories are both linked to pathological family patterns and inform the roots of modern psychiatry. Over half a century ago, Eric Wellisch argued very much the same thing:

> The very word "psyche" is Greek. The central psychoanalytic concept of the formation of character and neurosis is shaped after the Greek Oedipus myth. . . . Greek thinkers possessed an understanding of the human mind which, in some respects, is unsurpassed to the present day. . . . In ancient Greek philosophy, only a heroic fight for the solution but no real solution is possible. (1954, 115)

In the Greek world, humans feel trapped and desperate, with all hope still locked up in Pandora's box and unavailable. Their gods show little interest in them. Suicide offers itself as a way to gain freedom and security, whether through egoistic Promethean rebellion, altruistic self-sacrifice, or anomic confusion between the two. Far from providing a stopper, Greek thought seems to actually push the individual in his rush to self-destruction. The biblical person has a sense of being created and watched over by a concerned and caring God and of having a purpose and hope.[1] The rainbow in the sky after the flood reaffirms this relationship and gives the individ-

---

1. The work of Aaron Beck and his colleagues (1985) has pointed to the relationship between hopelessness and suicide.

ual hope (Gen. 9:12-14). Humans are important creatures with significant responsibilities, and they do not need to destroy themselves to please God. It is sufficient and expected that they show gratitude and make good use of the gift of life. They have no need to justify their existence beyond that: they are not pushed into deeds of impossible heroism or altruism.

The story of Jonah offers a prime example of this process. Jonah runs away in confusion because he is not able to answer God's command to go to Nineveh. But God provides a great fish to shelter him in his state of regressed confusion. Narcissus, by contrast, lacks protection in his confusion and falls to self-destruction.

Biblical intervention is often very simple. Elijah is given food and water, and Moses is offered help for his burden. In contrast, the Greek Ajax is left alone in his depression, with neither food nor emotional support. The biblical story of Naaman and Elisha (2 Kings 5:1-14) illustrates the importance of simple interventions. Naaman, a Syrian general stricken with leprosy, approaches the prophet Elisha for help. Elisha proposes a simple cure: "Go and wash in the Jordan seven times, and your flesh shall be restored to you, and you shall be clean." Naaman becomes angry that Elisha does not propose something grander, but his own servants criticize him for his disparaging attitude toward a simple intervention: "My father, if the prophet had told you to do something great, would you not have done it? How much more then, when he says to you, 'Wash and be clean'?" At their urging, Naaman dips in the Jordan and is cured.

Biblical Family Therapy

Effective psychotherapy must be two-pronged: it must provide for the restoration of the entire family when this is possible, and it must remove the individual from the family when the family cannot be restored. The unsalvageable family can actually promote self-destruction in the individual, and here the therapy must protect the individual from the family. An effective modern psychotherapy needs to avail itself of the biblical worldview. First of all, the individual is not abandoned, nor does she need to feel enmeshed. This is true even if her own family is deficient in these ways. Second, the individual's life improves when she realizes that she can recover from her mistakes. She must learn to hope. Finally, therapy must involve nurturing at both the symbolic and material levels.

The suicidogenic Greek family feels abandoned by the gods and is often hopelessly enmeshed. Generational boundaries are blurred, family members take sides against each other, and relationships between the genders are often fatally antagonistic. This impossible condition is agonizingly expressed in the Oedipus stories: "But now, I am forsaken of the gods, son of a defiled mother, successor to his bed who gave me my own wretched being" (Sophocles, *Oedipus the King*, 1359-61). Biblical families, by contrast, are neither abandoned by God nor hopelessly enmeshed. Generations are clearly differentiated from each other, and triangulation between the genders is discouraged. Further, the relationship between the genders is complementary rather than antagonistic: "Therefore a man shall leave his father and his mother and be joined to his wife, and they shall become one flesh" (Gen. 2:24).

The basic goal of covenantal family therapy is to transform suicidogenic families into hopeful families. This requires the redirecting of entire families from the enmeshed-disengaged axis onto a healthy axis that allows a genuine integration of individuation and attachment. Both Greek and biblical couples may face problems; the difference is in the response to those problems by the divine therapist. Zeus creates the entire context in which Prometheus must steal fire for mankind, and then he sends Pandora to entrap humans. Furthermore, Zeus actively intervenes to block a happy couple, Deucalion and Pyrrha, from achieving joint harmonious parenthood. He calls for male-female antagonism, with Deucalion throwing stones over his shoulder to create men and Pyrrha doing the same to create women.[2] On the other hand, the biblical God provides protection for Noah and his wife when he presents them with the instructions to build the ark. He does not force them into a Promethean rebellion to save themselves. Earlier, in the Garden of Eden, the biblical God interrupts the emerging narcissistic collusion between Adam and Eve; he provides them with protection to enable them to regroup and to rebuild their lives.[3]

2. In Greek mythology, aggression in cross-sex parent-child dyads occurs more than twice as often as aggression in same-sex parent-child dyads (Slater 1968, 403). Slater has pointed out that this finding runs counter to the cornerstone of orthodox psychoanalytic thinking. The pattern becomes understandable in light of our analysis. The ambivalent resolution of the Oedipal and Electra dilemmas available from the Greek perspective (Wellisch 1954) transfers parent-child conflicts from the same-sex arena to the cross-sex domain.

3. The biblical perspective provides unambivalent and full resolution of the Oedipal and Electra conflicts. This should drastically reduce cross-sex parent-child conflicts. Indeed,

A family approach to suicide prevention involves the transformation of a Greek family into a biblical family. Practically, this transformation must be divided into three phases: separation, protection, and integrated development.

Separation. The suicidal youth is trapped by his pathological family between enmeshment and disengagement. His parents perceive his attempts at individuation as abandonment, whereas he perceives the family attempts at unity as enmeshment. Each generation has its own symbols, and even potentially resolvable issues can lead to shattering crises. A graphic clinical experience serves as an illustration here. A rigidly homophobic Vietnam veteran was brought to treatment by his wife because he threatened to pull the earring out of the left ear of his adolescent son. The father thundered, "No son of mine is going to be a fruitcake!" The son, equally homophobic, responded, "Left is right, right is wrong." This response turned out to be the son's attempt to express, in the idiom of his generation, his self-assertion of being straight and not gay. Though neither party realized it at the time, the boy was very much his father's son. He dropped out of school (against therapeutic advice), enlisted in the army, and went with the American forces to Saudi Arabia. In such a case of family issues, the therapist must provide a temporary protective shield between the child and his parents, so that the child is protected from pathological family dynamics.

Protection. At this phase, the therapist must encourage both the child and the family to give up their shared polarity between individuation and attachment. The family must come to understand that the child must stake out his own identity. The child, in his turn, must come to understand the meaning and supportive functions of family. He must unlearn old behaviors and response patterns, and must incorporate new ways of transmitting and receiving symbols. This can be very confusing, but the therapist needs to help the child give up the illusory and dangerous temptations of premature autonomy or intimacy. The therapist must provide a protective shield to allow the child time to grow. The parents, too, must be weaned

---

the work of David Bakan (1971; 1979) has pointed to the involvement of fathers in biblical families; these fathers overcome their tendency to abandon their children, especially their daughters, which was a widespread practice in the Hellenistic world (Rostovtzeff 1964, 623-25, 1329, 1547). Even Tacitus, the anti-Semitic Roman historian, noted that Jews do not kill their newborn infants and thus provide for an increase in their numbers (Tacitus, *History*, 5.5).

away from the rigid choices between enmeshed loyalty and expulsion that they place on the family. They, too, will be confused, and the therapist needs to protect them as well.

Integrated Development. Until this phase, the therapist is dealing with the child separately from the parents. Now she brings them together, helping to create a shared agenda in which the parents do not see the child's needs for integrated development as abandoning, nor are parental responses designed to keep the child enmeshed. The child must perceive unconditional supports for his right to exist, to achieve, and even to surpass his parents. The therapist must now begin to withdraw from her role as a buffer between the youth and the parents and to solidify a new family environment based on harmony. The critical issues here are to elicit parental and family support for the youth to develop and for the youth to learn to differentiate himself in ways that maintain harmony. The therapist must seek to instill a sense of freedom that is not in opposition to the family but congruent with it. It is critical that the family learn to recognize this individuation-attachment conflict and to resolve it in a constructive way.

Biblical Individual Therapy

Sometimes a family is unsalvageable and may indeed contribute to the suicidal crisis. Findings from one recent study suggest that disturbed parents tend to be potentially suicidogenic for their children unless the children insulate themselves from the family dynamics (Kaplan and Maldaver 1990b).[4] Greek literature presents such a situation as hopeless. The child is enmeshed in the pathology of her family of origin with no concept of how

4. The Kaplan and Maldaver results suggest that the marital pathology score differentiates adolescent psychopathology independent of suicide and adolescent suicide independent of psychopathology. Further, reported adolescent psychopathology and suicide are largely independent of one another. In other words, pathological adolescents in dysfunctional families are not the ones who commit suicide; rather, it is the adjusted adolescents in these same dysfunctional families. The results in this sample suggest that some seemingly pathological defensive behaviors (e.g., communicative withdrawal) on the part of adolescents growing up in disturbed families actually serve a suicide-preventive function by protecting the adolescent from the pathological dynamics of the family. In other words, some defensive pathologies actually represent self-therapy on the part of adolescents in disturbed families. These results have strong implications for our family-therapy approach to adolescent suicidal behavior and are consistent with the work of Laing and Esterson (1970).

to escape. Oedipus's attempts to avoid his fate only sink him deeper into it: he flees from his adoptive parents in Corinth, hoping to spare them from the oracle's curse; but then he encounters his biological parents in Thebes and plays out the curse. There is no hope: "Pray thou no more, for mortals have no escape from predestined woe" (Sophocles, *Antigone,* 1336). For people so obsessed with tragedy, therapy is useless!

In the biblical world, even when a family seems irredeemable, all is not lost. "[D]o not leave me nor forsake me, O God of my salvation. When my mother and father forsake me, then the Lord will take care of me" (Ps. 27:9-10). Parents have been sent by God to do the job of rearing children. As the third partner in parenting, God himself offers children the security and respect they need. The parents must also recognize their reliance on God. One must not lose hope, no matter how desperate the situation. The prophet Isaiah foretells King Hezekiah's death because he has produced no offspring. Hezekiah responds: "The idea has been passed down from the house of my fathers: Even if a sword's edge lies on the neck of a man, he should not hold himself back from prayer" (*Berachot,* 10a).

A classic illustration of this theme is the story of Abraham. God commands him to leave the house and the country of his father and to go to a new land, where God will make of him a great nation (Gen. 12:1-3). Rashi has explained Abraham's need to separate himself from the corrupting influence of his family of origin: "In the land of idol worship, Abraham is not worthy to rear sons to the service of God" (Rashi on Gen. 12:1).[5] Several accounts in the Talmud illustrate the possibility of individuals overcoming the deleterious influences of their parents to become righteous people. The descendants of the wicked Haman teach the Torah in Bnei Brak, and the sons of the cruel Assyrian King Sennacherib (Shemaiah and Abtalyon) become the teachers of Hillel (*Gittin,* 57b).

Greek stories are filled with accounts of the destructive effects of families from which individuals never seem to escape. In the biblical narratives God intervenes by lifting the person above the limitations of his familial background. For example, Abraham leaves the house and land of his father, Terah, and is protected by God. But when characters in Greek literature return to their roots, they are overwhelmed by primordial forces.

---

5. Abraham does not allow Isaac to go back to his (Abraham's) ancestral homeland, but brings a wife from there to Isaac. Jacob does go, under duress, but he eventually brings his wives back to Canaan with him.

Therapeutic support can help to provide extraparental protection, and the therapist who offers it is acting in a biblical framework, whether he realizes it or not. He believes that he can help a patient overcome the tragic effects of a dysfunctional family: with secure support, that individual becomes free to change. The therapist is opting for a therapeutic, as opposed to a tragic, vision of life.

Individual therapy resembles the family approach, with one important difference: there is no reintegration between parents and child. The therapist must substitute for the parents, ultimately helping the patient find a parental substitute either within herself or in the extrafamilial environment. The three phases of this kind of individual psychotherapy are as follows:

Permanent Separation. The suicidal youth must be permanently separated from his pathological family. He must be taught to think in an untrapped manner and to free himself from the stark alternatives of enmeshment and estrangement that provoke his self-destructive tendencies.

Protection. The therapist must provide protection for the patient while she is vulnerable, so that the patient can strengthen herself without feeling threatened. This is a period of unlearning pathological ways of coping, and the individual needs to be protected.

Integrated Development. The therapist must guide and protect the individual in his integrated development. Such protection allows him to escape the destructive quick fixes of misdirected attachments and achievements. He must learn a repertoire of behaviors that provide both individuation and attachment.

A covenantal psychotherapy can free children and parents from narcissistic polarities and self-destructive tendencies. A healthy family assures protection and nurturing and allows and encourages a person to develop her own unique creativity. The therapist may provide substitute parenting to facilitate this process. Parents can use biblical concepts to protect their children and set limits for them, rather than simply permitting certain behaviors. They do this not to block the children, as in the typical Greek family, but to enable them to grow in ways that are not self-destructive. Freedom is instilled not in the Greco-Roman sense of escape but in the biblical sense of opportunity for commitment. The goal is to prevent suicide rather than promote it, to assist living rather than dying.

Hope can free the individual from the threat of a tragic, deterministic, and suicidal view of life. Further, it offers a therapeutic alternative to a fixation on impossible choices. The quest for the heroic "noble death" of the Greco-Roman tradition[6] becomes irrelevant as human life becomes more hopeful and possible. This has been the great insight of the biblical tradition.

Freud, Oedipus, and the Hebrew Bible

We conclude by investigating the question of why Freud, a Jewish man, used the Oedipus narrative rather than a biblical narrative thematic as a basis for psychoanalysis (Kaplan and Algom 1997). A widespread misconception notwithstanding, Yerushalmi's (1991) work makes it abundantly clear that Freud was no stranger to the Hebrew tradition. Freud's obsessive attempts to keep psychoanalysis from being seen as a "Jewish national affair" does not satisfactorily answer the question either. Finally, Freud claimed to observe the Oedipal configuration in his patients. But this also proves to be an incomplete explanation because his preoccupation with the Oedipus complex undoubtedly predisposed him to see it. Freud's fascination with the Greek Oedipus must have deeper roots.

Earlier in this book we discussed the Olympian story of creation. In the Greek theogony, nature exists before the gods, and Mother Earth colludes with her son to castrate her husband, Sky. The Oedipal conflict is born and ingrained through the Furies into the fabric of the natural world (Apollodorus, 1.4). Indeed, it seems to be an unchanging law of nature, foretold by Earth and Sky with regard to Uranus, Cronos, and Zeus (Apollodorus, 1.5; 2.1). In the biblical account of creation, God exists before nature; in fact, God creates the heavens and the earth. There is no sign of an Oedipal conflict here, nor is there the antagonism between man and woman that exists in the Greek story of creation. So we must repeat our question: Why was Freud influenced by the Greek view of creation rather than its biblical counterpart?

The radical biblical concept that a monotheistic God created nature and is thus able to change what seems to be immutable natural laws is in-

---

6. The therapeutic answer to the question posed by Hamlet, with which we opened the book, is "B": that is, to temporarily withdraw to a protected position (B), which avoids the suicidal dialectics of enmeshment and abandonment (the AC axis) that were likely to provoke the futile heroic gestures so common in the Greco-Roman world.

compatible with the much more deterministic Greek view that nature creates the gods and in fact governs them (Shestov 1966; Snell 1982/1935). Freud correctly understood that the latter deterministic alternative was immutably tied to an Oedipal conflict. But Freud had no ultimate faith in the transformative powers of the biblical God, and thus he was not able to use the Akedah, Abraham's binding of Isaac, as a model for resolving father-son conflict. Yerushalmi puts it this way: "Like Sisyphus pushing his rock, Oedipus and Laius must contend forever. At one point in the cycle the father must be slain by the son; at another, that of the return of the repressed, the father returns; the return is only illusion, for the cycle will begin again" (Yerushalmi 1991, 95). This ever-repeating cycle represents Freud's tragic understanding of the psychological processes intrinsic to a deterministic universe.

This is in marked contrast to the Bible's ringing and hopeful proclamation of an unambivalent resolution of the Oedipus complex:

> And He shall turn the heart of the fathers to the children,
> And the heart of the children to their fathers. . . . (Mal. 3:22-24)

References

Abraham, K. 1949. *Selected papers*. London: The Hogarth Press.

Abrahamsen, D. 1946. *The mind and death of a genius*. New York: Columbia University Press.

Abravanel, I. [15th century] 1964. *Perush al hatorah*. 3 vols. Jerusalem: Bnai Arbael.

Adams, J. 1700. *An essay concerning self-murder*. London: Privately printed for T. Bennett.

Aeschines. 1919. *The Speeches of Aeschines*. Trans. C. B. Adams. London: W. Heinemann.

Aeschylus. 1938. *The seven against Thebes*. In *The complete Greek drama*, vol. 1, ed. W. J. Oates and E. O'Neill, Jr., 89-122. New York: Random House.

Ainsworth, M. D. S. 1972. Attachment and dependency: A comparison. In *Attachment and Dependency*, ed. J. Gerwitz. Washington, DC: V. H. Winston and Sons.

Alighieri, Dante. 1977. *The divine comedy*. Trans. J. Ciardi. New York: W. W. Norton.

Alvarez, A. 1970. *The savage God*. New York: Random House.

Apocrypha of the Old Testament. 1965. New York: Oxford University Press.

Apollodorus. 1976. *The library*. Trans. M. Simpson. Amherst: University of Massachusetts Press.

Apollonius. 1912. *Argonautica*. Trans. R. C. Seaton. Cambridge, MA: Harvard University Press (Loeb Classical Library).

Appianus of Alexandria. 1912-1913. *Appian's Roman history*. Trans. Horace White. New York: Macmillan.

Aquinas, Thomas. 1981. *Summa theologica*. 5 vols. Trans. Fathers of the English Dominican Province. Westminster, MD: Christian Classics.

Aristotle. 1936. *The poetics*. Ed. and trans. S. H. Butcher. London: Macmillan.

———. 1976. *The ethics of Aristotle: The Nichomachean ethics*. Trans. J. A. K. Thomson. New York: Penguin.

Athenaeus of Naucratis. 1924. *The Deipnosophists.* London: Heinemann.

Augustine. 1955. *The problem of free choice.* Trans. Dom Mark Pontifex. London: Longman, Green.

———. 1957-72. *The city of God against the pagans.* 7 vols. Trans. Willima M. Green. Cambridge, MA: Harvard University Press.

———. 1960. *St. Augustine's confessions.* 2 vols. Cambridge, MA: Harvard University Press (Loeb Classical Library).

———. 1963. *The Trinity.* Trans. S. McKenna. Washington, DC: The Catholic University of America Press.

Aurelius, Marcus. 1964. *Meditations.* Trans. and ed. M. Stramforth. Baltimore: Penguin Books.

Avot, D'R. Nathan. 1887. Ed. S. Schechter, Vienna: n.p.

Babylonian Talmud. 1975. Vilna edition. Jerusalem.

Bachya Ibn Pakuda. 1965. *Duties of the heart.* Trans. M. Hyamson. Jerusalem: Boystown Publishers.

Baechler, J. 1979. *Suicides.* New York: Basic Books.

Bakan, D. 1958. *Sigmund Freud and the Jewish mystical tradition.* Princeton, NJ: D. VanNostrand.

———. 1971. *Slaughter of the innocents.* San Francisco: Jossey-Bass.

———. 1979. *And they took themselves wives: The emergence of patriarchy in Western Civilization.* New York: Harper & Row.

Battin, M. P., and D. J. Mayo. 1981. *Suicide: The philosophical issues.* London: Peter-Owen.

Bayet, A. 1922. *Le suicide et la morale.* Paris: F. Alcan.

Beavers, W. R., and M. Voeller. 1983. Family models comparing and contrasting the Olson circumplex model with the Beavers system model. *Family Process* 22: 88-95.

Beck, A. T., R. A. Steer, M. Kovacs, and B. Garrison. 1985. Hopelessness and eventual suicide: A ten-year prospective study of patients hospitalized with suicidal ideation. *American Journal of Psychiatry* 142: 559-63.

Beckerman, N. L. 1995. Suicide in relation to AODS. *Death Studies* 19: 223-43.

Ben Gurion, J. 1956. *Sefer yosippon.* Jerusalem: Hotstaat Hominer.

Berlin, M. 1943. *Rabban shel Yisrael.* New York: Histadrut Ha Mizrachi.

Bettelheim, B. 1955. *Symbolic wounds.* London: Thames and Hudson.

Blumenkrantz, A. 1969. *The laws of Nidah: A digest.* Far Rockaway, NY: n.p.

Bohannan, P. 1960. *African homicide and suicide.* Princeton, NJ: Princeton University Press.

Bowen, M. 1960. The family as the unit of study and treatment. *American Journal of Orthopsychiatry* 31: 40-60.

Bowlby, J. 1969. *Attachment.* New York: Basic Books.

———. 1973. *Separation: Anxiety and anger.* New York: Basic Books.

————. 1977. The making and breaking of affectional bonds: Etiology and psychopathology in the light of attachment theory. *British Journal of Psychiatry* 130: 201-10.

Brandt, R. B. 1975. The rationality of suicide. From "The morality and rationality of suicide." In *A Handbook for the study of suicide,* ed. S. Perlin. New York: Oxford University Press.

Breiner, S. J. 1990. *Slaughter of the innocents: Child abuse through the ages and today.* New York: Plenum Press.

Buehler, A. 1922. *Types of Jewish-Palestinian piety from 70 B.C.E. to 70 C.E.* London: Jews' College, Publication #8.

Camus, A. 1948. *The plague.* New York: Modern Library.

————. 1955. *The myth of Sisyphus and other essays.* New York: Alfred A. Knopf.

Caro, J. 1977. *Shulchan aruch.* Tel Aviv: n.p.

Cavan, R. 1928. *Suicide.* Chicago: University of Chicago Press.

Cicero. 1914. *De finibus bonorum et malorum.* Trans. H. Rackham. New York: Macmillan.

————. 1945. *Tusculan disputations.* Trans. J. E. King. Cambridge, MA: Harvard University Press (Loeb Classical Library).

Cohen, S. J. D. 1982. Masada, literature, tradition, archaeological remains, and the credibility of Josephus. *Journal of Jewish Studies* 33: 385-405.

Cohn, H. 1976. Suicide in Jewish legal and religious tradition. *Mental Health and Society* 3: 129-36.

Coleman, D. 2002. Not dead yet. In *The case against assisted suicide,* ed. K. Foley and H. Hendin, 213-37. Baltimore, MD: The Johns Hopkins University Press.

Conon. 1798. *Narrationes quinquaginta et parthenii narrationes amatoriae.* Göttingen: J. C. Dietrich.

Cyprian. 1951. In *The ante-Nicene fathers,* vol. 5, ed. A. Roberts and J. Donaldson. Grand Rapids: Wm. B. Eerdmans.

d'Holbach, P. H. T. [1770] 1821. *Système de la nature.* Paris: Etienne Ledoux.

Descartes, R. 1929. *A discourse on method.* London and Toronto: J. M. Dent and Sons, Ltd.

Dio Chrysostom. 1932. *Diochrysostrom.* Trans. J. W. Cohoon, London: W. Heinemann.

Diogenes Laertius. 1972. *Lives of eminent philosophers.* 2 vols. Trans. R. D. Hicks. Cambridge, MA: Harvard University Press (Loeb Classical Library).

Donne, J. [1608] 1984. *Biathanatos.* Ed. Ernest W. Sullivan II. Cranbury, NJ: Associated University Press.

Douglas, J. D. 1967. *The social meanings of suicide.* Princeton, NJ: Princeton University Press.

Droge, A. J., and J. D. Tabor. 1992. *A noble death: Suicide and martyrdom among Christians and Jews in antiquity.* New York: HarperCollins.

Durkheim, E. [1897] 1951. *Suicide.* Trans. J. A. Spaulding and G. Simpson. Glencoe, IL: Free Press.

Edelstein, L. 1943. *The Hippocratic Oath, text, translation, and interpretation.* Baltimore: The Johns Hopkins University Press.

Elwin, V. 1943. *Muria murder and suicide.* London: Oxford University Press.

Epictetus. 1890. *The discourses of Epictetus: With the Enchiridion and fragments.* Trans. G. Long. London: G. Bell and Sons.

Epstein, Y. M. (n.d.) *Aruch hashulchan.* Jerusalem: n.p.

Erikson, E. 1968. *Identity, youth, and crisis.* New York: W. W. Norton.

Euripides. 1938. *The Phoenissae.* In *The complete Greek drama,* vol. 2, ed. W. J. Oates and E. O'Neill Jr., 171-220. New York: Random House.

Faber, M. D. 1967. Shakespeare's suicides: Some historic, dramatic, and psychological reflections. In *Essays in self-destruction,* ed. Eishneldman. New York: Science Houses.

———. 1970. *Suicide and Greek tragedy.* New York: Sphinx.

Fedden. H. R. 1938. *Suicide: A social and historical study.* London: Peter Davies.

Finley M. I. 1959. *The world of Odysseus.* New York: Meridian.

Foley, K., and H. Hendin. 2002. The Oregon experiment. In *The case against assisted suicide,* ed. Foley and Hendin, 144-74. Baltimore: The Johns Hopkins University Press.

Frend, W. H. C. 1952. *The Donatist church: A movement of protest in Roman North Africa.* Oxford: Clarendon Press.

———. 1965. *Martyrdom and persecution in the early church: A study of a conflict from the Maccabees to Donatus.* Oxford: Blackwell.

Freud, A. 1936. *The ego and the mechanisms of defense.* New York: International Universities Press.

Freud, S. 1913. *Totem and taboo.* In *Standard edition of the complete works of Sigmund Freud,* ed. and trans. J. Strachey, 13: 1-161. London: Hogarth Press.

———. 1914. *On narcissism: An introduction.* In *Standard edition of the complete works of Sigmund Freud,* ed. and trans. J. Strachey, 14: 73-102. London: Hogarth Press.

———. 1917. *Mourning and melancholia.* In *Standard edition of the complete works of Sigmund Freud,* ed. and trans. J. Strachey, 14: 243-58. London: Hogarth Press.

———. 1923a. *The ego and the id.* In *Standard edition of the complete works of Sigmund Freud,* ed. and trans. J. Rivere, 19: 12-59. London: Hogarth Press.

———. 1923b. *The infantile genital organizations: An interpolation into the theory of sexuality.* In *Standard edition of the complete works of Sigmund Freud,* ed. and trans. J. Strachey, 19: 141-48. London: Hogarth Press.

———. 1924. *The dissolution of the Oedipus complex.* In *Standard edition of the complete works of Sigmund Freud,* ed. and trans. J. Strachey, 19: 173-79. London: Hogarth Press.

———. 1927. *The future of an illusion.* In *Standard edition of the complete works of Sigmund Freud,* ed. and trans. J. Strachey, 21: 1-56. London: Hogarth Press.

———. 1954. *The interpretation of dreams.* In *Standard edition of the complete works of Sigmund Freud,* ed. and trans. J. Strachey, vols. 4 and 5. London: Hogarth Press.

Fromm, E. 1950. *Psychoanalysis and religion.* New Haven: Yale University Press.

Gay, P. 1987. *A godless Jew: Freud, atheism and the making of psychoanalysis.* New Haven: Yale University Press.

Gayley, C. 1893. *Classical myths.* Boston: Atheneum Press.

Genesis Rabbah. (Vilna edition.) 1961. Jerusalem: n.p.

Goethe, J. W. von. [1774] 1957. *The suffering of young Werther.* Trans. B. C. Morgan. New York: F. Ungar.

Golden, W. W. 1900. Maimonides' prayer for physicians. *Transactions of the Medical Society of West Virginia* 33: 414-15.

Gordis, R. 1955. *Koheleth: The man and his world.* New York: Bloch.

Gottschalk, H. B. 1980. *Heraclides of Pontus.* Oxford: Clarendon Press.

Graves, R. 1955. *The Greek myths.* 2 vols. Baltimore: Penguin.

Greek Commentaries on Plato's Phaedo. 1976. Ed. and trans. L. G. Weserink. New York: North-Holland.

Greek Tragedies. 1960. Ed. D. Grene and R. Lattimore. Chicago: University of Chicago Press.

Haberman, A. 1946. *Sefer Gezerot Ashkenaz Ve Tsarfat.* Jerusalem: Mosad Ha Rav Kook.

Hadda, J. 1988. *Passionate women, passive men: Suicide in Yiddish literature.* Albany: State University of New York Press.

Haim, A. 1970. *Adolescent suicide.* New York: International Universities Press.

Halliday, W. R. 1970. *The pagan background of early Christianity.* New York: Cooper Square.

Hankoff, L. D. 1979a. Judaic origins of the suicide prohibition. In *Suicide: Theory and clinical aspects,* ed. L. D. Hankoff. Littleton, MA: PSG.

———. 1979b. Suicide and the after life in ancient Egypt. In *Suicide: Theory and clinical aspects,* ed. L. D. Hankoff. Littleton, MA: PSG.

Hardy, T. [1896] 1974. *Jude the obscure.* London: Macmillan.

Hartmann, H. 1964. *Essays in ego psychology: Selected problems in psychoanalytic theory.* New York: International Universities Press.

Heillig, R. J. 1980. Adolescent suicidal behavior: A family systems model. In *Research in Clinical Psychology, 1,* ed. P. E. Nathan. Ann Arbor, MI: UMI Research Press.

Hendin, H. 2002. The Dutch experience. In *The case against assisted suicide,* ed.

K. Foley and H. Hendin, 97-121. Baltimore: The Johns Hopkins University Press.

Herodotus. 1924. *The famous history of Herodotus.* Trans. B. Rich. London: Constable.

Hesiod. 1914. *The Theogony.* In *Hesiod: The Homeric hymns and Homerica,* trans. H. G. Evelyn White, 78-154. Cambridge, MA: Harvard University Press.

———. 1914. *The Shield of Heracles.* In *Hesiod: The Homeric hymns and Homerica,* trans. H. G. Evelyn White, 221-53. Cambridge, MA: Harvard University Press.

Hesiod and Theognis. 1973. *Theogony and Works and Days* [Hesiod] *and Elegies* [Theognis]. Trans. D. Wender. Middlesex, England: Penguin Classics.

Hill, T. E., Jr. 1983. Self-regarding suicide: A modified Kantian view. *Suicide and Life-threatening Behavior* 13: 254-75.

Hippocratic Writings. 1984. Trans. F. Adams. In *Great books of the western world,* vol. 10, ed. R. M. Hutchins. Chicago: University of Chicago Press.

Hirsch, S. R. 1976. *The Pentateuch.* 6 vols. Trans. I. Levy. Gateshead, UK: Judaica Press.

Hirzel, R. 1908. Der selbstmord. *Archiv. für Religionwissenchaft* 11: 75-104.

Hoche, A., and R. Binding. 1920. *Die Friegabe der Vernichtung Lebensunwerten Lebens* (Lifting constraints from the annihilation of life unworthy of life). Leipzig: Felis Meiner Verlag.

Holy Scriptures. 1955. Philadelphia: The Jewish Publication Society of America.

Homer. 1951. *The Iliad.* Trans. R. Lattimore. Chicago: University of Chicago Press.

———. 1967. *The Odyssey.* Trans. R. Lattimore. New York: Harper & Row.

Hooper, F. 1967. *Greek realities.* New York: Charles Scribner's Sons.

Huizinga, J. 1955. *Homo ludens.* Boston: Beacon Press.

Hume, D. 1984. *An essay on suicide.* With a historical and critical introduction by G. W. Foote. London: R. Forder.

Humphry, D. 1987. The case for rational suicide. *Suicide and Life-Threatening Behavior* 7: 335-38.

———. 1991. *Final exit: The practicalities of self-deliverance and assisted suicide for the dying.* Eugene, OR: The Hemlock Society.

Ignatius. 1968. *Epistles.* In *Early Christian writings,* ed. B. Radice. Baltimore: Penguin Books.

Ionesco, E. 1963. *Exit the King.* In *Plays,* vol. 5, trans. D. Watson. London: John Calder.

Jacobovits, I. 1959. *Jewish medical ethics.* New York: Bloch.

Josephus, Flavius. 1985. *Complete works.* Trans. W. Whiston. Grand Rapids: Kregel.

Jung, C. 1961. *The collected works.* Volume 4: *Freud and psychoanalysis.* Trans. R. F. C. Hull. London: Routledge and Kegan Paul.

Justinian. 1985. *The digest of Justinian.* Trans. A. Watson. Philadelphia: University of Pennsylvania Press.

Kant, I. 1788. *Grundlegung zur Metaphysik der Sitten.* Riga: J. F. Hartknoch.

Kaplan, K. J. 1987. Jonah and Narcissus: Self-integration versus self-destruction in human development. *Studies in Formative Spirituality* 8: 33-54.

———. 1988. TILT: Teaching individuals to live together. *Transactional Analysis Journal* 18: 220-30.

———. 1990a. Isaac and Oedipus: A reexamination of the father-son relationship. *Judaism* 39: 73-81.

———. 1990b. TILT for couples: Helping couples grow together. *Transactional Analysis Journal* 20: 229-41.

———. 1991-1992. Suicide and suicide prevention: Greek versus Biblical perspectives. *Omega* 24: 227-39.

———. 1998a. Shneidman's definition of suicide and Jewish law: A brief note. In *Jewish approaches to suicide, martyrdom and euthanasia,* ed. K. J. Kaplan and M. B. Schwartz, 78-79. Northvale, NJ: Jason Aronson Inc.

———. 1998b. *TILT: Teaching individuals to live together.* Philadelphia: Brunner/Mazel.

———. 2002. Isaac versus Oedipus: An alternative view. *Journal of the American Academy of Psychoanalysis* 30 (4): 707-17.

Kaplan, K. J., M. B. Schwartz, and M. Markus-Kaplan. 1984. *The family: Biblical and psychological foundations.* New York: Human Sciences Press.

Kaplan, K. J., and M. B. Schwartz. 1990. Walls and boundaries in rabbinic-biblical foreign policy: A psychological analysis. Presented at the 13th Annual Meetings of the International Society for Political Psychology, Washington, DC.

———. 1993b. *A psychology of hope: An antidote to the suicidal pathology of Western civilization.* Westport, CT: Praeger.

———. 1998. Watching over patient life and death: Kevorkian, Hippocrates, and Maimonides. *Ethics and Medicine* 14 (2): 49-53.

Kaplan, K. J., and M. Maldaver. 1990a. Parental marital patterns and adolescent suicide: A theoretical taxonomy and literature review. Presented at the 22nd Annual Meetings of the American Association of Suicidology, New Orleans, LA, April.

———. 1990b. Parental marital style and completed adolescent suicide: An empirical study. Presented at the 22nd Annual Meetings of the American Association of Suicidology, New Orleans, LA, April.

———. 1993. Parental marital style and completed adolescent suicide: A literature review and empirical study. *Omega: Journal of Death and Dying* 27: 131-54.

Kaplan, K. J., and S. Worth. 1992-1993. Individuation, attachment and suicide trajectory: A developmental guide for the clinician. *Omega: Journal of Death and Dying* 27: 207-37.

Kaplan, K. J., and N. A. O'Connor. 1993a. From mistrust to trust: Through a stage vertically. In *The course of life* (vol. 6), ed. S. I. Greenspan and G. H. Pollock, 153-98. New York: International Universities Press.

Kaplan, K. J., and D. Algom. 1997. Freud, Oedipus and the Hebrew Bible. *Journal of Psychology and Judaism* 21 (3): 211-16.

Kaplan, K. J., F. Lachenmeier, M. Harrow, J. C. O'Dell, O. Uziel, M. Schneiderhan, and K. Cheyfitz. 2000. Psychosocial versus biomedical risk factors in Kevorkian's first forty-seven physician-assisted deaths. In *Right to die versus sacredness of life,* ed. K. J. Kaplan, 109-64. Amityville, NY: Baywood Publishing Company. (Published simultaneously in a special issue of *Omega: Journal of Death and Dying* 40 [1, 1999-2000]: 109-64.)

Kaplan, K. J., J. C. O'Dell, L. J. Dragovic, M. C. McKeon, E. Bentley, and K. L. Telmet. 2000. An update on the Kevorkian-Reding 93 physician-assisted deaths in Michigan: Is Kevorkian a savior, serial killer or suicidal martyr? In *Right to die versus sacredness of life,* ed. K. J. Kaplan, 209-30. Amityville, NY: Baywood Publishing Company. (Published simultaneously in a special issue of *Omega: Journal of Death and Dying* 40 [1, 1999-2000]: 209-30.)

Kaplan. K. J., and M. Leonhardi. 2000. Kevorkian, Martha Wichorek and us: A personal account. In *Right to die versus sacredness of life,* ed. K. J. Kaplan, 267-70). Amityville, NY: Baywood Publishing Company. (Published simultaneously in a special issue of *Omega: Journal of Death and Dying* 40 [1, 1999-2000]: 267-70.)

Kaplan, K. J., and M. C. McKeon. 2000. Michigan versus Kevorkian. In *Right to die versus sacredness of life,* ed. K. J. Kaplan, 271-74. Amityville, NY: Baywood Publishing Company. (Published simultaneously in a special issue of *Omega: Journal of Death and Dying* 40 [1, 1999-2000]: 231-48.)

Kaplan, K. J., M. Harrow, and M. S. Schneiderhan. 2002. Suicide, physician-assisted suicide and euthanasia in men versus women around the world: The degree of physician control. *Ethics and Medicine* 18 (1): 33-48.

Kaplan, M. M. 1957. *Judaism as a civilization: Toward a reconstruction of American Jewish life.* New York: T. Yoseloff.

Kaufman, R. V. 1982. Oedipal object relations and morality. *The Annual of Psychoanalysis* 11: 245-56.

Kaufmann, Y. 1972. *The religion of Israel.* Trans. M. Greenberg. New York: Schocken.

Kazantzakis, N. M. 1960. *The last temptation of Christ.* Trans. P. A. Bien. New York: Simon and Schuster.

Kegan, R. 1982. *The evolving self: Problem and process in human development.* Cambridge, MA: Harvard University Press.

Keller, H. 1931. Comparison between Hippocratic Oath and Maimonides' Prayer in the ideal practice of medicine from the rabbinical point of view. In *Modern Hebrew Orthopedic Terminology and Jewish Medical Ethics,* ed. H. Keller. Boston: Stratford Co.

Kevorkian, J. 1991. *Prescription: Medicine, the goodness of planned death*. Buffalo, NY: Prometheus Books.

———. 1992, A Fail-safe model for justifiable medically-assisted suicide ("Medicaid"). *American Journal of Forensic Psychiatry* 13: 7-41.

Kissane, D. 2002. Deadly days in Darwin. In *The case against assisted suicide*, ed. K. Foley and H. Hendin, 192-209. Baltimore: The Johns Hopkins University Press.

Kohut, H. 1971. *The analysis of the self: The psychoanalytic study of the child*. Monograph No. 4. New York: International Universities Press.

Lachs, S. 1974. The Pandora-Eve motif in rabbinic literature. *Harvard Theological Review* 67: 341-45.

Lactantius. 1964. *The Divine Institutes (Books I-VII)*. Trans. Sister M. F. McDonald. Washington, DC: Catholic University of America Press.

Ladouceur, D. J. 1987. Josephus and Masada. In *Josephus, Judaism and Christianity*, ed. L. Feldman and G. Hata. Detroit: Wayne State University Press.

Laing, R. D., and D. Esterson. 1970. *Sanity, madness, and the family*. New York: Penguin Books.

Lebacqz, K., and H. T. Englehardt, Jr. 1977. Suicide and covenant. In *Death and dying and euthenasia*, ed. D. J. Horam and D. Mall. Washington, DC: University Publications of America.

Lewis, C. 1972. Jonah — A parable for our time. *Judaism* 21: 159-63.

Lewis, H. B. 1976. *Psychic war in men and women*. New York: New York University Press.

Libanius. 1969. *Selected Works of Libanius*. Trans. A. F. Norman. Cambridge, MA: Harvard University Press.

Lindell, K. 1973. Stories of suicide in ancient China. *Acta Orientalia* 35: 167-239.

Livy. 1909-1919. *The history of Rome*. Trans. D. Spillan, C. Edmons, and W. A. M'Devitte. London: G. Bell.

Lucian of Samosata. 1959, 1967. *Lucian*. 8 vols. Trans. A. M. Harmon. London: W. Heinemann.

Mahler, M. S. 1968. *On human symbiosis and the vicissitudes of individuation*. New York: International Universities Press.

Maimonides, M. [12th century] 1962. *Mishneh Torah*. 6 vols. New York: M. P. Press.

———. 1955. The oath and prayer of Maimonides. *Journal of the American Medical Association* 157: 1158.

Main, M., N. Kaplan, and J. Cassidy. 1985. Security in infancy, childhood, and adulthood: A move to the level of representation. In *Growing points of attachment theory and research*, ed. I. Bretherton and E. Everett. Chicago: University of Chicago Press.

Malbim, M. L. 1957. *Ha Torah ve ha Mitzva*. Jerusalem: n.p.

Maris, R. 1982. Rational suicide: An impoverished self-transformation. *Suicide and Life-Threatening Behavior* 12: 4-16.

———. 1983. Suicide: Rights and rationality. *Suicide and Life-Threatening Behavior* 13: 223-30.

Markus-Kaplan, M., and K. J. Kaplan. 1984. A bidimensional view of distancing: Reciprocity versus compensation, intimacy versus control. *Journal of Nonverbal Behavior* 8: 315-26.

McHugh, P. 2003. Annihilating Terri Schiavo. *Commentary* 119 (6): 27-32.

Melville, H. [1851] 1926. *Moby Dick*. New York: Modern Library.

Midrash Rahbah. 1961. Jerusalem: n.p.

Midrash Tanhuma. 1885. Vilna edition. Ed. S. Buber.

Minuchin, S. 1974. *Families and family therapy*. Cambridge, MA: Harvard University Press.

Napier, A. 1978. The rejection-intrusion pattern: A central family dynamics. *Journal of Marital and Family Counseling* 4: 5-12.

NASB Interlinear Greek-English New Testament. 1984. Grand Rapids: Zondervan.

Neuringer, C., and D. J. Lettieri. 1982. *Suicidal women: Their thinking and feeling patterns*. New York: Gardner Press.

Niebuhr, R. 1949. *The nature and destiny of man: A Christian interpretation*. 2 vols. New York: Charles Scribner's Sons.

Numbers Rabbah. 1978. Jerusalem: n.p.

Nussbaum, C. 1992. *Semblance and reality*. New York: KTAV Publishing House.

Oates, W. J., and E. O'Neill, Jr., eds. 1938. *The complete Greek drama*. 2 vols. New York: Random House.

Ohara, K. 1961. A study of main causes of suicide. *Psychiatric Neurology of Japan* 63: 107-66.

Olson, D. M., D. M. Sprenkle, and C. S. Russell. 1979. Circumplex model of marital and family systems: I. Cohesion and adaptability dimensions, family types, and clinical implications. *Family Process* 18: 3-28.

Optatus. 1917. *The Work of St. Optatus, Bishop of Milevis, against the Donatists, with appendix*. Trans. O. R. Vassall-Phillips. London: Longmans, Green.

Orbach, I. 1986. The "unsolvable problem" as a determinant in the dynamics of suicidal behaviors in children. *American Journal of Psychotherapy* 40 (4): 511-20.

———. 1988. *Children who don't want to live*. San Francisco: Jossey-Bass.

Orbach, I., S. Feschbach, G. Carlson, L. Glaubman, and Y. Gross. 1983. Attraction and repulsion by life and death in suicidal and normal children. *Journal of Consulting and Clinical Psychology* 51: 661-70.

Orbach, I., I. Milstein, D. Har-Even, A. Apter, S. Tiano, and A. Elizur. 1991. A multi-attitude suicide tendency scale for adolescents. *Psychological Assessment: A Journal of Consulting and Clinical Psychology* 3: 398-404.

Origen. 1954. *Prayer: Exhortation to martyrdom.* Trans. John J. O'Meara. Ancient Christian Writers, No. 19. London: Longmans, Green.

Orosius, P. 1964. *The seven books of history against the pagans.* Trans. J. Deferrart. Washington, DC: Catholic University of America Press.

Ostow, M. 1982. Judaism and psychoanalysis. New York: KTAV Publishing House.

Ovid. 1955. *The metamorphoses.* Trans. M. Innes. London: Penguin Classics.

Pascal, B. [1558] 1958. *Pensées.* New York: E. P. Dutton.

Pauly, A. F. 1916. *Real Encyclopaediae der classichen Alterrumswissenschaft.* Stuttgart: J. B. Metzler.

Pausanias. 1907. *The Attica of Pausanias.* New York: Ginn.

Pesikta Rabbati. 1885. Ed. M. Friedmann. Vienna: n.p.

Pfeffer, C. R. 1981. The family system of suicidal children. *American Journal of Psychotherapy* 35: 330-34.

Plath, S. [1963] 1986. *The bell jar.* New York: Bantam Books.

Plato. 1954. *The last days of Socrates* [including *Euthyphro, The apology, Crito, Phaedo*]. Trans. M. Tredennick. Middlesex, England: Penguin Classics.

———. 1955. *The republic.* Trans. D. Lee. Middlesex, England: Penguin Classics.

———. 1970. *The laws.* Trans. T. J. Saunders. Middlesex, England: Penguin Classics.

———. 1976. *Protagoras.* Trans. G. Taylor. Oxford: Penguin Classics.

Pliny the Elder. 1857. *The natural history of Plinius Secundus,* vol. 6. Trans. J. Bostock and H. T. Riley. London: Henry G. Bohn.

Pliny the Younger. 1963. *The letters of the younger Pliny.* Trans. B. Radice. Baltimore: Penguin.

Plotinus. 1918. *Complete works.* Trans. K. S. Guthrie. London: George Bell and Son.

Plutarch. 1932. *The lives of the noble Grecians and Romans.* New York: Modern Library.

Polybius. 1922-1927. *The histories.* Trans. W. P. Paton. London: W. Heinemann.

Pope, W. 1976. *Durkheim's Suicide: A classic analyzed.* Chicago: University of Chicago Press.

Quintilian. 1921-1922. *Institutiones oratoriae.* Trans. H. E. Butler. London: W. Heinemann.

Rank, O. 1936. *Will therapy.* Trans. J. Taft. New York: Alfred A. Knopf.

———. 1971. *The double.* Ed. and trans. H. Tucter. New York: New American Library.

Rashi. 1978. *Commentary on the Bible.* Mikraot Gedolot edition. New York: n.p.

Rashi on Genesis. 1961. Jerusalem: n.p.

Reik, T. 1961. *The temptation.* New York: George Braziller.

Richman, J. 1986. *Family therapy for suicidal behavior.* New York: Springer.

Rin, H. 1975. Suicide in Taiwan. In *Suicide in different cultures,* ed. N. Farberow. Baltimore: University Park Press.

Ringel, E. 1981. Suicide prevention and the value of human life. In *Suicide: The philosophical issues,* ed. M. P. Battin and D. J. Mayo. London: Peter Owen.

Robert, C. 1915. *Oidipus Geschichte eines poetischen Stoffs im griechischen Altertum.* Berlin: Weidmannsohe Buchhandlung.

Rosenburg, A. J., ed. 1976. *Samuel.* New York: Judaica Press.

Rosenstock-Huessy, E. 1969. *Judaism despite Christianity: The letters on Christianity and Judaism between Eugene Rosenstock-Huessy and Franz Rosenzweig.* New York: Schocken Books.

Rosner, F. 1970. Suicide in biblical, Talmudic, and rabbinic writings. *Tradition* 11: 25-40.

Rosner, F. R. 1998. Suicide in Jewish law. In *Jewish approaches to suicide, martyrdom and euthanasia,* ed. K. J. Kaplan and M. B. Schwartz, 61-77. Northvale, NJ: Jason Aronson Inc.

Ross, L. T., and K. J. Kaplan. 1993. Life-ownership orientation and attitudes toward abortion, suicide, doctor-assisted suicide and capital punishment. Presented at the 101st Annual Meeting of the American Psychological Association, Toronto, Canada, August.

Rostovtzeff, M. 1964. *Social and economic history of the Hellenistic world.* Oxford: Clarendon Press.

Rotenberg, M. 1992. *Dialogue with deviance: The Hasidic ethic and the theory of social contraction.* New York: Praeger.

Rousseau, J. J. [1761] 1925. *La nouvelle héloise.* Paris: Hachette.

Schneid, H. 1973. *Family.* New York: Leon Amiel.

Schwartz, M. 1985. Koheleth and Camus: Two views of achievement. *Judaism* 35: 29-34.

Schwartz, M., and K. J. Kaplan. 1992. Judaism, Masada, and suicide: A critical analysis. *Omega* 25: 127-32.

Schwartz, M. W., and K. J. Kaplan. 2004. *Biblical stories for psychotherapy and counseling: A sourcebook.* Binghamton, NY: Haworth Pastoral Press.

Seneca the Elder. 1974. *Oratorum et rhetorum sententiae divisiones, colores.* Trans. M. Winterbottom. Cambridge, MA: Harvard University Press.

Seneca the Younger. 1918-1925. *Ad lucilium epistulae morales.* 3 vols. Trans. R. M. Gummere. London: W. Heinemann.

———. 1979. *Seneca.* Cambridge, MA: Harvard University Press.

Servius. 1946. *Servianorum in Vergilii Carmina commentariorum editionis Harvardianae volumen Edwardas Kennard Rand confecerunt.* Lancaster, PA: American Philological Association.

Shafranske, E., and H. N. Maloney. 1990. Clinical psychologists' religious and spiritual orientations and their practice of psychotherapy. *Psychotherapy: Theory, Research, Practice, Training* 27: 72-78.

Shakespeare, W. 1959. *Hamlet.* Cambridge, MA: Houghton Mifflin.

Sherwin, B. L. 1998. Euthanasia as a halachik option. In *Jewish approaches to suicide, martyrdom and euthanasia,* ed. K. J. Kaplan and M. B. Schwartz, 80-97. Northvale, NJ: Jason Aronson Inc.

Shestov, L. 1966. *Athens and Jerusalem.* Trans. B. Martin. New York: Simon and Schuster.

Shneidman, E. 1981. *Suicide thoughts and reflections, 1960-1980.* New York: Behavioral Science Press.

———. 1982a. On "Therefore I must kill myself." *Suicide and Life-Threatening Behavior* 12: 52-55.

———. 1982b. The suicidal logic of Cesare Pavese. *Journal of the American Academy of Psychoanalysis* 10: 547-63.

———. 1985. *Definition of suicide.* New York: John Wiley and Sons.

Shneidman, E. S. 1968. Classifications of suicidal phenomena. *Bulletin of Suicidology* 1-9.

———. 1992. Rational suicide and psychiatric disorders. *New England Journal of Medicine* 326: 889-90.

Shneidman, E. S., and N. L. Farberow. 1957. The logic of suicide. In *Clues to suicide,* ed. E. S. Shneidman and N. L. Farberow. New York: McGraw-Hill.

Shoham, S. G. 1979. *The myth of Tantalus.* St. Lucia. Queensland: University of Queensland Press.

Siegel, K. 1982. Society, suicide and social policy. *Journal of Psychiatric Treatment and Evaluation* 4: 473-82.

———. 1986. Psychosocial aspects of rational suicide. *American Journal of Psychotherapy* 40: 405-18.

Sifre. 1957. Jerusalem: n.p.

Simon, B. 1978. *Mind and madness in ancient Greece: The classical roots of modern psychiatry.* Ithaca, NY: Cornell University Press.

Singer, P. 1975. *Animal liberation: A new ethics for our treatment of animals.* New York: New York Review/Random House.

———. 1979. *Practical ethics.* Cambridge: Cambridge University Press.

———. 1995. *Rethinking life and death: The collapse of our traditional ethics.* New York: St. Martin's Press.

Slater, P. 1968. *The glory of Hera: Greek mythology and the Greek family.* Boston: Beacon Press.

Smith, W. 1997. *Forced exit: The slippery slope from assisted suicide to legalized murder.* New York: Times Books, Random House, Inc.

———. 2000. Better off dead? *The Weekly Standard,* May 29, 2000, 25-26.

Snell, B. [1935] 1982. *The discovery of the mind.* New York: Dover.

Soloveitchik, J. 1973. *Bet Halevi.* New York: n.p.

———. 1983. *Halakhic man.* Trans. L. Kaplan. Philadelphia: Jewish Publication Society.

Sophocles. 1938. *Oedipus at Colonus.* In *The complete Greek drama,* vol. 1, ed. W. J. Oates and E. O'Neill Jr., 613-70. New York: Random House.

Sorasky A. 1982. *Reb Elchonon.* Trans. L. Oshry. New York: Art Scroll History Series.

Stael, A. L. De. 1796. *Sur l'influence des passions.* Paris: Charpentier.

———. 1814. *Réflexions sur le suicide.* Paris: Charpentier.

Stark, R., D. P. Doyle, and J. L. Rushing. 1983. Beyond Durkheim: Religion and suicide. *Journal for the Scientific Study of Religion* 22: 120-31.

Stephens, W. N. 1962. *The Oedipus complex.* New York: Free Press.

Stern, E. S. 1948. The Medea complex: The mother's homicidal wishes to her child. *Journal of Mental Science* 94: 321-31.

Stierlin, H. 1974. *Separating parents amid adolescents: A perspective on running away, schizophrenia, and waywardness.* New York: Quadrangle.

Stone, I. F. 1988. *The trial of Socrates.* New York: Anchor Books.

Street, A., and D. W. Kissane. 2000. Dispensing death, desiring death: An exploration of medical roles and patient motivation during the period of legalized euthanasia in Australia. In *Right to die versus sacredness of life,* ed. K. J. Kaplan, 231-48. Amityville, NY: Baywood Publishing Company. (Published simultaneously in a special issue of *Omega: Journal of Death and Dying* 40 [1, 1999-2000], 231-48.)

Szasz, T. 1971. The ethics of suicide. *Antioch Review* 31 (1).

Tacitus. 1942. *The complete works.* Trans. A. J. Church and W. J. Brodribb. New York: Modern Library.

Tanhuma Buber. 1978. New York: n.p.

Tatai, K., and M. Kato, eds. 1974. *Thinking of suicide in Japan.* Tokyo: Igaka-Shoiu.

Taylor, T. 1834. *Translations from the Greek of the treatises of Plotinus on suicide and the Scholia of Olympiodorus on the Phaedo of Plato.* London: Privately printed for T. Taylor.

Tendler, M. D. 1982. *Pardes rimonim: A marriage manual for the Jewish family.* New York: Judaica Press.

Tertullian. 1959. To the martyrs [Ad Martyres]. In *Disciplinary, moral and ascetical works,* vol. 40, trans. R. Arbeshann, E. J. Daly, and E. A. Quain, ed. R. J. Deferrari. New York: Fathers of the Church.

Thakur, Y. 1963. *The history of suicide in India.* Delhi: Musnshiram Manoharlal.

Tillich, P. 1959. The theological significance of existentialism and psychoanalysis. In *Theology of culture,* ed. R. C. Kimball, 112-25. New York: Oxford University Press.

Tuke, Rev. 1613. *A discourse on death.* London: n.p.

Urbach, E. E. 1979. *The sages: Their concepts and beliefs.* 2nd ed. Trans. I. Abrahms. Jerusalem: The Magnes Press, The Hebrew University of Jerusalem.

Valerius Maximus. 1823. *Valeri Maximi factorum dictorumque memorabilium liborinovem.* London: A. J. Valpy.

Van Hooff, A. J. L. 1990. *From autothanasia to suicide: Self-killing in classical antiquity.* London: Routledge.

Van Praag, H. M. 1986. The downfall of King Saul: The neurobiological consequences of losing hope. *Judaism* 35: 414-26.

Voltaire, F. M. A. 1973. *The selected letters of Voltaire.* Ed. and trans. R. A. Brookes. New York: New York University Press.

Washington v. Glucksberg, 521 U. S. 702, 117 S. Ct. 2258, 138 LEd. 2d 772 (1997).

Weininger, O. 1975. *Sex and character.* London: W. Heinemann.

Wellisch, E. 1954. *Isaac and Oedipus: A study in biblical psychology of the sacrifice of Isaac, The Akedah.* London: Routledge and Kegan Paul.

Werth, J. L. 1996. *Rational suicide? Implications for mental health professionals.* Washington, DC: Taylor and Francis.

Westcott, W. W. 1885. *Suicide: Its history, literature, jurisprudence, causation, and prevention.* London: Lewis.

Willi, J. 1982. *Couples in collusion.* New York: Jason Aronson.

Willis, G. C. 1950. *Saint Augustine and the Donatist controversy.* London: S.P.C.K.

Wynne, L. C., I. M. Ryckoff, J. Day, and S. I. Hirsch. 1958. Pseudo-mutuality in the family relations of schizophrenics. *Psychiatry* 21: 205-22.

Xenophon. 1854. *The Anabasis, or expedition of Cyrus, and the memorabilia of Socrates.* Trans. J. S. Watson. London: Henry G. Bohn.

———. 1857. *Minor works [including the Apology of Socrates].* Trans. Rev. J. S. Watson. London: Henry G. Bohn.

Yalkut Shimoni. 1876. Warsaw: n.p.

Yap, P. M. 1958. *Suicide in Hong Kong.* Hong Kong: Hong Kong University Press.

Yerushalmi, Y. 1991. *Freud's Moses: Judaism terminable and interminable.* New Haven, CT: Yale University Press.

Zeller, E. 1962. *The Stoics, Epicureans, and Sceptics.* Trans. O. J. Reichel. New York: Russell and Russell.

Zilboorg, G. 1967. *Psychoanalysis and religion.* Ed. M. S. Zilboorg. London: Allen and Unwin.

General Index

Abandonment, 56, 100, 105, 116-17, 124, 135, 145, 147, 152, 155-57, 168, 171, 177-78, 205, 209, 227, 231
Abimelech, 46, 107-8, 120, 123, 186
Abraham, 38-39, 159, 161-63, 165-67, 175, 181-83, 229, 232-33
Absorption, 135, 146, 157
Achilles, 15-17, 90, 102-3, 105, 150-51, 209
Adam, xv, 123, 132-34, 159, 181-82, 226
Adams, Reverend, 5-6, 233
Admetus, 33, 103-4
Aeschylus, 82, 97, 146, 179, 191, 233
Agamemnon, 16-17, 91-92, 100, 141, 150, 152-53, 174-75
Ahitophel, 46, 107-10, 113
Ainsworth, M. D. S., 138, 233
Ajax, 90-91, 94, 104, 111, 115, 225
Akedah, xv, 167-70, 232, 247
Akedah motif, xv, 167, 169
Akiba Ben Joseph, Rabbi, 37, 45-46, 49, 103
Alcestis, 83, 95, 103-4
Algom, N., 231, 239
Altruistic suicide, 9, 11, 62, 97, 100, 102-3, 113, 170, 175
Alvarez, A., xxi, 27, 35, 154, 233
Amram, 161, 173
Andromache, 83, 95, 105
Anima, 44

Anomic suicide, 9-11, 88, 96, 105, 113, 147
Antigone, 70, 81-83, 85-89, 94, 96-98, 139, 141-43, 153-54, 163, 190, 203, 223, 229
Antisthenes, 25
Aphrodite, 95-96
Apollodorus, 129, 130, 140, 146, 192, 231
Aquinas, Thomas, St., 54-55, 61-62, 233
Aristotle, 17, 22-23, 67-68, 81, 233
Athenaeus, 18, 201, 234
Attachment, xii, 9-10, 12-13, 24, 55, 76-79, 106, 123-26, 150, 155, 211, 226-28, 230, 233-35, 240-41
Attachment-detachment, 20
Augustine (Augustinus, Aurelius), St., 54-55, 60-62, 234, 247
Autonomy, xii, 9, 86, 124, 127, 129, 139, 214, 227
Aurelius, Marcus, 32, 234
Avodah Zarah, 47-48, 205

Bakan, D., vii, xi, xviii, 175, 224, 227, 234
Battin, M. P., 208, 234, 244
Beck, A., 224, 234
Beckerman, N. I., 208, 234
Bernadin, Joseph, Cardinal, 204-5
Bettelheim, B., 144, 234
Biblical intervention, 225
Biblical prohibition, 200-201

Biblical (covenantal) therapy: family
therapy, 192, 225-26, 228, 242-43; individual therapy, 228, 230
Body and soul: Biblical (Hebrew) view
of, 108; Christian view of, 80; Jewish
view of, 36, 43, 51; Platonic (Greek)
view of, 19, 43, 52
Boundaries, 76, 93, 95, 111, 125, 142, 226,
239. *See also* Walls
Bowlby, J., 138, 234
Brandt, R. B., 6, 235

Camus, A., 3-4, 67-68, 70-71, 235, 244
Cebes, 19-20
Child exposure, 198, 200
Christ, Jesus, 54-59, 62, 87, 170, 240; as
altruistic suicide, 62, 87, 170; as vol-
untary death, 54-55, 58-59, 62
Church councils on suicide, 61-62
Cicero, Marcus Tullius, 26-28, 48, 208,
235
Circumcelliones, 60
Circumstances, xxii, 24, 26-27, 32, 36,
47-48, 159, 215-16
Cleanthes, 24, 26
Clinical axis: couple, xv, 123-26, 137-38,
178, 226; individual, xv, 10, 12-13, 77,
106, 231
Clytemnestra, 16, 141, 150-51, 153, 155,
171-72
Cohen, S. J. D., 15, 235
Cohn, H., 35, 235
Control, 26, 32, 42, 47-48, 80-81, 88-89,
92, 94, 103, 129, 140, 143, 147, 167, 205,
208, 212, 219, 240, 242
Couples: Biblical, 123, 125, 132-35, 226;
covenantal, 134; disengaged, 123-24,
135; enmeshed, 123-24, 135; Greek, 123,
125, 126-31, 135, 145, 157, 226; narcissistic, 132, 136, 226; rejection-intrusion,
124, 130, 132
Covenantal, xiv, 7, 13, 77, 108, 110, 128,
131-32, 134, 168-70, 173, 176, 185, 226
Covenantal circumcision, 162, 168-69

Covenantal psychotherapy, 30
Covenantal purification, 177
Creation: Biblical story of, 36, 118, 132,
181, 231; Greek story of, 36, 45, 149,
231; Jewish view of, 36-37, 45, 176, 201
Creon, 81-82, 84, 86-89, 97-98, 141-43,
151, 153-54
Cross-generational reproducibility of
pathology: Electra Complex, 156-57,
178, 228-29; Oedipus Complex, 164,
228-29; suicidality, 146, 148-49, 157,
239
Curse of Oedipus, 14, 82, 98, 146, 164,
180, 186, 188, 190-92
Cycle, vii, xix, 10, 24, 41, 65-70, 74,
76-77, 81, 92, 105, 113, 135, 210, 232;
and development, 10, 65-66, 69, 74
Cynics, cynicism, 17, 24-25
Cyprian (Thascius Caecibus
Cyprianus), 58-59, 235

Dante, 4, 233
Daughters: Biblical (Hebrew), 37, 119,
160-61, 171-78, 184, 227; Greek, 85, 97,
100-102, 123, 130-31, 140-41, 147,
149-57, 173-75, 177, 190, 227
David, 81, 107, 109, 112-14, 116, 171-72,
186
Death with dignity, 214, 219
Deianeira, 83, 92-93
Demonax, 33
Depression, xix, 8, 32, 54, 90, 112, 151,
196; of Ajax, 8, 90, 225; of Hecuba,
151; of Phaedra, 96; of Saul, 112
Descartes, R., 218, 235
Despair, xx, 49, 71, 113, 115-18, 151, 173,
204, 209
de Stael, A. L., 5
Deucalion, xv, 126, 129-31, 134, 226
Development, vii, xv, xix, 10, 12-13,
65-66, 68-69, 71, 74, 75, 77, 91, 124,
130, 134, 142, 160, 167-69, 177-78, 186,
227-28, 230, 239-40; and cycle, 65-66,
69

Developmental axis, 13, 125, 137; couple, 125-26

d'Holbach, P., 4, 235

Diogenes Laertius, 15, 18, 24-25, 27, 31, 201, 207, 235

Disability, 196, 211, 217

Disease, 6, 20, 195-96, 199-203, 211-12, 218; views of, 20, 195, 199-202

Disengagement (isolation), 10, 85, 88, 123, 135, 227

Donatists, 56, 60-61, 236, 242, 247

Donne, J., 5, 15, 56, 61-62, 235

Droge, A., xx, 31-32, 48, 51, 53, 55-56, 207, 217, 235

Durkheim, E., ix-x, xxi-xxii, 9-10, 12-13, 23, 32, 49, 76, 82, 85, 100, 108, 113, 147, 236, 243, 246

Ecclesiastes (Koheleth), 49, 68, 69-71, 237, 244

Ecclesiastes Rabbah, 49

Edelstein, Ludwig, 197, 236

Egoistic suicide, 9-11, 82-83, 82, 83, 85, 89-92, 111-13, 147, 149

Das Ein ohne Leben (Existence without Life), 216

Elazar, Rabbi, 44

Electra, viii, 139, 141, 150-51, 154-55, 172, 176, 224

Electra Complex, xv, 150, 154-57, 177-78, 226

Elicitation of menstrual shame, 155-57, 176

Eliezer Ben Yair, 50-51

Elijah, 47, 107, 114-15, 117, 158, 225

Elisha, 115, 225

Elkanah, 159, 166

Englehardt, H. T., 6-7, 241

Enmeshment (embeddedness), xii, 10, 85, 88, 93, 96, 99, 123, 127, 135, 153-54, 167, 171, 178, 227, 230-31

Epictetus, 31, 206-7, 236

Epicureans, 17, 25, 247

Epicurus, 25-26

Epimetheus, xxiii, 126-30, 135

Er, myth of, 19

Erigone, 17

Euripides, 8, 80, 82-83, 94-99, 102-3, 105, 115, 139, 143-44, 150-52, 157, 167, 170, 175, 191, 200, 236

Eurydice, 83, 85, 89

Euthanasia, xiii, xxiii, 7, 197-98, 209-10, 212-13, 216, 218-20, 239-40, 244-46

Evadne, 83, 98-99

Eve, viii, xv, 123, 129, 132, 133-34, 181, 226, 241

Expendable (conditional, unwanted) child, 145, 147, 160-61, 176

Faber, M. D., 6, 82, 86, 92, 151, 236

Family: Biblical (Hebrew), 50, 109, 115, 117, 132, 136, 159-60, 163-64, 166-67, 170, 173-75, 178-81, 185-86, 192, 219, 225, 227-30, 239; Christian, 147; Greek, 50, 81, 83, 86-89, 94-98, 100-101, 104, 123, 130, 139-40, 143-44, 146, 150, 152-53, 155, 160, 164, 167, 173, 179, 186, 190-92, 224, 226-30, 245; Jewish, 49-50, 52, 149, 159, 246

Farberow, N., 8, 76, 243, 245

Fatalistic suicide, 9, 12, 24, 198, 203

Fate, xiii-xiv, 23, 29, 36, 42, 69-70, 81, 84, 89, 100, 103, 152-53, 160, 175, 200, 229

Family therapy, 192, 225-27, 242, 243

Fathers: Biblical (Hebrew), 107, 109, 115-16, 142, 158, 160-64, 167-78, 179-80, 186-92, 227; God as, 55, 58, 149, 170; Greek (Roman), 17, 67, 84-85, 87-102, 105, 123, 139-57, 159, 164, 168-70, 177, 179-80, 186-92, 227; Psychoanalytic (Freudian), 147, 149, 154-55, 157, 162, 168, 170, 176, 178, 187, 232

Fear (threat) of castration, 147, 162, 168

Fedden, H. R., xxi, 6, 17, 35, 61, 236

Finley, M. I., 17, 236

Fixation, 10, 12, 106, 231; at couple clinical axis, 124-25; individual clinical axis, 12, 124

Food and drink: not provided to Ajax, 80, 90, 115, 225; provided to Elijah, 115, 225; treatment of T. Schiavo, 215

Forward regression to next stage; couple developmental axis, 13; individual developmental axis, 126

Four hundred boys and girls who leapt into the sea, 48

Freedom: basic idea of, 7, 124, 228; Biblical (Jewish) view, xx, xxiii, 24, 26, 41-42, 51-52, 70, 108, 203-5, 230; Greek view, xx, 14, 23, 26, 29-30, 32, 41-42, 52, 68, 86, 100, 158, 198, 200, 203-5, 224

Freedom of choice, 211, 213

Freud, S., 154, 160, 168, 179, 187, 222, 231-32, 234, 236-37

Die Friegabe das Vernichtung Lebensunwertes Leben (Lifting Constraint from the Annihilation of Life Unworthy of Life), 216, 238

Fromm, E., 224, 237

Gamaliel, Rabban, 176

Gay, P., 237

Gender, 83, 108, 114, 144, 196, 226

Genesis Rabbah, 39, 49, 132, 134, 162, 175, 176, 183, 237

God (Biblical), xiii, xxii, 5, 7, 34-43, 45-48, 51-54, 57, 59-61, 65, 69-70, 73-74, 103, 107-19, 123, 132, 134-36, 147, 159, 161-63, 166, 172, 174-75, 178, 180, 181, 183-85, 191, 195, 201-3, 205, 207-8, 219, 223-26, 231; as Creator, 5, 36, 37, 201, 207, 208, 217, 219; loving, 36, 39, 42, 53-54, 217, 224; merciful, 74-75, 77, 202; as Parent, xxiii, 35, 37, 77, 107, 108, 223, 229; personal (relational), 56, 109, 114, 117, 118, 120, 147, 172, 217, 224; therapeutic, as Therapist, 47, 107, 114, 116

gods (Greek), 16, 18, 20, 22, 23, 27-28, 31, 36, 48, 55, 66-67, 84, 86, 90-91, 93, 95, 96, 98-99, 101, 103-5, 123, 127, 129-30, 134-35, 145, 188-90, 200, 207-8, 223-24, 229, 232; capricious (selfish), xxiii, 36, 95, 105, 108, 224; limited, 24, 36

Goethe, J. W. von, 4, 237

Golden, W. W., 202, 237

Golgotha, 170

Greek ambivalence toward self-knowledge, xx, 54, 84

Greek culture, x, xiii, xix, xxi, 13, 50, 197, 204

Greek society, xx, 17, 101, 130, 146, 168, 175, 197

Greek theogony, 36, 158, 180, 187, 189, 231

Hadda, J., 49, 50, 138, 237

Haemon, 83, 85, 87-89, 91, 94, 141-43, 154

Hagar, 167, 183

Hairsplitting, Talmudic, as an alternative to suicidally polarized thinking, 66

Hama, Rabbi, 183

Hamlet, 3, 21, 231

Hanina Ben Teradion, Rabbi, 47-48; versus Zeno the Stoic, 48

Hankoff, L. D., 7, 107, 237

Hannah, 48, 159, 161, 166-67

Hardy, T., 145, 237

Harrow, M., xvii, 211, 239, 240

Hecuba, 83, 95, 102, 141, 151

Hegesias of Cyrene, 26

Hendin, H., 211, 235, 236, 237, 238, 241

Heracleidae, 8, 83, 95, 101

Heracles, 83, 92-94, 101, 102, 187-90, 238

Hermione, 83, 105

Hero, heroic, heroism, xiii, xxiii, 15-18, 24, 39, 47-48, 64, 66-68, 70, 76, 80-83, 86, 100-105, 108-9, 111, 113, 127, 153, 163, 186, 199-200, 208, 212-13, 217, 219, 224-25, 231

Hesiod, xxiii, 18, 36, 45, 123, 127, 180, 187, 189-90, 238

Hezekiah, 186, 229

Hillel, 43, 45, 229

Hippocrates, viii, 195, 197-200, 202-3, 205, 239; *Treatise on Epidemics,* 195, 199, 200

Hippocratic oath, xiv, 195, 197-200, 206, 236, 238, 240

Hippolytus, 17, 83, 95-96, 139, 167, 200

Hirzel, R., 15-16, 238

Hobson's choice, 41, 66, 77, 80, 81, 84, 97-98, 101, 103-5, 107, 109, 119, 143

Homer, Homeric, 15-18, 204, 238

Hope, iii, v, xii, xiv, xxiii, xxiv, 28, 29, 58, 66-67, 109, 135, 151, 167, 204, 205, 224-26, 230-32, 239

Hopelessness, hopeless condition, xiii, xiv, xx, 32, 38, 66-67, 76, 81-82, 86, 104, 123, 127, 135, 151, 198, 208-9, 211, 214-15, 224, 226, 228-29, 234, 247

Hubris, xxiii, 66, 71, 72, 74, 77, 90, 100, 110, 115

Hume, D., 4, 238

Humphrey, D., 208

Hyllus, 92-94

Ibn Pakuda, B., 37, 234

Idealized, idealizing, 50, 75, 76, 86, 92, 104, 152, 153, 155, 157, 173, 175, 176

Ignatius of Antioch, 57, 58, 238

Individuation, xii, 9-10, 12-13, 76-79, 106, 123-26, 226-28, 230, 240, 241

Individuation-deindividuation, 10

Insecure parenting, 140 (see secure parenting)

Insoluble problem, 139

Intimacy, 104, 227, 242

Ionesco, E., 9, 238

Iphigenia, 8, 83, 95, 100-101, 103, 141, 150-54, 174-75

Isaac, viii, xviii, 119, 144, 158-59, 161-63, 165-67, 170, 175, 179, 181-84, 229, 232, 239, 247

Ishmael, 167, 179, 182-84

Isolated, isolation, 10, 85, 88, 111, 127, 149, 167, 217

Jacob, iv, viii, 119, 121, 159, 161-66, 179-85, 190-92, 229; Jacob's blessing, iv, 165, 179, 181-83, 185, 191-92

Jacobovitz, I., 218, 238

Jason, 143-45

Jephthah, 161, 173-75; daughter of, 161, 173-75

Jeremiah, 47, 114, 118

Jesus (Christ), 54-62, 117, 147, 170; as altruistic suicide, 62, 170; as voluntary death, 54-55, 60, 61

Job, viii, xiv, 47, 60, 107, 114, 117-18, 206-8, 217-19, 229

Jocasta, 82-85, 88, 97-98, 141-43, 145-56, 153, 190-91

Johanan, Rabbi, 44

Jonah, vii, xv, 47, 65, 71, 73-75, 77, 107, 109, 114, 119, 225, 239, 241

Joseph, Rabbi, 49, 165

Josephus, F., xxi, 47, 50-53, 235, 238, 241

Josiah, 186

Jotapata, 47, 50-51, 53

Judah, 160, 162, 136

Judeo-Christian principles, 197, 200

Jung, C. G., 66, 154, 238

Kant, I., 4, 238

Kaplan, K. J., iv, v, x, xii-xiv, xvii, 7, 10, 79, 112, 124, 137-38, 168, 195, 210-11, 224, 228, 231, 239-42, 244-46

Kevorkian, Dr. J., viii, 195-201, 203-6, 210-13, 239-41

Koheleth (Ecclesiastes), 49, 68, 69-71, 237, 244

Kohut, H., 76, 124, 241. *See also* Narcissism, Idealizing, Mirroring

Labdacus, 82, 86-87, 146, 160

Lactantius, 59, 251

Laius, 82-85, 141-42, 146, 232

Laws on suicide: Christian, 60-62; Greek, 23; Jewish, 35; Roman, 32

Leatherman, J., 204-5

Lebacqz, K., 6, 24

Left alone (isolated): Ajax, 91; Elijah not, 81; Moses not, 116
Leonhardi, M., 210, 240
Levi, 162, 185, 191-92
Libanius, 23, 241
Life as a banquet, 14, 30, 34, 43
Life belongs to: God, gods, self, state, xxii, 7, 36-37, 241
Life unworthy of life, 216, 238
Loss of control, 26, 32, 268
Lucian, 32-33, 241

Macaria, 8, 83, 101-3
Maimonides, viii, xxiv, 195, 197, 199, 201-6, 228, 237, 239-41.
Maimonides' prayer for physicians, 239
Main, M., 138, 241
Maldaver, M., 137-38, 228, 239
Male-female antagonism, 236
Manasseh, 163, 185
Marathon, battlefield of, 16. *See also* Pheidippides, death of
Markus-Kaplan, M., 242
Martyrdom, 8, 25, 35-36, 44-46, 49, 54-61, 94, 103, 159, 235-36, 239, 243-45
Masada, 29-53, 235, 241, 244
Mass (collective) suicides: Graeco-Roman, 15; Jewish, 47, 53
Mayo, D. J., 208, 234
McHugh, P., 214-17, 222
Medea, 143-45, 155, 164, 246
Medea Complex, 144, 246
Menelaus, 100, 105
Menoeceus, 83, 97-98
Minuchin, S., 124, 242
Miriam, 161, 171, 173
Misogyny, 88, 96
Modern society, xix, xxiii, 198
Moses, ix, 107, 114-16, 159, 173-74, 207, 224, 225, 247
Mothers: Biblical (Hebrew), 161, 164-65, 167, 171; Greek, 123, 139, 140, 141, 171
Mount Moriah, 164

Naaman, 235
Naomi, 45, 161, 164-65, 167, 171
Napier, A., 129, 242
Narcissism; idealizing versus mirroring, 75, 76, 149, 170, 178, 236. *See also* Kohut, H.
Narcissistic collusion in couples, 130, 131, 132, 226
Narcissus, vii, xv, xx, 65, 71-74, 76-78, 83, 84, 105, 186, 187, 224-25, 239
Nathan, 81, 186
Nehemiah, Rabbi, 183
Nemesis, xxiii, 65, 66, 68, 71, 72, 76, 77
Neoptolemus, 105
Nephesh, 43, versus *psychē* or *anima*, 44
Noah, xvi, 35, 69, 132, 134, 135, 136, 181, 226
Noble death, xxii, 86, 231, 235
Nonsentient, nonsentience, 218
Numbers Rabbah, 183, 242

O'Connor, N., 10, 138, 239
O'Dell, J., 211, 239, 240
Odysseus, 16, 18, 67, 90, 91, 92, 151, 236
Oedipus, iv, xiii, xv, xviii, xx, xxi, 41, 70, 81-85, 89, 91, 94, 96-98, 139, 141-43, 147, 148, 153-55, 164, 167-70, 179, 180, 182, 183, 185-91, 192, 223-24, 226, 228, 231, 232, 236, 247
Oedipus Complex, xv, xx, 146-48, 154, 155, 168, 169, 223, 231, 232, 236, 246
Orbach, I., 48, 79, 131, 242
Origen, 54, 253
Ovid, 65, 71, 76, 129, 130, 187, 189, 243

Pacurius, 29
Pandora, viii, xv, xviii, 123, 126-32, 135, 149, 224, 226, 241
Parable, 39, 48, 74, 81, 135, 137, 151, 162, 241; versus riddle, 81
Pascal, B., 68, 243
Paul, St. (Saul of Tarsus), 56
Peleus, 105
Peregrinus, 6, 25

Personal Creator, 36, 37, 201, 208, 217

Phaedra, 83, 95-96, 115

Pheidippides, death of, 16. *See also* Marathon, battlefield of

Phoenissae, 82-83, 95, 97-98, 191, 236

Plath, S., 66, 154, 243

Plato, 4, 17-24, 26, 38, 48, 51-52, 127, 147, 204, 208, 128, 237, 243, 246

Pliny, the elder, 32, 56, 57, 243

Pliny, the younger, 57, 243

Plotinus, 21, 24, 30, 243, 246

Polyxena, 83, 102, 103, 141, 151

Pontius, 59

Porphyry, 24

Prometheus, viii, xv, 67, 70, 123, 126-32, 135-36; Promethean rebellion (struggle), 127, 224, 226

Prophecy: Biblical (Hebrew), 109, 115, 185, 191; Greek, 15, 81, 141-42, 180

Psyche, xxi, 44, 220, 239

Psychology of hope, v, xii, xxiv, 220, 239

Pyrrha, xv, 126, 129-31, 134, 226

Pythagoras, 15, 17-18, 201

Pythagorean, -ism, 18, 197-98, 200-201

Quality of life, 185, 213, 218

Quintilian, 32, 243

Rabbinic thought on suicide, 35-50

Rainbow as sign of hope, 135-36

Rashi, 35, 116, 134, 160, 167, 172, 174

Rational suicide, 6, 31, 206-19, 238, 242, 245, 247

Rebecca, 114, 119, 134, 160, 165-67, 172, 174, 182, 184, 191, 239

Regression, 9, 13, 75, 126, 131, 133; forward regression, 13, 126

Richman, J., 123

Riddle, 39, 41, 72, 81-84, 92, 109, 111, 141; versus parable, 81

Right to die, 7, 195-96, 206, 208, 213

Right to life, 139

Ringel, E., 6

Roe v. Wade, 213

Ross, L. T., 7, 244

Rousseau, J. J., 4

Ruth, viii, 45, 158, 161, 171-72, 175, 176, 177, 202

Ruth motif, xv, 175, 177

Samson, 96, 108, 110-11

Samuel, 112, 161, 166-67

Sarah, 159, 183, 190

Saul, 46, 107-8, 111-13

Saul's armor bearer, 107-8, 113

Schiavo, T., 206-13

Schizophrenia, 72, 76, 246

Schneiderhan, M., 239-40

Schwartz, M. B., iv, 239, 244-45

Secure parenting, 138 (see insecure parenting)

Seneca, L. A., the younger, 14-15, 26, 28-32, 52, 101, 198

Sentient, sentience, 218

Shakespeare, W., 3

Shame of menstruation, 155, 157, 176

Sherwin, B., 218

Shestov, L., 232

Shneidman, E., 8-9, 35, 66, 76, 107

Sibling rivalry: Biblical, iv, viii, xxiv, 179-81, 192; classical, iv, viii, xxiv, 179-80, 187-89, 191-92; Freud, Sigmund, 187, resolution of, iv, viii, xxiv, 179, 181; *Totem and Taboo,* ix, 179, 187, 236

Siegel, K., 208-9, 245

Simeon, 185, 192

Simple interventions in the Hebrew Bible, 225

Singer, P., 218, 245

Sisyphus, 3, 18, 66-69, 71, 231

Slater, P., 17, 105, 140, 143, 131, 224, 226

Smith, W., 185, 209

Snell, B., 232

Socrates, 14-15, 17-22, 31-32, 38, 40, 53, 55, 206-7; gerophobia of, 21, 40; guard-post allegory of life, 20; and Hamlet, 21; and Jesus, death of, 55;

philosophy as "preparation for death," 14; suicidal aspects of defense plea, 21-22

Soloveitchik, J., 211

Sons: Biblical (Hebrew), 160-70; Greek, 140-49

Sophocles, 8, 16, 70, 80-86, 89, 94, 96-97, 99, 111, 115, 139, 142, 145, 153, 170, 190-91, 203, 223, 226, 229

Sound decision making, 209, 212

Specieism, 218

Sphinx, 41, 81-82, 84, 98, 109, 122

Stoic, 6, 17, 24, 26-32, 41-43, 52-54, 203, 206-7, 218-20

Stopper, 6, 9, 17, 37, 77, 81, 83, 95, 98, 99, 101, 103, 109, 114-19, 123, 127, 178, 224

Suppliants, 87, 97-98

Survivor guilt, 170

Suttee, 7

Szasz, T., 6

Tabor, J., 31-32, 48, 51, 53, 55-56, 217, 227

Tacitus, 227

Tamar, 184

Tarfon, Rabbi, 71

Terminality, 196

Tertullian, 54, 246

Teucer, 91

Thebes, 23, 81-82, 97-98, 141-42, 146, 170, 179, 187-88, 190-91

Theseus, 17, 95, 98-99

Threat (fear) of castration, 147, 162, 168

Trachinae, 82-83

Tragedy: Aristotelean definition of, 81; distinguished from therapy, 224-25, 230; Greek distinguished from Hebrew Bible, xxiv, 63; versus hope, 230-31; and noble death, 231; and suicide, iii, iv, vii, viii. xv, 230, 231, 236

Triangulation in families, 226

Tuke, Reverend, 6

Urbach, E., 43-44

Vagina dentata, 146

Van Hooff, A. J., 9

Van Praag, H., 12

Voltaire, F. M. A., 14

Washington v. Glucksberg, 214

Wasserman, E., Rabbi, parable of, 39, 51

Weininger, O., 49, 78-79, 149

Wellisch, E., 144, 163, 167-68, 224, 226

Wichorek, M., 210-12

Willi, J., 129, 247

Worth, S., 10, 138, 240

Xenophon, 21-22, 48

Yerushalmi, Y., 241

Yossipon, 50

Youk, T., 216

Zelophehad, daughters of, 173-74

Zeno the Stoic, 15, 24, 27, 31-32, 48, 206-20; death of, 47-48

Zenoism, 208

Zeus, 16, 36, 82, 123, 127-35, 140, 145, 187-90, 226, 231

Zimri, 47, 107-8, 110, 113

Index of Selected Classical Writings

Aeschylus
Seven against Thebes
11.785-86   146, 179
11.879-924   191

Apollodorus
The Library
1.1   146
1.1.1   140
1.1.4   140
1.4   231
1.5   231
1.7-2   129
1.7-3   130
2.1   231
3.2.2   192

Aristotle
Ethics
3.7   22
5.11   22

Poetics
Chapter 6   81
Chapter 13   81

Cicero
De Finibus
3.60-61   27, 208
15.49   26

Tusculan Disputations
1.18   27
1.34.83   26
1.71-75   28
1.84   28

Diogenes Laertius
*Lives of eminent philoso-
phers*
6.18   25
6.76   24-25
6.95   25
6.100   25
7.20   27
7.28   24, 207
7.87   27
7.130   24, 27
7.176   27
8.45   201
10.120   25-26
10.125   25
10.128   25

Epictetus
Discourses
1.29   31, 206-7
3.24   31
10.41   31

Euripides
Alcestis   103-105
Andromache   105
Electra   139, 141, 150,
154-55
Hecuba   102, 103, 141, 151
The Heracleidae   8, 101-2
Hippolytus   95, 96, 139,
200
Iphigenia in Aulis   8, 100,
141, 150, 151-53, 175
Medea   141, 143-45
The Phoenissae   97-98,
191
The Suppliants   98-99

Hesiod
Shield of Heracles
11.35   190
11.56   190
11.80   190

Theogony
11.155-210   187
11.504-5   189

11.587-93   123

11.591-94   127

11.616-20   127

11.629-725   189

Works and Days

60-86   127

87-90   127

90-96   127

Hippocrates

Hippocratic Oath   195,
    197-98, 200, 203, 205

Treatise on Epidemics
Section 11 — 2nd
constitution   195, 199

Homer
Iliad

1   17

9.320   33

18.95-96   15

24.505   16

Odyssey

1.59   16

26.61   16

Josephus
Wars of the Jews

3.514-16   51

7.598-603   51-52

Marcus Aurelius
Meditations

5.29   32

8.47   32

10.8   32

Ovid
Metamorphoses

1.381-98   129

3.347-59   72

3.366-475   65

3.379-92   72

3.405-6   72

3.414-54   72

3.463-75   72

3.497-502   72, 187

Plato
Apology

29a   21

40c-e   21

41a-42a   18

Laws

8.838   20

9.12   20, 23

Phaedo

62a-c   20, 208

64a   19

64b   19

66e   19-20

68a   20

68d   20, 52

83a   19

Protagoras

320-22   127

Republic

1.614   19

3.406d   20

10.3   19

Pliny
Letters

Book 10   57

Natural History

3624   32

Seneca
Controversiae

5.1   28

8.4   28

9.4   28-29

10: preface   29

De Ira

3.15-34   30, 198

Epistle

12.8-10   29, 30

24   52

24.12-15   29

24.23   26

24.24   26, 29

58.36   30

65.22   29

70.5-6   30

70.11   30

71.15-16   29, 30

77.6   30-31

117.23-24   30

120   29

Sophocles

Ajax 8, 15-16, 80-81, 90-91

Antigone   81, 85-89, 139,
            141-43, 153-54,
                  223, 229

Oedipus at Colonus   190

Oedipus Rex   70, 83-85,
        141-42, 145, 153, 190,
                  223, 226

The Trachinae   92-94

Xenophon
Apology

6   21

7   21

14   22

23, n.1   22

27   22

31   22

Scriptural Indices

THE TANACH/
HEBREW
SCRIPTURES/
THE OLD
TESTAMENT

Genesis

1:28	37, 181
2:7	34, 159
2:16-17	132
2:18	123, 132
2:24	158, 226
3:1-7	132
3:8-10	132
3:11-12	132
3:17-20	132
3:20-21	132
3:22-23	132
4:6-7	181
5:1-32	134
6:13	135
6:17	134
6:18-22	135
8:15-19	135
9:1	135, 181
9:5	35
9:6	35
9:12-17	xxiii, 135, 224-25
12:1-3	229
17:9-11	161
17:18	183
17:20-21	183
19	160
21:16	167
22	162
22:11-12	162
24:12-20	165
25:23-24	184, 191
27-28	114
27:13	165
27:28-29	165
27:39-40	184
27:41	184
27:42-45	119
27:46	119
28:1-4	119, 166
28:5	164
28:9	184
30:1-2	59
33:4	184
37	163
38	160
42-45	163
48:20	185
49:5	185
49:28	164, 179

Exodus

1-2	173
4:19	44
19:4	37
20:13	60

Leviticus

18:5	36
18:26	160
21:5	35

Numbers

11	114
11:11-15	116
11:16-19	116
23:9	176
27	173-74

Deuteronomy

5:17	60
6:7	161
30:19	34, 42
32:39	61

Judges

9:53-57	110
9:54	46, 108
11:30-31	174
11:35	174
11:39-40	175
13	111
16:28-30	110-11
16:30	46, 108

1 Samuel

1:17	166
1:20	166
2:9	167
15:7-9	112
15:10-23	112
22:13	112
22:18-19	112
28:6	112
31:4	108, 111-12
31:5	108
31:14	46
31:15	46, 113

2 Samuel

1:6	46, 108
1:9-10	113
1:13-16	113
17:23	46, 108, 109

1 Kings

1:6	186
16:18	47, 108, 110
18–19	114
19:4-8	107, 115
19:9-14	115
19:10	44

2 Kings

5:1-14	225

Jeremiah

20:14, 18	118

Jonah

1–4	114
1–2	65
1:1-3	73
1:12	73
2	73
3:1-10	73
4:1-3	73
4:6	74
4:7-8	74
4:9-11	74

Malachi

3:23-24	158, 232

Psalms

22	114, 116
22:1-3	117
22:9-11	117
22:24	117
27:9-10	223, 229

Proverbs

31	39, 164
31:10-11	158
31:27-28	158

Ruth

1:16-17	172
2:11	172
4:15-17	172

Job

1:21	207
2:9-10	207, 219
7:15-16	118
9:21	118
10:1-2	118
13:15	118, 206, 207
13:22	118

Ecclesiastes (Koheleth)

1:3-7	69
1:3-10	70
1:17	70
2:13	70
2:24	70
3:1-8	69
4:12	70
9:9	70

1 Chronicles

10:4	46, 108
10:5	46, 108

APOCRYPHA

1 Maccabees

6:46	47

2 Maccabees

10:22	47
14	60
14:41-42	47
14:43-46	47

THE NEW TESTAMENT

Matthew

27:3-5	54
27:46	56, 117, 147
27:50	55

Mark

15:34	56

Luke

10:18	55
14:26	55
18:33	55

John

2:4	147
3:16	55, 170
10:18	54, 55
12:25	56
15:13	55

2 Corinthians

5:6-8	56

Philippians

1:21	56
1:23-24	56
3:20	56
3:21	56

1 John

2:15	55
3:16	55

THE BABYLONIAN TALMUD

Berachot

5b	44
10a	229
17a	165
23a	49
61b	45

Eruvin

13b	45
45a	46

Yoma

22b	113

Taanit

29a	48

Ketubot

62b	165

Sotah

12b	173
37	163

Gittin

57b	48, 229

Kiddushin

30a	161
31b	165

Baba Kamma

91b	35

Baba Batra

3b	48
119b	174

Sanhedrin

74a	36, 45

Makkot

49	109

Avodah Zarah

11a	205
18a	48
18b	48

Avot

2.16	71
2.21	38
3	37
4	38, 43
4.21-22	34, 43
4.29	42
6.2	34, 42, 203

Hullin

94a	49

Avot de Rabbi Nathan

2.33	43

Semachot

2, 5	49

MIDRASH

Sifre (on Numbers 27:7)

	174

Genesis Rabbah

34:13	112
19:12	132
20:8	134
26:4	176
56:8	162
58:9	39
59:2	39
60:3	175
61:6	183

65:9	39
65:22	49

Ruth Rabbah

2:22	112

Lamentations Rabbah

1.45	48
1.50	40

Ecclesiastes Rabbah

10:7	49

RABBINIC SOURCES

Rashi (on Genesis 12:1)	229
Rashi (on Deuteronomy 34:8)	160
Rashi (on Ruth 1:16)	172

Tosafot Avodah Zarah

18a	47, 48
18b	48

Maimonides (Prayer for Physicians)	195, 197, 201-3, 205

Daat Zekenim (on Genesis 9)	46

Shulchan Aruch

Orach Chaim

329.6	46

Yoreh Deah

345.3	112

Malbim (on 1 Samuel 1:8)	159

CHURCH FATHERS

Aquinas, Thomas
Summa Theologica
2.2.64.5   61
3.47.1   54-55, 61

Augustine
City of God
1.17   60
1.19   60
1.20   60, 61
1.22   60
1.24   60
1.27   60

Epistles
185.2.7   61

The Trinity
4   54

Cyprian
Letters
55.3   59

*On the Glory of
Martyrdom*
29   59
54   59

Ignatius
*Epistle to the
Magnesians*
8   58

Epistle to the Romans
1   57
4   57, 58
9   58

*Epistle to the
Smyrneans*
3   58

Lactantius
Divine Institutes
89   59-60
90   59-60

Origen
*Exhortations to
Martyrdom*   54

Pontius
*A Life and Passion
of Cyprian*
7   59
9   59
10   59

Tertullian
To the Martyrs
4   54